NAMING SECURITY – CONSTRUCTING IDENTITY

MANCHESTER 1824

Manchester University Press

New Approaches to Conflict Analysis

Series editor: Peter Lawler, Senior Lecturer in
International Relations, Department of Government,
University of Manchester

Until recently, the study of conflict and conflict resolution remained comparatively immune to broad developments in social and political theory. When the changing nature and locus of large-scale conflict in the post-Cold War era is also taken into account, the case for a reconsideration of the fundamentals of conflict analysis and conflict resolution becomes all the more stark.

New Approaches to Conflict Analysis promotes the development of new theoretical insights and their application to concrete cases of large-scale conflict, broadly defined. The series intends not to ignore established approaches to conflict analysis and conflict resolution, but to contribute to the reconstruction of the field through a dialogue between orthodoxy and its contemporary critics. Equally, the series reflects the contemporary porosity of intellectual borderlines rather than simply perpetuating rigid boundaries around the study of conflict and peace. *New Approaches to Conflict Analysis* seeks to uphold the normative commitment of the field's founders yet also recognises that the moral impulse to research is properly part of its subject matter. To these ends, the series is comprised of the highest quality work of scholars drawn from throughout the international academic community, and from a wide range of disciplines within the social sciences.

PUBLISHED

Eşref Aksu
The United Nations, intra-state peacekeeping and normative change

M. Anne Brown
Human rights and the borders of suffering:
the promotion of human rights in international politics

Lorraine Elliott and Grame Cheeseman (eds)
Forces for good:
Cosmopolitan militaries in the twenty-first century

Richard Jackson
Writing the war on terrorism:
language, politics and counter-terrorism

Tami Amanda Jacoby and Brent Sasley (eds)
Redefining security in the Middle East

Jan Koehler and Christoph Zürcher (eds)
Potentials of disorder

Helena Lindholm Schulz
Reconstruction of Palestinian nationalism:
between revolution and statehood

David Bruce MacDonald
Balkan holocausts?
Serbian and Croatian victim-centred propaganda and the war in Yugoslavia

Jennifer Milliken
The social construction of the Korean War

Ami Pedahzur
The Israeli response to Jewish extremism and violence:
defending democracy

Tarja Väyrynen
Culture and international conflict resolution:
a critical analysis of the work of John Burton

Naming security – constructing identity

'Mayan women' in Guatemala on the eve of 'peace'

MARIA STERN

Manchester University Press
MANCHESTER AND NEW YORK

distributed exclusively in the USA
by Palgrave

Published by Manchester University Press
Oxford Road, Manchester M13 9NR, UK
and Room 400, 175 Fifth Avenue, New York, NY 10010, USA
www.manchesteruniversitypress.co.uk

Distributed exclusively in the USA by
Palgrave, 175 Fifth Avenue, New York,
NY 10010, USA

Distributed exclusively in Canada by
UBC Press, University of British Columbia, 2029 West Mall,
Vancouver, BC, Canada V6T 1Z2

British Library Cataloguing-in-Publication Data
A catalogue record for this book is available from the British Library

Library of Congress Cataloging-in-Publication Data applied for

ISBN 0 7190 7116 X *hardback*
EAN 978 0 7190 7116 4

First published 2005

14 13 12 11 10 09 08 07 06 05 10 9 8 7 6 5 4 3 2 1

Typeset
by Helen Skelton, Brighton, UK
Printed in Great Britain
by Biddles Ltd, King's Lynn

Contents

Acknowledgements

There have been too many people who have helped me during the prolonged process of completing this work to name them all. I will limit myself to those who have read and commented on my work at various stages, as well as those who have directly aided me in my research.

First of all, Cynthia Enloe, Svante Karlsson, and Björn Hettne deserve a very special mention. Thank you for your support and wise guidance.

Several other people have read my work in its entirety: an anonymous reviewer, Elisabeth Abiri, Maria Eriksson Baaz, Ann K. Gollin, Peter Lawler, Helena Lindholm Schulz, Merritt Polk. I thank you all for your careful reading and helpful comments. Ann K. Gollin, Merritt Polk and Djordje Zarkovic have also helped me immeasurably with the arduous process of copy-editing: thank you!

Many more have read and commented on my work at various stages of its completion: Brooke Ackerly, Hans Ambrahamsson, Michael Baaz, Andreas Behnke, Lena Bjurving, Gunilla Blomqvist, Barry Buzan, David Campbell, Edmé Reyes Dominguez, Monica Erwér, Marita Eastmond, Kathy Ferguson, Mats Friberg, Linda Green, Gail Greiner, Ulla Holm, Peter Johansson, Bent Jørgensen, Naila Kabeer, Ane Kirkegaard, Mona Lilja, Adriano Manuel Malache, Heidi Moksnes, Iver Neumann, Henrik Norberg, Camilla Orjuela, Jane Parpart, Spike V. Peterson, Lester Edwin J. Ruiz, Eduardo Simón Brynnel, Michael Schulz, Finn Stepputat, Daniel N. Stern, Kaia Stern, Michael Stern, Ralph Pettersson, Ann Tickner, Jacqui True, Marie Tynell, Stellan Vinthagen, Rob Walker, Joakim Öjendahl. Thank you all for your thoughtful comments and criticism.

Several other people have aided me with their astute and incisive advice when I was revising this book for publication: Véronique Pin-Fat, in particular, deserves a very special mention (and many thanks) for her insightful comments, rigorous feedback, and wise council. I am also extremely grateful to an anonymous reviewer, Maria Eriksson Baaz (and her brutal delete button), Peter Lawler, Gillian Youngs, and Vivienne Jabri. Thank you!

Acknowledgements

Three main academic environments have been meaningful in different and important ways for the intellectual work that has gone into this book: 1) the World Order Models Project (WOMP) introduced me to the many-faceted world of 'globalized' political theorizing. 2) The Department of Peace and Development Research, Gothenburg University (Padrigu) – especially Femfo (Feminist Research Group) and the Seminar for the Study of Identity Politics and Conflict Resolution, provided a safe haven for intellectual imagination and discussion. 3) The International Studies Association (ISA), particularly, the Feminist Theory and Gender Studies Section, and more recently, the Post Structural Politics Working Group of BISA, served as welcoming forums for the development of my research. Thank you all who have supported me in my work.

Thank you also to Chatrine Butler, Jóhanna Jónsdottir, Ann-Sofie Steén and to my students at Padrigu and the Institution for Gender Studies, Gothenburg University.

Many colleagues and friends in Guatemala aided me during my fieldwork. Clara Arenas Bianchi, Gustavo Palma Murga, Emma Chirix, Matilde González, Alfredo de León, Deborah Díaz, and Alejandrina Alvarenga at AVANCSO and Jorge Solares at the University of San Carlos provided me with an invaluable base for my research, as well as friendship and support. Thank you.

Marise Guindon has earned a special acknowledgment for assisting me so completely in my fieldwork and sustaining me in numerous ways during my visits in Guatemala. Merci-Thank you-Gracias!

Most importantly, thank you to the women who took the time and shared their life stories with me. It is understood that I could not have written this book without your ample confidences.

I would also like to thank Padrigu, FRN (Swedish Council for Planning and Coordination of Research), and the Knut and Alice Wallenberg Foundation for their generous support of my research.

I am also deeply grateful to my family, friends, colleagues, and my children's pre-school teachers who have all helped me throughout this long and bumpy process. You know who you are. Your support has been invaluable.

Lastly, I thank Eduardo Simón Brynnel for helping me in so very many ways and for living with this book! Alexander Erik Stern-Pettersson and Andreas Daniel Stern-Pettersson: among all else, thank you for your questions (e.g. 'Mommy, why did the Guatemalan army hurt the Mayan women? Aren't they supposed to be on the same team?') For you: 'larger than the whole wide world and more than infinity.'

For my parents:
Ann K. Gollin and Daniel N. Stern

Part I

Rethinking security studies

1

Introduction: exploring in/security

We are women, poor, indigenous; we are ... triply discriminated against.
(Onelia, born 1972)[1]

The PACs[2] always threaten the women, always they try to find out who is organizing the women ... [They ask] 'Why don't you have husbands, where do you get these bad ideas?' ... Several days ago even [some one told me] that they raped four women.
(Carmen, born 1955)

Many Mayas have stopped wearing their traditional clothes so that the other society ... the *Ladinos*[3] will accept them ... The group doesn't view them anymore as Mayas, because they do not speak the language, don't wear the clothes, as if they devalue themselves, devalue the culture. But they can't be *Ladinos*: they are forming another group without identity, without culture ... There are women who have done this ... and it is dangerous, dangerous to devalue [us]. The majority of women are [already] devalued ... The Mayan culture is starting to decay ... and we women are those who supported it the most ... It is not necessary to arrive at this ... losing being Mayan.
(Elena, born 1962)

THE ABOVE TESTIMONIES reflect the experiences of many politically active Mayan women in Guatemala at the close of over thirty years of armed conflict, and at a moment when peace was being negotiated and a desirable future seemed possible. Among other things, these testimonies evoke urgent questions about security and identity – questions which guide the subject matter of this book: how do people such as 'Onelia', 'Carmen', and 'Elena' speak about their experiences of insecurity and their struggles for security and identity? What might their words imply for rethinking security and insecurity in terms of Global politics?

Prompted by questions such as these, this book is motivated by two related concerns: first, that experiences like those reflected in the above citations (with the exception of a few 'dissident sites'[4]) rarely figure in the articles, books, conferences, and policy papers that make up Security studies. How can it be that these experiences are not included in a conceptualization of insecurity that – ultimately – is about people and their being in the world? Second, security presents a conundrum, or paradox.[5] As is arguably evident in the harmful realities of conflict, the promise of security implies both supplementary insecurity and a logic of violence: how can we better understand and thereby seek to contest the seemingly self-perpetuating politics of producing danger in the name of security? These puzzles moved me to re-examine the limitations of security as we commonly 'know' it by closely exploring security and insecurity as they are articulated in the discourses of politically active Mayan women in Guatemala. Inspired by these concerns, this book, therefore, offers a reading of what may be at stake in the seemingly inherent conundrum, or paradox, of security.

Based on partial life-history interviews that I conducted with leaders of different organizations within the popular/Mayan movement in 1995, the book explores the notions of danger and harm that were meaningful to, and constituted the lives of, many Mayan women. In particular, it considers how the narrators 'pinned down' their identities in order to achieve security in a context riddled with different, yet related, forms of violence. Hopefully, by so doing, it can offer possible ways of understanding the struggles for security of many people in disparate parts of the world.

I propose that although there have been increasing challenges to a narrow state-centric notion of security, the logic of sovereignty and the ensuing delimitations of politics continue to impede alternative conceptualizations of security.[6] Throughout the chapters of this book, I therefore seek to show how the narratives of the Mayan women I interviewed unsettle sedimented understandings about insecurity and identity – understandings which govern policy, delimit political imaginaries, and cast a blind eye to the insecurities of many. I aim to disrupt such imperial moves through revealing contestations in Mayan women's security narratives. Primarily, the book will explore how Mayan women's security narratives – as discourses of resistance – both rearticulate and disrupt the main story of security imbedded in the modern 'paradox of sovereignty' (Connolly, 2004: 23). By paying careful attention to Mayan women's anomalous accounts of insecurity, it aims to contribute to a profound rethinking of the concepts and practices of security and identity, and to take into account the disparate articulations of insecurity in a post-Cold War, post-colonial, and globalized world. Ultimately, it is one reading that may offer possible ways to understand better – and therefore address – how political bodies name danger and threat and identify strategies for procuring safety.

In broad strokes, this book will engage in rethinking security and identity through two main sites of exploration. First, in Part I, I query into the underlying logic of security as it has come to be understood in modern politics through reading different ways security has been conceptualized in the field of security studies. Central to this discussion is an exploration of the abiding logic imbedded in the belief in a sovereign subject and in modern articulations of sovereignty. My intent is to unpack this logic in order to reveal how it both underpins dominant understandings of security, and informs those sites of resistance contesting its violent effects, such as Mayan women's narratives. Second, in Part II, I draw insights from closely reading Mayan women's narratives and from considering security as it is written in sites otherwise marginalized or silenced in security studies.

Mayan women's security narratives

From the beginning of the 1990s, many Mayan women trained their voices and articulated publicly that they were insecure in multiple ways: as women, as members of an oppressed ethnic group, and as members of a socio-economic class which struggled to attain the basic requirements for survival. Many also expressed that they felt threatened in different and related manners in the various contexts of their lives: such as their family, the *Ladino* society, their organizations, or the Guatemalan nation-state project. Similarly, those who threatened these persons might, in a different context, be their closest allies. Many Mayan women therefore, represented their security and insecurity as contingent and multiple – even hybrid.

Despite (and because of) their subaltern positions, many Mayan women began in the late 1980s and early 1990s explicitly to act politically.[7] They publicly protested against their self-defined triple discrimination within their own communities and organizations, nationally and globally.[8] For the first time in Guatemala's history, Mayan women were making claims for security and identity *as Mayan women*, and negotiating their struggles in simultaneous sites of subjugation and resistance. They forged a vision of a more secure existence, and redefined who they were in relation to those who threatened them, thereby altering the very relations of power which rendered them insecure. They reconstructed both what the identity, 'Mayan women' and what security and insecurity meant in the different contexts of their lives. They also made it increasingly clear that they, too, were subjects in the remaking of the society in which they were living.

Indeed, the multiple insecurities articulated in Mayan women's narratives cannot be understood separately from their claims to political identity: what they considered threats and envisioned as promising safety and security depended upon *who they were*. They did not identify themselves with the particular articulation of Guatemalan national identity that prevailed at the time; instead they identified themselves, in part, in opposition to the homogenizing claims of Guatemalan nationalism, stating that their culture and identity (*being Mayan*) were placed at risk by this violent national project. They identified themselves as Mayan *women* whose femininity was defined in part by their roles as guardians and transmitters of the Mayan culture. As women, however, they were particularly vulnerable both to the harms of sexism within their communities (and households) and to the sexualized violence of military tactics. They also identified themselves as poor peasants (*campesinas*) whose connection and therefore access to cultivatable land was vital for their cultural and physical survival. In this regard, poverty related to the neo-liberal economic policies of an export economy and consequent national land distribution was a great threat to their security. In sum, Mayan women's insecurity was hybrid, contingent, defined in terms of their identity, and tied to many interlocking systems of oppression and domination.

Revisiting security as we 'know' it

Given the above, how then can we understand or redress Mayan women's insecurity? It can be argued that Mayan women's experiences of insecurity are drastically different from insecurity as it was conceived by the security elite in Guatemala, as well as by most theorists of security in the study of modern global politics.

As much feminist scholarship has revealed, women and members of marginalized groups (although seemingly assumed to be included as members of the state[9]) have been denied adequate consideration in the formation of security policies.[10] According to dominant readings, security has traditionally revolved around the nation-state: the state has been cast as both the agent and the referent object of security; other states have acted as the source of possible threat (as well as temporary allies). People, like Mayan women, who do not feel represented or protected by the state, or whose political identities reside elsewhere (such as in ethnic or women's movements) have therefore rarely graced the pages of most writings about security, and their voices have not been included in the formulations of what has been considered a threat and therefore relevant under the label 'security'. Moreover, 'security', arguably, remains a specific concept within global politics that poorly reflects complex confluences of identity and power (Jabri and O'Gorman, 1999). It follows then that the insecurity experienced by many like 'Onelia', 'Elena', and 'Carmen', does not neatly *fit* into the prevailing security discourses.[11]

Furthermore, 'security' has been shown to be inadequate in explaining or prescribing solutions for many of the most pressing and violent conflicts within states, between states, and beyond states. The growing salience of the discourses of 'identity politics', as well as the implications of the globalization and deterritorialization of danger (in the form of an ever-growing threat from globalized terrorism), have placed in high relief such failings. Reconceptualizing security, I propose, is therefore crucial if security policies are to respond to the very real needs of bodies (both people's and political) that clamor for attention in the world today.

Reconceptualizing security

Taking my departure in the critical challenges posed by reading the representations of insecurity in the narratives of Mayan women, I propose that security and identity are concomitant. In light of this, one must take seriously – and critically rethink – the inter-relationship between security and identity in order to make sense of the security articulated in the narratives of the Mayan women I interviewed. In short, I suggest that it has become increasingly clear that *who (we say) we are* matters in how we conceive of, strive for, and practice security. Similarly how we 'speak' security, name danger and threats, as well as safety and well-being, implies (and indeed informs) a particular expression of our identity, which serves to represent 'us' – or, in other words, the supposedly sovereign subject of security (Waever, 1995; Walker in Krause and Williams, 1998).

The manifestations of the hegemony of national security can be seen, in effect, as a source of insecurity for Mayan women. Guatemalan national security policy during the 'dirty war' certainly silenced Mayan women's voices, sanctioned the acts which threatened them, and obscured relations of power which placed them in marginalized positions within many different and interfacing systems of domination. Indeed, the grammar, or logic, of security (as it has been written in dominant as well as marginal security policies/discourses), produces danger and threat, and spins an intricate web of abiding violence and harm. In brief, the Guatemalan state, although multi-ethnic and multi-cultural, has engaged in a particularly violent form of nation-state building; pervasive and brutal national security policies have been designed to homogenize the population, even if this meant killing a large number of them, including many Mayan women (Bastos and Camus, 1995: 148).

Mayan women's security narratives prompt consideration of whether the people who live within the geographical borders of states, 'citizens', necessarily concede the direct connection between their identity and the claims about sovereignty expressed as national security (Youngs, 1999: 88). Like many others marginalized by the policies of state security, Mayan women do not invest in the definition of political identity implied in their status as Guatemalan citizens; instead, they see these security policies and their implicated notions of acceptable political identity as extreme threats to their well-being. They invest in their 'triple identity' as 'Mayan, women, and poor'. This tripartite identity can be read as an identity in resistance to the delimiting and harmful meanings given to these very identity labels through, among other discourses, Guatemalan national security policies. However, Mayan women's triple identity and struggles for security should not be seen as only a reflective, albeit subverted image of these subjugated identity positions. Although certainly formed in relation to dominance and discrimination – to insecurity – their identities also supersede these framings, offering more.

The above arguments invite a return to a slightly different angle of the puzzle I raised in the beginning of this chapter, namely: the narratives of Mayan women, as well as those of many other peoples struggling for security within the geopolitical and discursive confines of a nation-state system, cannot altogether escape the dominant discourses which produce them as subjects under (or in relation to) a state. I suggest that the discourses and practices of modern sovereignty by necessity circumscribe the struggles against its violent manifestations and delimit the landscape of political possibility for the security of peoples and communities.[12]

In light of this reframing of the conundrum of security, I will explore how modern articulations of state sovereignty delimit the realm of political possibility and imply certain notions of security. Any attempt to rethink or unpack security to 'include' or 'make room for' new variables (such as women or ethnic groups – Mayan women) risks repeating the logic of security as it has been written by the assumed story of the modern state system. This story has led to much violence and harm, and, arguably, its pretense of reflecting reality has recently come under much consideration. There have indeed been many attempts within international relations (IR) theory to query into the ontology of the concepts/practice of security.[13] Nevertheless, as it is generally practiced and understood, 'security' arguably remains imbedded in a 'grid of intelligibility' in which modern sovereign power – commonly assumed to be the possession of the state – circumscribes the space for political imagination (Dillon, 2004: 43).

Given the above line of reasoning, chapter 2 offers a site of exploration into the dominant 'grid of intelligibility' which inscribes security – both the articulations of security which pose Mayan women as threats or imply their harm, and the articulations of security which underpin Mayan women's discourses of resistance. The main arguments I propose in chapter 2 are as follows: according to the logic of sovereignty, the state acts as the ultimate subject of security and therewith its existential survival becomes paramount and supercedes any other claim. The very existence of the state as subject demands continual reinforcement as 'foundational' and beyond question (Edkins and Pin-Fat, 1999: 6). For instance, discourses of nationalism and the expressions of sovereign power (i.e. both the inscription of laws and the ability to suspend these laws in a state of national security emergency) perpetually reinstate the state-as-subject. Importantly, the supposed sovereignty of the state rests on the notion of the possibility of a sovereign subject – a reasoning subject which is whole, cohesive, and transcendent. For this narrative to work, the state must ostensibly 'possess' subjectivity – subjectivity which shall be represented through national identity, insofar as identification is understood as the naming of a subject position, as a 'picture', or representation of the subject.[14] This reasoning subject can name threat and danger and identify strategies for the assurance of its security and for the continued hegemony of national identity. Security can therefore be seen as a discursive practice which operates in order to 'secure' the subject of the state. Security then becomes both named and enacted through the working of 'discourses of danger', which discern self from Other (Campbell, 1992; Dillon, 1990–91; 1996).

This story implies that people invest in the picture of the subject (national identity) that is evoked. I suggest that identity (or the process of identification) is constructed through difference. Identity also depends upon a striving for similarity – what many have referred to as the 'Janus face' of identity politics (most specifically, nationalism and ethnicity) (Eriksen, 1993; Yuval-Davis, 1997). Identification requires a continual construction of the image of wholeness, of similarity on the 'inside', which gains presence through the erection of boundaries that distinguish the inside from the outside and, thus, similarity from difference. This move is part of a whole series of distinctions which produces a representation of the self (subject) in relation to the Other, as well as those like me (us) from those that are different (them).

Yet, instead of accepting identity as a somewhat stable or tangible level or entity that could be named and secured, critical scholars trying to unpack these logics have carefully shown how, in various contexts, sovereign power constructs itself through the workings of discourses of danger and insecurity – through the naming of threat, of enemy, of Other, thus producing the very identity that is intended to be secured (Campbell, 1992; Dillon, 1990–91, 1996; Weldes et al., 1999). The (impossible) securing of a subject relies upon the myth of the subject as already existing (and in need of security). Yet, instead of the subject of security being separate and existing prior to the act of 'speaking' or writing security, it is through the very naming of threat and danger that the 'subject of security' is formed (Campbell, 1992). This 'subject' gains the semblance of presence through its evocation in a temporal narrative where danger and threat from the Other makes sense in a story with a clear beginning and origin (the past), middle (now) and the promise of a happy ending (security).

Central to such an understanding of security, and the inevitable production of its subject, is the intimate and 'indissoluble relation' of security with insecurity. Dillon explains, for instance, that 'the not-secure of security is the radical excess of security that continuously contours security' (Dillon, 1996: 127). This statement suggests that the relationship between security and insecurity is more complex than is commonly understood. It is generally accepted within realist IR theory that one state's security implies another's insecurity. Furthermore, efforts at securing one's state (or other referent object of security) inspires similar efforts in the 'enemy' state, thus spurring more threats and greater insecurity (the so-called 'security dilemma'). Yet Dillon's claim involves understanding insecurity as the inevitable *supplement* to security. The concept of security bears with it 'insecurity'. When one defines or names security, a notion of insecurity is also implied. Simply, if one were totally 'secure', then one would not need security, there would be no threat. Edkins' explanation of the workings of supplements in discourse offers insight into how seemingly opposing concepts/practices (security and insecurity) are integrally dependent upon each other for their definition and their enactment. She explains that supplements are undecidables:

> They contain *within themselves* an ambiguity, a duplicity of meaning. They are *neither* one thing *nor* another, at the same time they are simultaneously *both* [...] They cannot be resolved [...] 'added in order to complete, to compensate for a lack in what was supposed to be complete in itself' [...] [They are] both inessential and essential. (Edkins, 1999: 70)

The first term (security) can only exist in relation to the second. Moreover, insecurity always 'haunts' any notion of security or act of securing, making it both necessary and impossible.[15] Hence security always carries with it its own undoing, thus ensuring that the act of securing must endure. Threat and danger will always loom and are indeed integral, as a 'constitutive outside' to security and safety.[16] Security and insecurity can therefore be seen as intrinsically so inter-related that a co-operative concept, 'in/security', can be helpful in connoting the complexity of naming (and implying) both threat and safety. I therefore will use the term 'in/security' throughout this book.

In sum, I suggest that despite disparate attempts to open or widen its scope, 'security' – as it is generally practiced and understood – remains imbedded in a 'grid of intelligibility' written by modern sovereign power (Dillon, 2004: 43). Dominant representations and practices of security therefore close off terrains of meaning and being, even in sites of resistance. I therefore propose that attention to the underlying logic of in/security is crucial in identifying and exploring 'vital sites of contestation' in Mayan women's security narratives (Edkins and Pin-Fat, 2004: 2).

Part II of the book will consider how Mayan women's struggles for in/security rearticulate the logic of in/security as described above. Mayan women's narratives, written in resistance to an unusually violent nation-state project,[17] offer a particular site from which to understand the seemingly inherent conundrum of security, and to glimpse possible venues for resistance against its delimiting logic. These narratives reject the security story written and enacted by the Guatemalan state as violent and dangerous, yet clearly cannot completely escape the confining grammars, or logic, of its plot. They thus simultaneously rearticulate and disrupt in/security as it has been written in modern accounts of politics. To recap: attention to how dominant power relations resonate in attempts at resisting them (while not promising complete emancipation), offer crucial opposition and thereby open up the possibility for alternatives.

Focusing on multiple struggles for safety, security, and indeed identity, Mayan women's narratives suggest that the inter-relationship between security and identity must be seen as complex and contingent. As noted above, by including Mayan women's security narratives as valid sites from which to theorize security and identity, this book is intended as a contribution to envisioning a political imaginary that redresses fundamental questions about community, safety and harm (Shaw, 2004).

Because of the extent and pervasiveness of the violence of the society in which Mayan women live, security and insecurity are *explicit* organizing principles in their construction as political subjects. Violence that is poorly understood through the lenses of the dominant logic of security could be better understood if we began asking questions about the damage that can occur at the confluence of competing identity claims and the efforts at securing subject positions. Mayan women's narratives are specifically compelling in this light because their self-defined political identity is multiple: they are 'Mayan women', not just Mayan, not just women. (Most also identify themselves as Mayan *campesina* women.)[18] They have lived in a situation of extreme violence and hardship in a war-torn society where they have been, and continue to be, victimized because they are women, Mayan and poor, and thus 'triply oppressed'.

Importantly, the narratives imply that identity cannot be seen as a 'level' or 'sector', or tangible thing that can ever be secured, no matter how detailed or multiple one's attempts at representing it may be. Instead, one might rethink identities as formed through (among other mechanisms) the discursive naming of in/security.[19] In this sense, identity can be seen as attempts to pin down a subject in order to secure it. The subject of security is named, called forth, or 'hailed into place' through the process of naming danger and threat, as well as safety and well-being (Hall, 1996). Yet, as we will see in Part II of the book, Mayan women's narratives suggest that this process can never be complete, because a subject can never be fully represented or 'safe'. Identity and its centrality to security, therefore, can be seen as an impossible promise for the successful securing of a subject, be it nation-state or marginalized community. Security, as well as identity, the narratives tell us, is thus necessarily haunted by the ghosts of its own undoing and therefore forever elude those who seek it.

Methodological considerations

This book also offers an attempt to begin theorizing from some of the methodological quandaries I faced in my efforts at investigating what in/security can mean to Mayan women. I therefore make explicit the challenges I faced while engaging in a study informed by feminist theorizing with the theoretical and methodological tools of a discipline (IR) that has paid little attention to questions of gender or to the multiple violences implicated in practices of security. Why has it been so difficult to find a way to address Mayan women's in/security in a manner that does not reduce them to universalized (male as norm) individuals or citizens of a state?

As is surely unsurprising to many feminist thinkers, 'bringing Mayan women's experiences of in/security in' to security studies poses some difficult methodological as well as theoretical puzzles (Ackerly, Stern and True, 2005). Attempts to redefine security to take into account the perspective of marginalized sites (such as that of Mayan women) risk repeating the traditional logic of security described above, or are left flailing about in search of an alternative conceptual apparatus. In chapter 3, I therefore retrace the methodological journey my research took in order to contextualize my subsequent readings of Mayan women's texts. In particular, I explore the methodological implications of treating in/security as a discursive practice in a 'marginalized site' among people whose voices have been silenced in both the context where they are living, and in terms of the dominant conceptualizations of security. Central to these explorations, lays a discussion of the method I employed to co-create an in/security narrative and then to read in/security in these texts. Through my method of reading, I sought to avoid predetermined or essentialized definitions of in/security which would foreclose openness to the meanings that were imbued in the narrators' texts.

Exploring in/security in spatio-temporal contexts

As we will see in Part II of the book, the very multiplicity, hybridity, and contingency of the insecurities that the narrators name, as well as the implicit connection between these in/securities to the triple identity they embrace call attention to the simple yet critical notion that in/security is far more complex and contingent than most theories about security would lead us to believe. In different ways in each of the ensuing chapters, I will consider the very 'untidiness', and multiplicity of the narrators' representations of their in/security. These chapters explore how in multiple, often conflicting ways, Mayan women's insecurity narratives both adopt the logic of security inscribed by sovereignty, and contest and resist the imperial moves imbedded in such logic.

In order to best address the complexity of Mayan women's in/security, the chapters in Part II are divided into the *spatio-temporal contexts* that organized the (transcribed) narratives. These spatio-temporal contexts act as the guiding frame of the individual chapters and are composed of particular spaces (such as the family) during particular moments *in the narrative*, as well as all the discourses of power and relations which inform these spaces and moments (i.e. nationalism, sexism, racism, classism). These contexts necessarily flow into each other, although they remain sufficiently separate so that the chapter categorizations do not disrupt the logic of the narratives. I limit my depictions to how they appear in the texts, although when necessary I provide a very brief background description to situate the narratives in the historical moment of the time of the interview (1995). The narrators have corroborated that the spatio-temporal contexts which comprise the different chapters coincide with the important contexts in their testimonies. In some cases, however, I will conflate several of the original contexts into broader ones so that I can arrive at some commonalty between texts.

Introducing conclusions/concluding introductions

In the following chapters of this book I will raise questions about how it may be possible to rethink in/security in order to take into account the experiences of those who neither identify nor situate themselves in the ways prescribed by the architects of security policies, or according to the ways one commonly thinks about modern politics. This implies querying into the conundrum of in/security as I have introduced it in the above sections.

Through reconsidering in/security in two inter-related sites of exploration: the theoretical body of security studies, and the in/security narratives of Mayan women, I will argue that Mayan women are valid subjects of security whose positions of vulnerability and resistance cannot be seen as separate from the dominant concepts and practices of security in global politics more generally.[20] In particular, the various ways in which the different chapters query into Mayan women's articulations of in/security help to reveal the limitations of political imaginaries which do not adequately address the contingency and multiplicity of the ways in which people identify themselves and seek security. Importantly, these chapters explore how discourses of danger also resound in marginal sites and show how attention to the ways in which the narrators navigate their multiple and often contradictory in/securities offers possible openings for reimagining in/security and identity. Indeed, the following chapters of this book will together trace how the very act of placing these (contingent) texts in the context of thinking about in/security sheds light on the very contingency of accepted descriptions of 'reality' – and of in/security and identity.

Notes

1 The names of the narrators are fictitious. Additional information in the narratives has been changed to protect the narrators' anonymity and safety. The interviews were conducted in Spanish; I bear full responsibility for all translations from Spanish to English.

2 The Guatemalan army forced civilians to serve in Civil Patrol Units (PACs) in order to discourage guerrilla activity in the communities. The PACs act as an extended arm of the army and a key counter-insurgency strategy (REMHI/ODHAG, 1999: 45–6).

3 *Ladino* refers to the dominant population, which typically has mixed Spanish and indigenous heritage. It also refers to anyone who is not indigenous. *Ladino*ization is a term for the process whereby an indigenous (Mayan) becomes assimilated into the *Ladino* culture.

4 Those works which explicitly reflect over security and (gender-cultural) identity include: Hansen (2000); Hoogensen and Rottem (2004); Jabri and O'Gorman (1999); Peterson (1992); Sylvester (1994). Feminist accounts of security include: Blanchard (2003); Cohn (1993); Elshtain (1987); Enloe (1988, 1990, 1993); Peterson and Runyan (1993); Pettman (1996); Reardon (1985, 1993); Tickner (1993, 2001); Wibben (2002).

5 The 'paradox' of security is also addressed in e.g. Campbell (1992), Der Derian in Lipschutz (1995); Dillon (1990–91, 1996); Mowitt in Weldes et al. (1999); Sylvester (1994).

6 For critiques of state-centric view of security see e.g. (fn. 4–5); Booth (1998); Falk (1995); Jahn (1987); Johansen (1982); Krause and Williams (1997); Lipschutz (1995); Stephenson (1988); Stern (1990); Terriff et al. (1999).

7 Conavigua, the national widow's organization, was founded in 1988.

8 Mayan women's 'triple oppression: as women, Mayan, and poor' was a common description made by members of popular/cultural movements. See *Majawil Q'Ij* (1995).

9 Feminist political theory has shown how the seemingly gender-neutral basic grammar of 'modern' political imaginaries masks the gendered workings of power which cast the masculine as the norm. See e.g. Brown (1988); Carver in Randall and Waylen (1998); Flax (1987); Okin (1989); Pateman (1988); Spelman (1988).

10 See fn. 4.

11 I use the term 'discourse' to connote the production and re-presentation of meaning which delimit the realm of understanding, action, and imagination within a certain framework. In any given society, there are always many different – often competing – discourses, which organize life in varying ways (Weldes et al., 1999: 19). The power of discourses lay in the way we accept their framing and representation of reality as descriptive; their prescriptive/productive power remains often obscured from our vision (Eriksson Baaz, 2004).

12 Shaw addresses the 'ambivalent potential' of sovereignty as follows: 'the ambivalent potential of sovereignty is expressed with unusual clarity in the lives and politics of indigenous peoples ... the lives, politics and selves of indigenous peoples thus express intricate terrains of power produced by discourses and practices of sovereignty. This is not to say that indigenous peoples have only been victims of sovereignty, on the contrary. Although produced as marginal by sovereignty discourse, indigenous peoples have creatively engaged their situated-ness through complex rearticulations of selves, communities and power in and through these discourses and practices. Their struggles illustrate in very concrete ways both the potential and constraints embedded in them. Insofar as we seem to be living through a period characterized by the rearticulation of political possibility, through and in relation to discourses of sovereignty, this renders the struggles of these peoples, in, through, and against these discourses a vital site for thinking about the future of politics. In particular, the struggles of indigenous peoples provide a critical lens on sovereignty, revealing and politicizing the violences that have been its conditions of possibility' (Shaw, 2004: 165–6).

13 See e.g. Dillon (1990–91, 1996); Der Derian in Lipschutz (1995); Campbell (1992); Connolly, (1991); Krause and Williams (1997); Sylvester (1994); Wæver (1995); Walker, (1993); Weldes et al. (1999).

14 For a discussion of the term 'picture of the subject', see Pin-Fat (2000: 667) and Edkins and Pin-Fat (1999: 11).

15 I am borrowing the term 'haunting' in the way it is used here from Pin-Fat (2000: 663–74).

16 For discussion of the term 'constitutive outside' see Edkins (1999: 70); Hall (1996: 15); Pin-Fat (2000: 663–74); Pin-Fat and Stern (2005).

17 The role of the US in this formation of this project is undeniably crucial. See, e.g. Brignoli (1985); Garcia (1988); La Feber (1993); Jonas (1991); Karlsson (1996).

18 *Campesina* means 'peasant' in Spanish. It has also become a political identity among the poor peasant population that is struggling for a just distribution of land. I have not focused specifically on this identity because the majority of Mayan women make clear that their *campesina* identity is an integral component of their Mayan identity and is therefore included in their identification as 'Mayan woman'. This will be further addressed in chapter 7.

19 See e.g. Dillon (1990–91, 1996); Campbell (1992); Connolly (1991); Krause and Williams (1999); Weldes et al. (1997).

20 The repetition, 'mirroring' (Chow, 1993) or mimicry of hegemonic practices in marginal sites is surely not a novel insight. Fanon, for example, contended both with the appeal and the limitations/exclusionary potential of 'identity politics' in resistance as early as 1952. Fanon's work eloquently addresses a puzzle that has informed much post-colonial and feminist theorizing: namely the seeming foreclosure of political imaginaries through the workings of hegemonic (or colonial) discourses of domination and alterity. Fanon (1952).

2

Theorizing security and identity

> Power relations entail resistance ... 'there are no relations of power without resistances ... formed right at the point where relations of power are exercised.' (Foucault, 1980: 142)

> It is through the analysis and unpacking of these intricate relationships of power and resistance that forms of domination produced by sedimented power relations can be understood and vitally contested. (Edkins and Pin-Fat, 2004: 2)

Reading Mayan women's narratives as valid sites of in/security discloses the delimiting grammars imbedded in 'sedimented' understandings of security and identity and hints at possible mechanisms for alternative, less violent political practices. As the citation above affirms, resistance and contestations are an integral part of dominance. Therefore, these narratives, which can be seen as complex discourses of resistance, offer a particular site from which to rethink the paradox of in/security. Much then can be learned by turning our attentions towards the ways Mayan women's narratives both refute and rearticulate security as it has been inscribed through modern state sovereignty (Shaw, 2004: 165).

Such a reading, however, implies first laying some ground work. Primarily, it is necessary to explore and unpack the underlying logic of security as it has largely come to be understood in modern politics. Without such an exploration, it would be difficult to consider how Mayan women's security narratives oppose the violent expressions of security enacted by the Guatemalan state – and how they both rearticulate and resist the seduction and power of the dominant narrative of security. In the first section of this chapter, I will therefore read some of the different ways security has been conceptualized in the field of security studies, briefly focusing on the main storyline of security, as well as the sequels that it has spurned.

Additionally, Mayan women's narratives underscore how articulations of in/security also imply articulations of identity. This connection has also not gone unnoticed: an increasing recognition of the centrality of identity to understanding in/security has prompted many scholars to explore the theoretical bases of this crucial inter-relationship; much of this work focuses on reconsidering sovereignty.[1] In sum, this work suggests that in/security is a discursive practice inseparable from, and concomitant to, processes of identification, and circumscribed by sovereignty. In the second section of this chapter, I will therefore also consider some of the main lines of reasoning supporting this claim as both helpful tools for unpacking the logic of in/security, and as a critical basis for understanding Mayan women's in/security, which I address in Part II of the book.

Security as we know it

National security: a fairytale[2]

In traditional IR (dominated by so-called 'realists'), the (liberal) state is the predominant if not the sole recipient and agent of security; the modern state system provides the playing field in which sovereign states 'act' in order to ensure their survival through the guaranteeing of national security. That security is about threats, danger, and a struggle for safety seems to be well established. Buzan's definition of security as the 'pursuit of freedom from threat' is now perhaps the most widely used and accepted among IR security scholars (Buzan, 1991: 18). Later, he updated that definition to read: 'Security means survival in the face of existential threats' (Buzan, Waever and de Wilde, 1998: 27).

According to dominant accounts, security is attendant upon the primacy of a certain (oversimplified) understanding of modern state sovereignty (Walker, 2004: 240). This notion reads roughly as follows: state sovereignty serves as the cornerstone of the international system; anarchy rules on the outside of states, and law and order reign inside the geopolitical territory of state borders. 'National' security is paramount because states compete in a hostile international system characterized by belligerent 'others'. Security means that the state, as such, survives. Danger resides 'outside' the borders of the state in aggressive ambitions of similar, yet significantly different, political bodies – i.e. other states. Security demands, above all, clear distinctions between an inside and outside, whereby borders can be secured, danger kept at bay, and safety ensured domestically. Consequently, any perceived threat to the sovereignty of the state must be countered, lest anarchy and chaos enter into the domestic domain and thereby blur the dividing lines that clearly demarcate friend from foe, 'here from 'there', 'then from now', 'norm from exception' (ibid.: 246). In sum, state sovereignty cannot be sustained unless national security is achieved; consequently security is the linchpin of state survival as a sovereign entity and therefore takes precedence over all other functions of the state.

Weber's well-cited claim that the state enjoys the 'monopoly over the legitimate use of force' has weathered extremely well and remains a succinct expression of the dictates of state sovereignty (Weber, 1994). The 'state' enjoys a monopoly over the use of 'legitimate' violence in both the 'domestic' and the international environment. 'National' security is predominantly viewed in military terms, where security signifies military defense and the strategies designed for this. According to this logic, the state does not pose a threat to 'its' people, but instead is their protector. 'National' security depends upon keeping danger on the 'outside'; when 'danger' is located in the 'inside' in the form of 'outlaws' and criminals they are properly punished and therewith disarmed and incarcerated in prison. In addition to a strong military defense, the assurance of a safe, familiar, and lawful inside rests upon the continual reinforcement of national identity (and the hierarchy of identities it generates) as 'natural' and ultimately hegemonic. This is achieved through nationalism. According to this logic, national identity predominates and incorporates all other political identifications (difference); any challenges to its hegemony are thereby waylaid.

Arguably, there is an increasing realization that the nature of state sovereignty has fundamentally changed (or has lost the pretense of ever having existed). This is usually attributed to the increasing evidence of globalization and exemplified in the terrorist attacks against the US on 11 September 2001 (Booth and Dunne, 2002). Nevertheless, despite the seeming increase in recognition of the challenges contemporary global politics pose to modern state sovereignty, I propose that the accounts of security attendant to its grammar continue to prevail in both the conceptualization and practice of security – among Guatemalan security elites, and globally. Ironically, in Guatemala, instead of its scripted role as official protector, the army posed the main direct threat to the Guatemalan population, especially to the Mayan *pueblo*[3] and Mayan women.

Reproducing security as we know it?

> To the extent that we have an idea of a specific modality labelled 'security' it is *because* we think of national security and its modifications and limitations, and not because we think of the everyday word 'security'. The discourse on 'alternative security' makes meaningful statements not by drawing primarily on the register of everyday security, but through its contrast with national security. (Waever, 1995: 49)

Much of the field of (so-called) 'alternative' security has been about deepening or widening security beyond the state to include different threats, and referent 'objects'.[4] There has also been a move to make claims about the condition of security that rejects the minimalist notion of the military security of state borders.[5] 'Alternative' notions of security promised a better framework (than that provided by a traditional focus on the state) for redressing a wide range of insecurities – such as those experienced by Mayan women.[6] Critics of traditional understandings ruminated over what should be included as the 'subject' of security[7] (e.g. the state, the individual, the globe; humans, women, the environment), what should be included as threats (e.g. military attack, human rights abuses, environmental damage, economic dependence), and what should be considered proper strategy (military deterrence/common security, intervention, economic sanctions, the enforcement of human – and women's – rights).[8]

These original delineations of security categories have been further developed by the addition of culture and identity as vital to contemporary considerations of security, arguably because of the changing 'art' of armed conflict. Kaldor's influential writings on the centrality of identity politics to the processes of 'New Wars', for example, has gained significant attention in a wide array of academic and policy circles (Kaldor, 1999). In general, there has been a call for the inclusion of identity as an important sector or condition which demands securing (Von Busekist, 2004, Hoogensen and Rottem, 2004; Laffey, 2000).[9]

Additionally, in reaction to such reasoning, and in order to address the seeming 'infinite expanding of the concept to imply all that is good', scholars included in what is known as the Copenhagen School argued against reifying (and expanding) security and therewith divesting it of meaning and political currency (Waever, 1995: 47; Buzan et al., 1998; Guzzini and Jung, 2004).

Although certainly very important for recognizing many of the limitations of a state-centric view of security, I propose that many of these approaches reflect a political imaginary that hinders us from adequately considering the harm and vulnerability that Mayan women's narratives express, and for querying into the paradox of in/security that figures in their narratives. My contention follows two main simultaneous lines of critique: first, these approaches, in different ways, do not adequately address Mayan women's hybrid, multiple, and contingent articulations of in/security. Second, they do not sufficiently challenge – and may even unwittingly repeat – the violent logic of the fairytale of security described above. Instead of offering an exhaustive reading of the rich scholarship[10] that makes up these avenues in the broad terrain of security studies, I will critically consider two very different ways of conceptualizing security that are helpful to a reading of Mayan women's narratives, yet, I suggest, fall short in engaging with the concerns set out above: human security and security as a 'speech act'. I choose to look more closely at these approaches precisely because they *do* offer much in terms of addressing in/security as articulated by Mayan women. However, revealing some of their limitations may further disclose the delimiting power of 'in/security' as we have been taught to imagine it.

Humanizing security?

In response to the state-centric view, scholars and policy makers looked to employ a discourse of 'human security' as a sort of 'catch-all' for an approach to security that would address all people's security needs (Security Dialogue, 2004). This approach emphasizes individuals as people, instead of as citizens as the referents of security (e.g. Falk, 1995; King and Murray, 2002). The impetus is to dislodge the stronghold the state enjoys on defining threats as well as identifying the threatened, especially since many of the conflicts occurring globally figure the state as the main threat against its people (as was the case in Guatemala), instead of the state as the official protector of the people. In 1994, the Human Development Report from the United Nations Development Program (UNDP) officially 'launched' the concept of human security as a viable alternative:

> For too long, the concept of security has been shaped by the potential for conflict between states. For too long, security has been equated with threats to a country's borders. For too long, nations have sought arms to protect their security. For most people today, a feeling of insecurity arises more from worries about daily life than from the dread of a cataclysmic world event. Job security, income security, health security, environmental security, security from crime, these are the emerging concerns of human security all over the world. (UNDP, 1994: 3)

Behind this concept lies an idea of a transnational humanitarian responsibility for human welfare (Hettne, 2003). According to this analysis, the state no longer needs to act as the sole agent, provider, or recipient of security. Instead, human beings should become valid units of analysis and indeed of security policy – not only in terms of their status as individual citizens within a state, but because of their inherent value as humans. This goes hand in hand with an increasingly widely adopted move to speak of the globe (or the international community) as the appropriate realm through which to guarantee security and human rights (Falk, 1995). It is implied then that modern state sovereignty and its attendant expressions of security would no longer completely determine the terms of politics; instead a more peaceful and co-operative 'global society' might emerge.[11]

The notion of human security has offered many advocates of marginalized groups and 'women's' security an important venue for highlighting the particular vulnerabilities of peoples who suffer violence *from* representatives of the state.[12] Often, human security is intimately connected to the 'discourse of human rights' (Abiri, 2000). As a policy overview report on 'Gender and Armed Conflict' states: 'The human security approach is based on the assumption that "all people have basic human rights and should enjoy these rights regardless of *who* and *where* they are" (UNDP, 1994, cited in El Jack, 2003).

How might this be problematic as a lens through which to read Mayan women's in/security narratives? In concert with the substantial work for 'women's rights as human rights', feminist analysis has asked the questions: 'which individuals (or humans?), in which contexts?', and has thus revealed security to be a gendered construct that disregards many women's experiences.[13] Indeed, feminist scholarship has pointed out in myriad ways that the prevailing discourse of 'human' rights (and arguably, human security) rests on an idea of the 'enlightenment' sovereign subject – a particular, gendered notion of being human that, as Pin-Fat reminds us, is universalizing, yet hardly universal.[14] Butler, for instance, posits:

> the terms by which we are recognized as human are socially articulated and changeable. And sometimes the very terms that confer humanness on some individuals are those that deprive certain other individuals of the possibility of achieving that status, producing a differential between the human and the less-than-human. (Butler, 2004: 2)[15]

Following Butler and Pin-Fat, I suggest that the discursive shift from individual *qua* 'man-citizen' to 'human', although arguably important, does not significantly alter the underpinning ontology. Although feminist interventions, such as those noted in El Jack (2003), have wrested a notion of individual (*qua* man-citizen[16]) security from a stance that explicitly ignores gender, women, and other marginalized groups, they neglect adequately to address questions of identity, power, and context – sites of inquiry that are arguably crucial for understanding Mayan women's in/security. Indeed, Mayan women's narratives suggest that it is precisely *who* and *where* we are that matters in the production and practice of in/security (Peterson, 1992: 32). Obscuring, then, the assumed location (within a state), and identity (human as man-citizen) which underpin the concept of human security, I propose, reproduces the political imaginary presented through the 'idiom' of state sovereignty. The paradox whereby the state must serve as the 'protector' or guarantor of human rights provides just one persistent and problematic example.

Perhaps most importantly, in spite of the incisive critiques of conceptions of mainstream security accounts offered by analysts and activists adopting human security as their framework, security in these accounts is conceived as (more or less) a *thing*, or a determined condition that could be applied to different objects, and procured by different agents – as long as its definition is wide or deep enough to be inclusive. According to such reasoning, as long as one identifies carefully enough what the referent of in/security *is*, such as 'human', 'women', or 'ethnic group' or 'women ethnic minorities', then security could surely be achieved. Yet, as I will argue in section 2 of this chapter, it is perhaps this very notion of the possible deliverance of security to a knowable and namable ontologically prior 'referent', that is attendant to the continuing production of violence.

'Speaking' security

Arguing against the conceptualization of security as a 'thing' or 'condition', and against the deepening and widening of the valid referent objects of security, Waever initially claimed that security has two meanings, an everyday one, which is an un-analytical term, and one that has been crafted in the specific discourse of IR, and is thus limited to 'nation-state' security (Wæver, 1995: 48–9). The everyday meaning of security signifies 'being secure, safe, not threatened' (ibid.:

49). The label 'security', on the other hand, 'has become the indicator of a specific problematique ... Security is, in historical terms, the field where states threaten each other, challenge sovereignties, try to impose their will on others, defend their independence' (ibid.: 50). He states that security therefore does not have 'an independent, stable, context free meaning' (ibid.: 50). The everyday meaning can not just be applied to the nation-state, but instead nation-state security means the *specific* conversation within IR theory and practice: one remains outside of IR theory – and within 'another language game' – if one does not engage security from 'within the discourse', meaning that the security logic ('the mode of thinking, a set of rules and codes from the field of 'security'') must remain consistent (ibid.: 51). In this logic, 'the images of challenges to sovereignty and defense have remained central' (ibid.: 50).

Wæver therefore criticizes the alternative security discourse for 'infinitely expanding the concept' and for reifying security and having it mean 'all that is politically good, or desirable' (ibid.: 47). By so doing, he explains, security comes to mean something 'true', universal – pre-textual, and thus outside of the security discourse. Security, as defined outside of this discourse, has little, if any, bearing on the security of IR theory and politics. Wæver suggests, then, that security is a *speech act*, uttered by official representatives of the state and in reference to nation-state security.

> With the help of language theory, we can regard 'security' as a *speech act*: In this usage, security is not of interest as a sign that refers to something more real; the utterance *itself* is the act. By saying it, something is done ... By uttering 'security' a state-representative moves a particular development into a specific area, and thereby claims a special right to use whatever means are necessary to block it. (Ibid.: 55)

It can only be defined and conceived *within* this discourse; there is no security outside of this discourse. He defines a security problem rather narrowly, saying that:

> Security problems ... can undercut the political order and thereby 'alter the premises for all other questions' ... [They] must therefore be addressed prior to all others because, if they are not, the state will cease to exist as a sovereign unit and all other questions will become irrelevant. (Ibid.: 52–3)

Wæver also questions the positive value assigned 'security', suggesting that, because of its status as a tool of language, it does not have a value of its own. Instead of striving for security (which inherently implies insecurity) one should struggle for de-securitizing an issue (ibid.: 57).

In Waever's later work with Buzan, the stringency with which they tie security to the nation-state softens (Buzan et al., 1998: 37). The emphasis on the state as basically the *only* referent of security that is relevant for IR has indeed shifted to make room for a 'sectoral analysis of security' and which addresses other 'security-identity' constellations than the state. The societal sector, for example, is understood as follows: 'the referent objects in the societal sector are whatever larger groups carry the loyalties and devotion of subjects in a form and to a degree that can create a socially powerful argument that this "we" is threatened' (ibid.: 119).[17] They offer an elegant and seemingly inclusive framework for analysis: 'security means survival in the face of existential threats, but what constitutes as existential threat is not the same across different sectors' (ibid.: 27).

Could Mayan women's in/security be understood through such analysis? I will address this question primarily by borrowing from Hansen's critique against the 'Copenhagen School' for silencing the workings of gender in their development of their framework of analysis (Hansen, 2000). Hansen points to the limitations in a framework which neglects to account for the security of those whose voices are silenced in official discourses, be they state discourses or other recognized security-identity constellations. She thus raises questions of voice, power and privilege which are familiar to students of feminist and post-colonial theory (Spivak, 1987). Who *can* speak security, and if it is only security elites, can we expect a 'trickle-down' effect (Hoogensen and Rottem, 2004: 161)? Are then 'people's' security (if indeed they *can* speak) circumscribed by the 'more important issues pertaining to national or international security (ibid.)? If so, how?

Hansen also raises the crucial question of identity as plural (Hansen, 2000: 287). If we accept Weaver's claim that security is about existential threats and 'survival' of 'self-determined', self-sustained communities, how can one pay attention to multiple identities and to how gender informs other 'self-sustained' communities (Waever, 1995: 53)? According to this logic, gender-specific threats can only be articulated when they are separate from other existential threats, such as those identified by 'self sustained' religious communities (Hansen, 2000: 287). Following this reasoning, we can surmise that rape poses a security problem – and may be securitized – in terms of Mayan women as members of the collective 'women', *or* of the 'Mayan community', but not both. Yet, as introduced in the previous chapter, Mayan women's in/securities crisscross such dividing lines. As I will show in the following chapters of this book, Mayan women's 'naming' of their in/securities – and the attendant constructions of their identities – is informed simultaneously by many different intersecting relations of power and belonging.

In sum, I suggest that the analytical framework for making sense of the relationship between security and identity in Buzan et al. (1998) does not adequately take into account the peoples whose identities are multiple and in flux. Although Buzan et al. are wary of reifying 'we' communities in their analysis (ibid., ch. 2), their focus on self-sustaining communities as constituting the actors in the societal sector may serve to reproduce these entities as somehow sovereign and foundational. Moreover, I suggest that their focus on the practice of security as a speech act largely neglects attention to *how* these identities (institutions, actors), are produced through the naming of security, and the violence imbedded in such practices.

Nevertheless, Wæver's emphasis on in/security, the speech act, as constructed within discourse powerfully discharges the idea of security as a thing, which can be applied to different bodies at different times, and should therefore not be underestimated. Indeed, the notion of security-identity as a speech act proves to be a helpful analytical tool in reading security-identity in the speech-acts (of a sort) of Mayan women's narratives.

I will now therefore turn to an exploration to how the logic of security is delimited by the 'grid of intelligibility' through which sovereignty operates (Connolly, 2004; Marcus, 1999). The following sections of this chapter, however, will return to fill in many of the lines of critique sketched above.

Security and identity

As we will recall, the concerns prompting this book involved the inability of security studies to reflect the multiple harms that Mayan women experience at the confluence of different and competing identity positions, and the manifestations of the paradox of in/security that resound in their struggles for safety. How do particular articulations of modern state sovereignty inform hegemonic understandings and practices of in/security as well as attempts at resisting these practices? Another way of asking this question is: what might be some of the hidden assumptions about people and their being in the world that both underpin the violence that Mayan women experience – and demarcate their struggles for safety and well-being. These questions warrant further reflection as groundwork for reading Mayan women's narratives.

This section of this chapter will therefore consider some connections between security, sovereignty, subjectivity, and identity. I will first argue that security can be seen as a discursive practice, which operates in order to 'secure' the 'subject' of security – usually the state. I will then further probe into notions of subjectivity and identity in order to explore how discourses of danger/safety work in the attempts to secure identity – in sites of resistance, such as Mayan women's narratives, as well as in sites of dominance, such as the Guatemalan state. In short, I propose that security, as we know it, is attendant upon the primacy of state sovereignty as the ordering principle (claim) of politics. This supposition is based on several moves which read as follows (and which I will develop further below). The modern articulation of state sovereignty dictates that the security of the state is paramount. The analogy between individual bodies and states enables a turn whereby the state is assumed to possess 'subjectivity' in a similar way that individual people have subjectivity. Wendt's much disputed claim that 'states are people too' succinctly summarizes the basic assumptions (Wendt 2004). National identity becomes the resulting picture of the (sovereign) subject of the state – a picture that must be secured. If not, then, the state is existentially at risk. The subject of the state as 'real' must then be continually reinforced. This occurs through, among other things, the workings of nationalism, which establishes a hierarchy of identities and a sense of community and belonging among its members.

Much of the initial scholarship examining in/security as a discursive practice has focused on analyzing the state's enactments of in/security (e.g. Dillon, 1990–91; Campbell, 1998; Weldes et al., 1999). Although there has been little work examining security as a textual practice in contesting discourses, the insights proffered by research in dominant sites is helpful in understanding the dynamics of security in sites 'procured as marginal by sovereignty discourse' (Shaw, 2004: 167). These sites, as Shaw points out, are peopled by those like the Mayan women I interviewed, who, instead of benefiting from and assuming the 'necessity of sovereignty' in its modern articulations, 'have politicized it and are seeking to rearticulate it as a terrain of political possibility' (ibid.). The following arguments should therefore also be read as invitations to query further about in/security in the narratives of Mayan women – sites of resistance which both contest and reinvent the logic of securing a sovereign subject.

Sovereignty and the state

Many IR theorists have argued convincingly that sovereignty – commonly assumed to be the possession of the state – informs possible notions of power, security, identity and indeed political imagination.[18] Edkins and Pin-Fat, for instance, refer to sovereignty as a 'master signifier' which provides the 'nodal point' around which 'meaning is articulated' in modern politics:

> ... Subjectivity can only exist, or rather be constituted, in relation to a particular social or symbolic order. The social order itself, is brought into existence, supposed or posited, in relation to a particular signifier, which covers the whole or lack in the social or symbolic order and provides a nodal point around which meaning is articulated. In modernity, one of the signifiers that performs this function, is *sovereignty*. The concept of sovereignty is central to discourses of politics and the international. It informs conventional notions of what political power might be. [...] 'Sovereignty' as a master signifier is not free and autonomous here but stands implicated and embroiled in questions of 'subjectivity' ... Sovereignty performs this task [as master signifier] for the social reality that is taken to be modern politics. (Edkins and Pin-Fat, 1999: 6–7)

The principle or the 'master signifier' of sovereignty inscribes both 'politics' and 'the political'. Politics can be understood as 'the sphere of activity and institutions that is called 'politics', as opposed to 'economics', or 'society', whereas 'the political' 'refers to events in which politics of the first sort and its institutions are brought into being' (Edkins, 2004: 12; Edkins, 1999). Taking the above seriously suggests that sovereignty forecloses possible alternatives to basic questions of subjectivity, ethics, and belonging – and most importantly for the purposes of this book: in/security.

Although sovereignty as a concept certainly has served different purposes throughout history, it is assumed to be the foundational concept/practice for modern political thought, providing answers to questions about power and authority, as well as subjectivity and location (Bartelson, 1995). Sovereignty can be seen as an explanation of who and where we are. It defines the locus of legitimate authority, responsibility, power, identity, and behavior – so much so that the threat of its dissolution becomes a call to action to ensure its continuance at all costs. Sovereignty – especially when reduced to mean state sovereignty – is assumed to be a known, albeit slippery, condition of, and for, modern political life. However, a growing number of critical scholars remind us that, unlike its reified status in the mainstream fairytale (and its reiterations) sketched above, sovereignty escapes distinct definition: It can be seen as a paradox (Connolly, 2004: 23), an 'idiom of power' (Dillon, 2004: 41), as 'simultaneously a principle, and institution, and a practice (Walker, 2004: 242). Sovereignty, according to Walker, acts as a claim about reality (and lives) – as a solution to problems about power and authority, rather than as something somehow real, concrete and present. Sovereignty, working both as an abstraction and a material social form, therefore necessarily changes, 'mutates', reflecting and producing the cultural particularities and discourses of power at play in specific 'modern' societies (Walker, ibid.).

Sovereignty depends upon a notion of a sovereign, cohesive whole subject (be it 'reasoning, political man', kingdom, or nation-state (Edkins and Pin-Fat, 1999; Edkins 1999). As it has come to be understood through the heritage of Western political philosophy, sovereignty signifies supreme (moral) authority. The story reads as follows. A sovereign subject enjoys the capability to know: 'to construct a coherent representation [of the world and what is important in it] that excludes contesting interpretations and controls meaning' through (his) 'word [which] is the origin of truth beyond doubt' (Ashley and Walker, 1990: 261). The promise of transcendence is critical to the idea of the sovereignty. This promise involves the possibility of reaching above, beyond, and outside of the particular limits that frame one's existence. The sovereign is able to see the whole picture – the picture that the sovereign subject defines through 'true' observations and knowledge. The sovereign reasoning man creates language, sets the conditions of knowledge, makes history, and acts as the source of truth and meaning (ibid.). This is also the promise that legitimizes the violence of the modern state (in contract with this reasoning man) (ibid.: 262).[19] From a 'serene and stable context of self-identity' the state is able to discern an undeniable good from an undeniable bad, foe from friend (Connolly, 1991: 19).

In modern political thought in general and IR theories about security in particular, sovereignty has come to be assumed to be synonymous with the state and the international state system. The discursive move from man to state has been one of the central foundations of much theory about the way the working of 'international' political relations function (RIS, vol. 30, n. 2, April 2004; Tickner, 1993). In order to sustain its status as somehow natural, it is important that the sovereign subject (the state) be continually reinforced as 'foundational' and a given (Edkins, 1999: 5). Indeed, the very 'given-ness' of the state is continually reinforced through the expressions of sovereign power (i.e. laws, state institutions, national security policies, borders, the 'sovereign ban', etc., and discourses of danger) that seemingly derive from its status as sovereign.[20] Yet, one could instead see these practices as constituting the state as a subject, thus concealing its construction and contingency; states, as we may recall, are founded, defined and reproduced through violence.[21] For example, the Guatemalan state's security policies designed to protect 'Guatemala' from insurgents involved also enforcing a 'sovereign ban' whereby laws were suspended and 'citizens' killed; these policies aimed to 'secure' certain articulations of the state as given, as inherently sovereign, and concealed the violent historical production and contemporary reproduction of Guatemala as a state at all.

Sovereignty works not only by concealing its violent inception, but through being able to make distinctions between 'self' and 'enemy'. This critical function of modern 'idioms' of sovereign power renders the hegemony of national security policies indispensable. Importantly, the naming of the enemy (and therewith naming the self under threat) is also crucial for clarifying the particular nexus of sovereignty and the attendant understandings of in/security that, as we shall see, resonate in Mayan women's narratives.

Contemporary claims about sovereignty delineate a 'we' with a particular history and locate this community in a somehow naturally ordained demarcated space: the state (Walker, 1993: 154). The relations between university and diversity (inside and outside) are resolved through the drawing of territorial, as well as cognitive borders which delineate self from other (ibid.; Kearney, 1991). The solution of state sovereignty implies an over-riding unity within the geographical territory – the political body – and the individuals within the territory, thus creating an 'imagined community' (Anderson, 1991: 6). As we shall see in Part II of the book, the nation-state is certainly not the only imagined community which is produced according to the above logic. Other communities, such as the Mayan *pueblo*, are constructed through similar mechanism of inclusion/exclusion. Similar enactments of in/security ensue.

Political bodies, so the story goes, similar in form, yet significantly different in identity, reside outside the borders of the community. Thus, the reality of diversity receives a spatial solution in the designation of an internal and an external, in the inscribing of boundaries between an inside and an outside (Walker, 1993).

Political identity is also determined by these spatial locations. The system of nation-states enables man-citizen to be both different from others (as significantly marked by his national identity) as well as connected to humanity at large through the relations between these different, yet contained and ordered identities. Walker further explains:

> As a response to questions about whether 'we' are citizens, humans or somehow both, state sovereignty affirms that we have our primary – often over-riding – political identity as participants in a particular community, but retain a potential connection with 'humanity' through participation in a broader international system. (Walker, 1993: 154)

The story of the sovereign state assures that by ascribing unity to the people within a specific territory, and designating that territory as something natural and rooted in the evolution of history (and through 'forgetting' the violence of its very construction), a stable base for a political community is constituted (ibid.). Through designating this state as the proper home for the nation – or the 'authorized We's' who make up this community – the survival of the state can become conflated with the survival of 'us'. The same logic, as we shall see, resounds in other identity communities, such as the Mayan *pueblo*. According to this logic, the community enjoys a common and particular history – a history with an organic beginning and evolution and an ordained place among (or over) other groups (Anderson, 1991: 7).

Through the gendered kinship ideology of the nation, the citizen's heritage lives on in a predictable future (McClintock, 1993: 66). Gender differences enable a 'unified' cultural identity to look both backwards (to ensure the rootedness and thus naturalness of the community) and forward, to embrace 'tradition', while meeting 'modernity'.[22] 'Man's' resentment against 'his' inevitable demise finds a (semi) solution in the consolidation of political identity in sovereign man as member of the secular nation-state with a nameable past, present, and future in controllable and reliable linear time. Through the reliable continuation of the nation, 'we' need not die. The imagined community thus carves out its place in time, taming the arbitrariness of history, and (partially) overcoming the necessity of human mortality (Anderson, 1991: 36; Connolly, 1991: 18–19). This might help explain why the survival, or seeming security, of the community as such often takes precedence over the survival of its members: the promise of national security, in this sense, also assures immortality.

State sovereignty thus establishes parameters by which we conceive of, and act in, political life. Political identity can be seen as intimately linked to understandings of nation (the many as one) that ground sovereignty. The political identities privileged by state sovereignty (the 'authorized We's') become the legitimate agents and the targets of security policies and theories. In the prevailing security discourse, different in/securities are consequently placed into a fixed hierarchy determined by the over-riding 'existential need' to secure the 'us' which is supposedly represented by the state. However I suggest that the subject of the state elides into *being* 'us' (the nation), which in turn encompasses 'us' (the people). Man-citizen forfeits 'his' sovereignty to the authority of the community in exchange for both identity (as national citizen) and protection from danger – for security.[23] (He maintains, however, authority in the private realm; 'Women-the-feminine' have simply been seen as part of man-citizen-state's jurisdiction (Tickner, 1993). Thus the survival and protection of the state becomes discursively translated into the protection of 'us'.

Furthermore, the primacy of national identity sculpts the meanings we give to other social identities. Surely, a hierarchy of identities with national identity superseding all other identity positions seldom is without friction and conflict; certain articulations of citizenship may involve, and indeed be premised upon, oppression and marginalization from a center of power, (as, we shall see, is the case with the Mayan *pueblo's* relationship with Guatemala). Nevertheless, the hegemonic script written by the logic of state sovereignty implies that one must relate to, and be partially defined by, the fact that one happens to reside within the geographical borders of a state, and one's (gendered) location in that state (Connolly, 1991: 205; Jabri and O'Gorman, 1999: 2).

Despite considerable challenges to the primacy of the nation-state as the fundamental unit of global politics, the nation-state project, as forever becoming, can be still seen as the hegemonic political project of the modern era.[24] The different terrains in which people resist, refute, redefine, and rebuild nations in relation to states make a universalized nation-state impossible (Nelson, 1999; Shaw, 2004). Nevertheless, a dominant imaginary of the nation-state as cast by the story of modern sovereignty persists (Dillon, 2004). This imaginary involves a certain measure of homogenization of the internal community in order to clearly delineate a unique 'we', which is the nation (Jonas, 2000 and Nelson, 1999). Hence despite what might be a 'weak' or 'failing' nation-state project (such as was arguably the case in Guatemala), the need to create a homogenous and over-riding political identity supersedes all other claims to political identity. Subsequently, attempts to 'secure' the nation, arguably, involve violently reinstating a clear hierarchy of identity whereby a particular, and heavily guarded, interpretation of national identity must replace any alternative and competing articulations of identity through national security measures. Similarly, those subjugated by violent or failing projects often attempt to rearticulate sovereignty along the drawing of different lines of inclusion/exclusion as a form of resistance (Edkins and Pin-Fat, 2004). Elena's words which introduced this book eloquently exemplify such moves. As we recall, she warned against the danger of decaying the Mayan culture through the wearing of non-traditional dress.

In the following paragraphs, I will further consider what assuming an identity of 'we' might imply and how the discourses that construct this representation of the subject might work in Mayan women's narratives of resistance, as well as in the dominant narratives of the national security policies that have so threatened their survival. I will therefore turn to an exploration of subjectivity and its relations to identity in order to understand better how the basic logic of modern sovereignty is successfully seductive, and how discourses of danger (and safety) are so powerful and pervasive even in Mayan women's texts.

Representations of being human

As evidenced in Elena's citation above, paying attention to who Mayan women say they are is crucial for understanding how they articulate in/security. Yet, in the dominant logic of security, who 'we' are, is often assumed to be already resolved; indeed the dominant logic of security names identity and subjectivity as 'ontologically prior objects' (Edkins and Pin-Fat, 1999: 11–12). Reading against these assumptions, I suggest that part of the limitations of security (as we know it) can be attributed to the preclosure of the question of who we might be or become. These suppositions can find support in the work of critical theorists who have stubbornly asked questions about the production of subjectivity, its relation to identity, as well as the limitations of our political imagination, and how such limitations affect 'human being' (or 'being human') as well as how we envision in/security (Dillon, 1996, 2004).[25] In the following section I will therefore briefly explore possible ways of understanding the connection between subjectivity, identity and security as necessary groundwork for the reading of Mayan women's texts.

Subjectivity

I am not attempting to arrive at a definition of the subject or subjectivity here. Nor do I wish to sketch an overview of the vast literature that is devoted to querying into the nature of the subject from various disciplinary perspectives (ibid.). The broad understanding I portray here takes its point of departure in a now well-established body of literature that explores subjectivity and discourse as co-constitutive and finds the notion of a sovereign subject, which precedes discourse, as deeply problematic.[26]

Subjectivity in the most profound sense can be seen as ineffable; it cannot be adequately or fully represented or 'spoken' and therefore cannot be secured. Instead, subjectivity can be seen as being in excess or an excess of being (Edkins, 1999: 32; 2004: 12). There is always something left over when a subject is articulated and interpellated into discourse (Hall, 1996). In the body of work known as post-structuralism within IR, a range of scholars have theorized subjectivity and the implications of its 'excess' for politics and ethics.[27] In sum, these theorists largely agree that subjectivity is neither foundational, containable, nor neatly fitted into the symbolic order. Subjectivity is too large, excessive, messy, fluid, changing, contradictory, and unbounded. It is always 'becoming', and therefore cannot be pinned down in a single representation or even a series of multiple repetitions within the temporal confines of language (Edkins and Pin-Fat, 1999: 11; Edkins, 1999: 15).

We can surmise, therefore, that a representation of the subject can never be complete or finished. Any picture (i.e. representation) of the subject that we may compose will inevitably require a frame marking its presence. Furthermore, there are always many different discourses (sometimes contradictory) at play at a certain time. This leads to the notion that a person occupies many different subject positions – that a person has multiple subject positions or even multiple selves.[28] Yet, I propose, no matter what notion of multiple selves we may evoke to capture or stand for who we, as a person or a movement or 'a people' may be, attempts to secure these selves depend on a picture being painted of 'us'. Such a picture demands boundaries and a content that resides within its contours, even if these boundaries shift and recompose themselves.

THE POLITICS OF NAMING: IDENTITY

If the answer to the question of subjectivity can never be complete or satisfactorily represented, identification then becomes the resulting naming – in discourse or language – of what it means or feels like to be a particular human among other humans (Stern, 2004). This is not to say the subject pre-exists the (constructed) identity categories that he/she then 'chooses' to occupy or fill, as it is argued in many 'sociological' accounts of subjectivity (Woodward, 1997). Instead, the picture of the subject gains presence through the process of interpellation and articulation within discourse (Hall, 1996). Identification refers to the naming process of the subject positions called forth to represent the subject – which is, as I have argued above, unrepresentable.

Hall provides the richest explanation of identities that I have found, and I will cite him at length. He explains that he uses 'identity' to refer to:

> the meeting point, the point of *suture* between on the one hand the discourses and the practices which attempt to 'interpellate', speak to us or hail us into place as the social subjects of particular discourses, and on the other hand, the processes which produce subjectivities, which construct us as subjects which can be 'spoken'. Identities are thus points of temporary attachment to the subject positions which discursive practices construct for us ... They are the result of a successful practice of 'chaining' into the flow of the discourse ... The notion that an effective suturing of the subject to the subject-position requires not only that the subject is 'hailed', but that the subject invests in the position, means that suturing has to be thought of as an articulation, rather than a one-sided process, and that, in turn, places *identification*, if not identities, firmly on the theoretical agenda. (Hall, 1996: 5–6)

Following Hall and many others, I theorize identities as constantly being recreated; they shift and change, even instantaneously.[29] In the workings of everyday life, we may move in out of subject positions depending on context. Our/other's representations of these subject positions take form as our identities, which might be quite wide and fluid. Identities can be seen as *an expression of* multiple and constantly changing relationships, orders, discourses: they are a repository, a reflection, a product, as well as (re)creator of our surroundings (Butler, 1990, 1993). Identification, as a continual process, works both in response to material circumstances and discursively (Ferguson, 1993: 161, 175).

Each identity position, such as that of 'woman', is produced out of a confluence, or 'intersection' of inter-relating power relations in a complex and dynamic play of power also imbuing other identity positions (such as 'poor', 'Mayan', 'Guatemalan') with meaning. Indeed, identity must be seen as multiple, hybrid and ambivalent. One's gender, national, class, religious, sexual identities, for instance, are co-constructed out of confluent and even contradictory or competing discourses. The identity category of 'Mayan' therefore cannot just be a complement to that of 'woman', 'peasant', etc. It would be understood as continually reformed in interaction with these other categories, and in relation to the shifting boundaries that differentiate self from Other, marking an inside from an outside.[30] I therefore conceive of the nexus of different mutually constructed and constructive identity positions as *identity constellations* – a term which I use throughout this book. Crucially, I suggest that identity must not be seen as an (albeit constructed or even multiple) add-on to a 'core' subject; subjects are not inherently separate from the identities which serve to represent them. Therefore, it would be a mistake to think of subjects as choosing or being inflicted with an identity – as if they were separate entities. Butler has argued that despite the seeming 'naturalness' of certain identities, they are reproduced through the performance of a script drafted in discourse and defined by relations to an Other, to difference. She explains that 'there is no gender identity behind the expressions of gender; that identity is performatively constituted by the very "expressions" that are said to be its results' (Butler, 1990: 25). Hall explains that 'above all, and directly contrary to the form in which they are constantly invoked, identities, are constructed through, not outside difference' (Hall, 1996: 4).

> Butler makes a powerful case that all identities operate through exclusion, through the discursive construction of a constitutive outside and the production of abjected and marginalized subjects, apparently outside the field of the symbolic, the representable ... (Hall, 1996: 15)

Many theorists within the studies of ethnic and national identity have also focused on the importance of boundaries and markers of difference between ethnic groups: we know who (and where) *we* are depending upon who and where *they* are. Returning to the work of Barth, we find arguments that ethnic identity emerges in relation to an Other against whom one can define who one is (as opposed to who one is not); that 'ethnic groups only persist as significant units if they imply marked difference in behaviour, i.e. persisting cultural differences' (Barth, 1969: 205). This is not to say that that which one may consider as symbols or manifestations of 'culture' and 'tradition' within a group do not exist prior to a meeting with an Other.

Importantly, subjects must invest in the identities into which they are 'hailed into place'. Therefore, despite their fluidity and mutability, we should not make the mistake of believing that the processes of identification are frivolous or arbitrary. When a subject is 'hailed in to place', this place is also where other similar subjects also dwell, and from where other like subjects also articulate their identity. Drawing on Ricoeur, Hekman explains that 'identity is necessarily about sameness and difference; it is about the intensely personal and the necessarily social' (Hekman, 1999: 6). It is also, I suggest, about the promise of safety and security. Indeed, if one were to regard the space between similarity and difference as a binding hyphen (as a bridge which binds one to the other and gives presence to the place in between) then we might begin to see that not only do identity/difference (or inclusion/exclusion) inscribe each other, but similarity/difference are also concomitant, or mutually constitutive.

The meaning given to markers, which help distinguish between the similar and the different, play a decisive role in identity formation. Although these markers can be perceived and deeply experienced as primordial, I argue that they are constructed within discourse, and performed. Hence, even though the significance of the 'marker' of difference, and even the difference itself, may be socially constructed, the power of the indicator of difference usually lies in its being experienced and perceived as given, fixed, natural – especially when much is at stake in identity claims, as was the case with the women who spoke their claims to me (Lindholm Schulz, 1999).

Furthermore, understanding identities as necessarily incomplete representations of a subject which are produced by discourse does not imply that all identities can change easily or quickly, or that they are not deeply imbedded in the histories and experiences of people's lives.[31] Connolly, for instance, distinguishes between entrenched elements of identity, and those less obdurate, warning that it is a mistake to assume that because they are constructed, all identities can easily be changed (Connolly, 1991: 176). Hekman calls for an attention to the 'necessary distinction between the epistemological analysis of identity and the experience of identity in everyday life' (Hekman, 1999: 18). She argues that often the distinction between the 'experiential' dimension of identity and its epistemological analysis become confused. In criticizing Rorty's claim that embracing a non-essentialist position need not be problematic, she counters:

> Individuals do not, in fact die for principles they regard as contingent, much less constructed, fluid, or fictional. On the contrary, they die for beliefs that they know to

> be linked to their deep selves, that are connected to who they know themselves to be. Contingency will not bring me to the barricades. (Hekman, 1999: 19)

Discourses of power determine the assignment of the social and political meaning of the markers of identity (Hekman, 1999: 22). For instance, one can dispute the extent to which race or ethnicity is genetically determined or even the importance of posing this distinction. The significance given to the difference in 'racial' physical attributes however depends upon the matrix of power relations that determine social relations. 'Black' means different things in New York than in Nairobi. '*Ladino*' means different things in Miami than in Guatemala (Appiah, 1992).

Recalling how the primacy of modern articulations of sovereignty delimit claims to political identity, it is not difficult to imagine how markers of identity can become highly politically charged as signs of those who 'belong' within the nation-state and those who threaten the hegemony of (certain articulations of) national identity. Through discourses of danger (as we shall see below), markers of difference can come to determine enemy from 'friend' – and serve as the 'reason' for killing (as was arguably the case in Guatemala's national security policy during the 'dirty war'). How might discourses of danger – both those that placed Mayan women at risk, as well as those which informed their struggles for security – work?

Discourses of danger/safety

In/security can be seen as a discursive practice that operates in order to 'secure' the 'subject' of security: be it 'the state' or 'the culture'. In/security becomes both named and enacted through the working of 'discourses of danger', which discern self from Other (Campbell, 1992; Dillon, 1990–91, 1996). The naming of identity is crucial in this process. Campbell explains, for example, that by 'telling us what to fear', the operations of 'discourses of danger' have been able to 'fix where we are' and even who we are (Campbell, 1992: 195).

In the following paragraphs, I will explore how discourses of danger and in/security serve continually to reconstitute the subject of security through naming the enemy and re-establishing the identity of 'us' in opposition to the dangerous 'Other'. I suggest that the workings of discourses of danger (and safety) are central to the production of the subject of security, as well as the marking of that subject from its various constitutional others. In the following section, I will therefore consider how the dominant logic of security (as inscribed through sovereignty) necessitates and informs such discourses in order to reveal how this logic might be reproduced in the in/security narratives of Mayan women.

In his early work, Dillon draws our attention to how danger, fear and threat are employed in power discourses to secure sovereign identities and to imperil identities that challenge the sovereign subject's hegemony (Dillon, 1990–91). He describes the power/knowledge mechanisms which ensure sovereignty by 'legislat(ing) fear; shaped, disciplined, and civilised by authorised articulations of danger' as an 'in/security discourse' (ibid.: 108). Dillon explains that this discourse is a self-securing process that constitutes legitimate political subjects. Through maintaining the exclusive rights to define the 'enemy' – who is within the realm of politics and who is outside – the principle of state sovereignty controls the definitions of, as well as the use of danger. Therefore, in Dillon's argument, the primacy of the state, and the definition of what 'stateness' means vis-à-vis other states (and vis-à-vis the people and institutions which make up the state) is also assured through what he names the 'in/security discourse'. As is the meaning of the Other.

Within in/security discourses, norms of identity are created through the decision of who/what is excluded. '[I]t is the distinctive competence of the sovereign power (man/Leviathan) to be able, always, to draw the necessary distinction; or else it would not be sovereign [...] sovereignty is the power to invest all circumstances with threat' (ibid.: 108). Dillon argues that Hobbes' emphasis on casting out the stones which do not fit in the 'building of an edifice' is a primary theme in the reproduction of certain political orders: a particular community maintains its salience from the perpetual need to protect itself from different, challenging orders. Notions of threat and survival can become the legitimizing reason for sustaining the order, and can even be seen as constructing the order (Hobbes, quoted in ibid.: 106).

As noted above, the prevailing modern fairytale of in/security rests on a hierarchy of identities where the nation-state and the individual (man-citizen) in contract with the state are seen as rational and legitimate political subjects. The hegemony of the state, and the invested definition of man-citizen, is thus perpetuated. Dillon explains that when read through the lens of sovereignty, Kant's question about the nature of 'man' is translated into 'Who is the enemy?', or 'What must we fear?'; the answer, says Dillon, is: 'the exception' (ibid.: 108).

According to the prevailing logic of security, when a nation-state (ethnic group, or other collective identity category) is threatened from the 'outside', coherence becomes even more crucial for group survival (for the supposed security of the 'sovereign' subject); deviance from the norm is then often considered apostasy. In the face of perceived threat, the explicit 'politicization' of identity provides a more fixed or static representation than those depicted in the identities we assume, transform, and discard in the rhythms of everyday life – a representation that promises to be easier to secure. For example, when politicized, a particular representation, such as that of 'Mayan woman' at the time of the interviews (1995), became a less fluid, more stable picture (although never static) than it might have been before the identity 'Mayan woman' gained a particular political currency in light of the peace negotiations. In the capacity of her 'politicized' identity, this person should (as the story goes) think and act from a relatively stable site – together with other like subjects – in order to achieve certain aims. The naming of in/security – especially when an identity is 'politicized' – is integral to this process.

Edkins incisively points out that the process which is commonly called 'politicization', can actually be referred to as a 'depolitizisation', or an abandonment of 'the political' and an ensuing technologization: the enactment of a script that is no longer open to political contestation, but is rather followed as more or less given (Edkins, 1999, 1–16). The invested identity (and its attendant strategy for being and doing as already decided) is reproduced through continual and varied performances or representations (i.e. the enactment of national security policy or the telling of one's life-history narrative) which further perpetuate the processes of identification. Nonetheless, the option to engage in mimicry and 'ironic' alterations or subversions of the differences that matter must also exist (Butler, 1990; 1993). As argued above, identities can never offer a complete representation of subjectivity and must therefore ultimately always be becoming and never complete.

In the processes of politicization (or in Edkins' terms: 'depolitization'), elites and others making claims based on a collective identity often presume and work towards creating a sense of 'unity' and coherence within the collectivity. This presumption (which, can be exemplified in Elena's words cited above) discourages changes or variance within this identity category. Regulatory practices of locating and naming danger externally in the Other also tame, discipline, and in effect, produce, the 'self'. Dominant claims to identity then act as what Butler calls a 'normative ideal instead of a descriptive feature of experience' (Butler, 1990: 16).

Discourses of danger are then directed 'inwards' as a mechanism for reproducing a 'self': a subject that can be securely named and thereby secured. Deviance may come to be interpreted as disloyal or even dangerous to the political goals of the collectivity (Butler, 1990: 14–15). Established norms become internalized in the workings of society and in the world-view of individuals; members of a collective are expected to adhere to these norms. Power – both 'capillary power' and overt force – ensure the coherence of the dominant identity by making precautionary examples out of the danger of deviance (Foucault, 1980: 39, 78–133). Danger, therefore, resides in any threat to the coherence of identity – to the invested representation of the subject of security. If, for example, the coherent identity of 'man-citizen' depends upon certain norms which regulate its expressions (and therefore the meaning of the 'masculine' national subject) then any deviance from this norm endangers that very identity's right to hegemony and questions its very existence as such (Connell, 1995; Connolly, 1991: 205).

It is surely unsurprising to feminist or post-colonial scholars that the workings of similar in/security discourses to those at play in nation-states are integral to the construction of all sorts of collective identities, including women's movements as well as 'ethnic groups', nations, or religious communities (Jabri and O'Gorman, 1999).[32] The international women's movement, for example, has been riddled with exclusionary mechanisms, which cast certain groups of women as 'outside', dangerous, etc. (Alvarez and Escobar, 1991; Erwér, 2003). Furthermore, feminist readings of 'identity politics' often attest to the inherently violent ramifications of this drive for unity.[33] Many studies have indicated that women's behavior and bodies often become the sites of violent 'border crossings' and 'border guarding' in times of conflict.[34] As we shall see in the chapters in Part II, the 'grid of intelligibility' offered by the notion of a sovereign community often results in women's behavior within the communities being carefully guarded, lest 'foreign' ideas and bodies enter into the community as dangerous viruses.

FOREIGN POLICY

Campbell's play on the term 'foreign policy' is helpful in further exploring how differentiating between self and Other sculpts their meanings, and for considering how such mechanisms play out in Mayan women's in/security narratives. He explains the constitutive workings of discourses of danger and 'in/security' by exploring alternative narratives about US foreign policy. He describes foreign policy as:

> All practices of differentiation or modes of exclusion (possibly figured as relationships of otherness) which constitute their objects as 'foreign' in the process of dealing with them [...] [It] applies to confrontations between self and other located in different sites of ethnicity, race, class, gender, or geography. (Campbell, 1992: 76)

Campbell offers alternative readings of particular moments in the making of US 'foreign policy', explaining how the colonizers of the 'New World' first constructed their identity – as well as the definition of the Other – in the distinction between the native/savage 'Indians' and the civilized/moral selves of the colonizors. Later the defining difference between self and Other were constructed around new distinctions, which followed similar patterns. These categorizations overlapped and were implicated in each other, all sharing a certain mode of representation (ibid.: 145). Importantly, these representations made that which the legitimate, moral, correct, sane, and familiar compared with and fashioned itself against. Campbell explains:

> The construction of the 'foreign' is made possible by practices that also constitute the 'domestic' ... one of a range of practices that make up the discourses of danger which serve as 'art of domesticating the meaning of man by constructing his problems, his dangers, his fears' (ibid.: 69).

Hence, ironically, the regulative practices of the discourses of in/security and danger compose both a necessary complement and a menace to the dominant identity in the forming of an Other. Like Campbell, Connolly remarks that if difference and the drive to identity are inevitable, and if the claim to a natural or true identity is always an exaggeration, then:

> a powerful identity will strive to constitute a range of differences as intrinsically evil – as other. It does so in order to secure itself as intrinsically good, coherent, complete, or rational and in order to protect itself from that other that would unravel its self-certainty and capacity for collective mobilization if it established its legitimacy. This constellation of constructed others now becomes both essential to the truth of the powerful identity and a threat to it. The threat is posed not merely by actions the other might take to injure or defeat the true identity but by the very visibility of its mode of being as other. (Connolly, 1991: 65–6)

Parker et al. explore this doubleness, emphasizing how the formation of national identity relies on binary oppositions such as the creation of the self of the nation in relation to the others who are not us. 'Nations are forever haunted by their various definitional others' (Parker et al., 1992: 5). Read through this light, Nelson's claim that 'struggles over culture and history, over modernity and tradition, and over Mayan and national identity articulate the state, modify its identity and penetrate the apparent boundaries between state and civil society' take on even more meaning (Nelson, 1999: 76–7).

As denoted by the term 'in/security', that which threatens is integrally part of that which is to be rendered safe and acts as the 'constitutive outside' to the subject being secured. Whether implicitly, or explicitly, what is on the inside not only implies what shall be defined as dangerous, but more importantly, what shall be kept at bay, excluded, as the 'outside' (Pin-Fat and Stern, 2005). Thus, the significance of the presence of the threat is integral to the composition of the subject. Explicit discourses of danger, such as those enacted in times of war and violent conflict to secure the state, serve to veil this constitutive dynamic by casting the 'outside' as inherently evil, and the anomaly as deviant. The enemy, the dangerous, the excluded, serve as the 'constitutive outside' to the establishment of the subject of security, and the safe, the included. Hence, following this logic, discourses of danger must also be seen as discourses of safety or: danger/safety (Connolly, 1991: 64–5).

Crucially, as Hekman reminds us and as we shall see in Mayan women's narratives, the regulatory practices of discourses of danger would not work if people did not believe in their identities as integral to who they are – individually and as members of a collective (state, nation, etc.) – so much so that many are willing to 'not so much to kill but to die for these limited imaginings' (Anderson, 1991: 144). Norms are established not only by what is excluded, but also by imitation of that which is included. Power resides in the authority and legitimacy to establish and maintain these norms, and gains legitimacy from the drive to adhere to these: to be like others, feel attached, belong and feel safe. Anderson ascribes this phenomenon to a love for an interest-less and pure brotherhood and horizontal comradeship (ibid.: 144). Muppidi refers to the need for people to recognize articulations, and affirms the dual process of producing insecurity 'imaginaries' through 'interpellation and articulation' (Muppidi, 1999: 123–5). He explains that people (or the public) must accept the systems of meaning being presented by those who are doing the 'imagining' in order successfully to reproduce security imaginaries. The public must then also engage in mimicry of the 'imagining' (much like in Anderson's nationalism), thus reproducing the meaning of security proposed, and presented as 'natural', and the identity as rendered 'safe'. Hence, highlighting the drive to be similar to others may shed light on the overwhelming potency and attraction of identity politics as a venue for safety. Identity politics' promise of safety might be as especially tempting to peoples who are marginalized and alienated in the societies where they are living. This promise, we shall see, figures as a central organizing theme in Mayan women's discourses of danger/safety. Furthermore, I suggest that this promise is integral to the continuing perpetuation of in/security as paradox.

Through many of the mechanisms described above, in/security discourses give substance to political subjects in marginal as well as dominant sites. When the boundary lines between the 'inside' and the 'outside' (the dangerous and the secure) blur, and the difference between the self and the other diminish, discourses of danger/safety reinstate the crucial dividing lines which promise a secure identity – that is, ensure the security of a subject. The assignment of 'foreign' threat pretends to safeguard the identity of the community in question. Dominant identities are therefore fashioned, in part, as a response to the danger/threat implied by difference. Similarly, marginal identities are, in part, constructed for the Others by groups in power in order to secure their own dominance and legitimacy (i.e. to imbue their identity with meaning). Yet, as noted above, contesting discourses do not simply present mirror images of identity, which give presence to the subject of reflection; As Butler has taught us, repetitions leave room for difference as a form of resistance (Butler, 1990; Nelson, 1999).

Resistance?

> The taking place of power also circumscribes the space of the possible for political understanding and political being as well as for a regime of rule. Such a space of the possible is what we might call a political imaginary [...] Like every idiom of power, sovereign power provides a 'grid of intelligibility' for why power is ordered as it is, how it is to be enacted and passed on as well as why it should be obeyed. But again, like every idiom of power, expressions of sovereign power are themselves subject to changing grids of intelligibility ... imbricated with other grids of intelligibility. (Dillon, 2004: 42)

Throughout this chapter I have argued that despite a move away from an eclipsing state-centrism, the articulations of modern state sovereignty delimit not only how in/security is understood, but also how it is practiced. Perhaps most importantly, through unpacking some of the processes through which the dominant logic of security is produced and reproduced I aim to reveal how highlighting the very 'constructed-ness' of in/security, identities and indeed subjects, might give students of security entry into how the violent conflicts fought in the name of identity politics and security are produced, and hint at how they could be produced differently.

In light of the above, I propose that Mayan women's in/security narratives – as contesting discourses – can not occupy a place 'outside' (nor do they reside purely apart from) the masculine-dominated discourse of nation-state security, thus offering a new model or point of entry into unearthing true or somehow better strategies for offering safety. Their in/security discourses can be seen as 'codes of intelligibility' that are indeed contesting but that necessarily include relations to the Guatemalan nation-state, as well as to myriad of other locations such as *Ladino* society, and to 'men'. Mayan women's in/security discourses are also constructed out of the dominant logic of security and political imaginary circumscribed by modern state sovereignty. Hence, not only are Mayan women's experiences of insecurity and struggles for security informed by the specific political context of the Guatemalan state, but their narratives are constructed in relation to dominant understandings of what is politically possible.

Yet, Weldes et al.'s attention to the 'internal contradictions and lacunae' in discourses offers a venue for locating possible strategies for resistance:

> The fact that cultures are composed of multiple discourses or codes of intelligibility, and that the world therefore can be and is represented in different, often competing ways, has significant implications. In particular it means that any representation can potentially be contested and so must actively be reproduced. Meanings are not given, static, or final; rather, they are always in process and always provisional. The production of insecurities thus requires considerable social work – of production, reproduction, and possibility of transformation. Dominant discourses must constantly reproduce themselves to answer challenges to their constructions of the world and their identifications of those insecurities worthy of a response. Defining security and insecurity requires considerable ideological labor. Contesting discourses, in turn, attempt to re-articulate insecurities in ways that challenge the dominant representations ... In addition, discourses themselves are not perfectly coherent but always entail internal contradictions and lacunae. (Weldes et al., 1999: 16)

As we have seen, through unpacking the sedimented relations of power imbedded in the often uncritically accepted building blocs of modern politics, critical interventions have steered the course of security studies away from blindly accepting as natural the conception of in/security that follows the logic of state sovereignty. Importantly, such work has cleared space for addressing the contingency and hybridity of in/security-identity constellations and their constructions in contesting discourses (Jabri and O'Gorman, 1999: 10). If taken seriously as valid texts of politics, both contestations and rearticulations, such as Mayan women's, remind us of what has been left out – kept at bay, excluded – from dominant readings of security (such as multiplicity and hybridity). As Dillon reassures us, grids of intelligibility mutate, change and indeed are open ended. Although 'sovereignty remains central to the political imaginary of the modern', the modern must not be seen as forever determined, and therefore doomed to repeat its injuries into infinity (Dillon, 2004: 46).

The following chapters of this book are devoted to looking into the lacunae and contradictions of in/security and its relations to identity that Mayan women's narratives offer. More precisely, I will explore the marginalized and dissident discourses of danger/safety that organize the narrator's texts. Through my reading, I will attempt to denaturalize secure representations of security and subjectivity in these narratives as well as in those that they challenge. My intention is to explore the hybridity and contingency of the representations of in/security and subjectivity that compose these discourses in order to open up terrains of meaning and enable thinking of in/security differently. Through this reading, I hope to reveal some cracks in the security imaginaries that perpetuate the violence which harms Mayan women, and which perpetuates the paradox of in/security as we know it which resound in their texts.

Notes

1 See e.g. Dillon (1990–91, 1996); Campbell (1992, 1999); Edkins, Persram and Pin-Fat (1999); Sylvester (1994); Walker (1993).

2 This is based on the 'classic' understandings of 'security' in the international state system. See e.g. Bull (1977); Carr (1939); Morgenthau (1973); Walt (1991); Waltz (1979).

3 The term *pueblo* in Spanish means people, nation or even village. In this context it connotes a strong sense of cultural and political belonging.

4 In his ground-breaking book, Buzan (1991) discussed security in terms of 'levels' of analysis. Although he maintained that nation-state security was indeed paramount, Buzan's work was important in displacing the absolute centrality of military state security in IR thinking. In his more recent work, the state has given way (at least ostensibly) as the ultimate site of security; instead, he and Waever argue for analysis at the 'regional level' (Buzan and Waever, 2003).

5 See e.g. Brundtland (1987); King and Murray (2002); Falk (1995), Imber (1994); Security Dialogue (2004).

6 The 1980s saw an expansion of writings on 'alternative security', in policy circles as well as academia, e.g. Brundtland (1987); Palme Commission (1982).

7 Walker discusses the notion of the 'subject' of security in Krause and Williams (1997: 78).

8 See fn. 4, 5 (this chapter) and fn. 6 (chapter 1).

9 See Albert et al. (2001); Lapid and Kratochwil (1996); Jabri and O'Gorman (1999) for a discussion of culture and identity in IR theorizing. Huntington's notion of the 'Clash of Civilizations' is also worth noting in this context (1998).

10 See fn. 4, 5 (this chapter) and fn. 6 (chapter 1).

11 Walker argues that such a move does not proffer seriously rethinking 'about political life that is somehow different from the one that they assume to be in place within and between modern states' (Walker, 2004: 369).

12 Bouta and Frerks (2003); El Bushra (2003); El Jack (2003); UN Security Council Report 2004 (S/2004/814).

13 See fn. 4 (chapter 1).

14 Another example of the universalization of the 'universal' can be found in feminist accounts of the discourse of human rights. The notion of human rights rests on a notion of the 'human' that masquerades as universal, yet which is built on a particular 'picture' of humanity (see Pin-Fat, 2000 for further exploration of this point. See also Fraser, 1999; Peterson, 1990).

15 See also Pin-Fat (2003).

16 See Lister (1997) for an excellent feminist critique of 'citizenship'.

17 For a critique of Wæver's notion of society, see Hoogensen and Rottem (2004); McSweeney (1999); Shaw (1994).

18 See Walker and Mendlovitz (1990); Bartelson (1995); Edkins, Persram and Pin-Fat (1999); Edkins, Pin-Fat, and Shapiro (2004).

19 Sylvester describes the gendered history of sovereignty through a rereading of the realist heroes Machievelli, Hobbes, and realism's 'sweetheart' Morgenthau (Sylvester, 1994: 81–2). See also Tickner (1993); Youngs (1999: 3).

20 Following Georgio Agamben, Edkins and Pin-Fat call attention to a critical distinction between sovereignty as 'synomonous with sovereign statehood' and sovereign power. Sovereign power, they argue, involves 'grammars of power and resistance, irrespective of the site or sites in which they are located' (Edkins and Pin-Fat, 2004: 3).

21 'The foundation of authority can not rest on anything but itself, that it is violence without a ground [the grounds constituted in the *coup de force*]. Although the multifarious discourses surrounding the state that invoke its name and declare its purpose give the appearance of simply reflecting a reality awaiting apprehension, such discourses in actuality constitute that reality, for when pursued, the forces of authority upon which these discourses rest can be considered 'mystical'. In consequence, the founding moment that institutes the law, a constitution, or the state involves an interpretive and performative force, a *coup de force*' (Campbell, 1999: 24). See also Pin-Fat (2005).

22 Women often act as the guardians of tradition and the transmitters of culture. See Yuval-Davis (1997) for an excellent discussion of these processes.

23 Peterson's feminist reading of the state/man's 'protection racket' provides another take on this seemingly reasonable exchange (Peterson, 1992: 49).

24 A detailed discussion around the differences between states, nations, and nation-states lies outside the scope of this book. See e.g. Eriksen (1993). For further discussion of how nationalism, national identity, and ethnicity are gendered constructs, see e.g. Anthias and Yuval-Davis (1989); Anzaldúa (1987); Jayawardena (1986); Kandiyoti (1991); Moghadam (1994); Peterson (1994); Radcliffe and Westwood (1993, 1996); Trinh, T. Minh-ha (1989); Wilson (1992); Yuval-Davis (1997).

25 See also Edkins and Pin-Fat (1999); Edkins (1999); Jabri (1998); Jabri and O'Gorman (1999).

26 Foucault (among others) has taught us about how discourses of power/knowledge construct subject positions and the subject of a particular discourse. (Foucault, 1980). See also Butler (1990, 1993).

27 See Edkins (1999) and Edkins, Persram and Pin-Fat (1999) for an excellent overview of this work.

28 Ferguson has coined the term 'mobile subjectivities' to portray a representation of the multiple (and even contradictory) subject positions/identities that a person 'has' (Ferguson, 1993).

29 Butler (1990, 1993), Eriksen (1993) and Hall and du Gay (1996) offer excellent accounts of the processes of identity formation.

30 The identity 'Mayan-women' can therefore be seen as 'hyphenated' (see p. 205 for a further discussion of this). However, throughout this book I write 'Mayan women' separately, without the hyphen marking the linkage between the identity positions 'Mayan' and 'women', because this is the way the Mayan movement (and many of the narrators) write it (see also Anzaldúa, 1987: 77 and Ferguson, 1993).

31 When addressing the question of choice and agency, it is helpful to recall Butler's analysis regarding the possibility of agency (Butler, 1990: 142–3).

32 See fn. 24.

33 Ibid.

34 Systemized rape in wartime whereby the enemy uses women's bodies as vessels for the marking of their trespasses is just one of the many manifestations of the specific 'role' allotted 'the feminine' in struggles between different communities. See Niarchos (1995).

3

Reading Mayan women's in/security: a framework for analysis

> Narratives select episodes of life and mark them in time: before, after, again, and so on. These episodes are then rearranged, not necessarily in historical order, but to tell the most coherent story about what life felt like. The narrative aims at life verisimilitude, not historical truth. In this way, narrative gives us back the feeling of continuity in life. They tame *chronos*, make the passage of time seem familiar and tolerable, and make us feel coherent along this infinite dimension. (Stern, 2004: 6)

IN THE PREVIOUS CHAPTER I argued that identity and security were concomitant and that in/security can be seen as a discursive practice, which is necessarily contested, and constantly being reproduced and reconstructed. Through the naming of danger and threat (and safety and well-being), discourses of danger (safety) inscribe the meaning of both self, and other, thus re-establishing the subject of security.

Taking seriously the above arguments implies certain directions of inquiry: for instance, asking what in/security means for Mayan women must also involve, at the very least, asking what in/security means in terms of the identities they located and named. It also means exploring how they speak of the interwoven systems of power relations that informed their lives, how they name threat and danger as well as safety and well-being – exploring the very multiplicity or hybridity of their in/security.

In this chapter I will discuss how I undertook this challenge, and make visible my methodological framework for reading Mayan women's in/security. As noted in the introduction, this book addresses how in/security is represented in the discourse of eighteen politically active Mayan women during the period June–October 1995.[1] My intention here is to reveal the methodological scaffolding upon which the subsequent analytical chapters rest. I do this for two mains reasons: first, I aim to offer the reader tools with which better to understand the context of both the narrators' words and my analysis; second, because the study of security has traditionally focused primarily on the state and the relations between states, it has presented little discussion of methodological tools for studying other subjects – especially silenced or marginalized ones. By explaining the groundwork upon which I built my analysis, I intend to invite others to make use of the methodological underpinnings of my study.

In order to comprehend how the narrators were situated and whose voices might resonate in their testimonies, I will first briefly give an account of the basic context in Guatemala. I will then explore the Mayan movement and the main points of the Mayan(ist) discourse at the time of the interviews before I turn to my methodology for reading their security narratives. I will then briefly outline what the narratives are about before turning to a description of how the narratives were written. Next I will address *how* I perceive the content of the narratives, as well as explain my method for reading in/security in the texts. I will conclude with a brief discussion on some of the ethical conundrums posed by my research.

Historical background

The term 'Mayan' served as a unifying pan-identity, which included twenty-one different, more local ethnic identities. The Mayan people reside in an area of Central America that spans four countries: Mexico, Belize, Guatemala, and Honduras. The modern-day Mayans share a common culture and spirituality. Language and clothing mark the differences between the different ethnias. Besides Spanish, twenty-one Mayan languages are spoken; these can be divided into six main language groups.

Guatemala boasts by the far the largest percentage of its population as Mayan. Most estimate that the indigenous population (mostly 'Mayan') comprised 55–70 percent of Guatemala's entire population in the 1990s. However, the assessment of how many indigenous lived in Guatemala is a highly charged question. Mayan activists tended to cite the larger proportions, while the Guatemalan government claims that only 43 percent of the population is indigenous (thus keeping the numbers below 50 percent.)[2] The category of 'Mayan', which can be read as a site of resistance against the violent national project, has only recently been included in contemporary accounts of the political-economic situation in Guatemala. In this sense, one can surmise that 'Mayan culture', as it is understood today, has been fashioned since the late 1980s and narrated differently by divergent factions.[3]

Despite their numbers, the Mayans of Guatemala have historically been marginalized and repressed by different regimes since colonialization. For centuries, hierarchical power relations between those who were considered *Ladino* and the indigenous population characterized social, political, and economic life in Guatemala. Guatemala's recent history features a '*Ladino* state', where an insidious and violently overt racism pervaded society. The dividing lines between *Ladinos* and Mayans, however, were porous and blurry; they therefore became even more politicized in attempts both to homogenize the population on the part of the army/state, and to make political claims based on cultural identity, on the part of the Mayan *pueblo*. How directly the indigenous culture had been inherited from the ancient pre-Colombian Mayan civilization is still a point of contention among anthropologists, archeologists, and historians. Towards the end of the 1980s, the Mayan of Guatemala (and in the rest of Central America) increasingly saw themselves as belonging to the same culture that existed before the invasion of Columbus. In the political conjuncture of 1995, the social boundaries between '*Ladinos*' and 'Mayans' became increasingly politicized and marked.

Between the years 1960–96, an insurgency–counter insurgency 'civil' war officially took place in Guatemala. Together with the legacy of colonialism and US imperialism, the brutal policies of the 1980s to the early 1990s formulated and institutionalized a modern society largely characterized by killing, fear, oppression, poverty, and crime. During the thirty-six years of civil war, violence served the interests of national security and national identity.

Throughout the insurgency, the guerrilla forces were based in the rural poor, mostly indigenous populations. However, a portrayal of the uprising as 'ethnic' or indigenous misrepresents both the initial impetus of the conflict, and the identification of the warring parties. For example, a large majority of the Guatemalan foot soldiers and civil patrollers in the indigenous-dominated regions were indigenous, as were many of the *guerilleros* (guerilla soldiers) (Nelson, 1999: 81).[4] The revolutionary movement, however, never upheld any form of equitable representation or distribution of power between *Ladinos* and Mayans, nor did it adequately take into account the specific needs of the indigenous communities (Jonas, 1991: 69, 140). Within the literature on the history of the conflict, there seems to be a dominant consensus that *Ladino* intellectuals from Guatemala City who espoused Marxist ideology led the original revolutionary movements. The initial struggle was articulated in the language of class-based revolts (Jonas, 1991: 67–8). It was not until the salience of the Mayan movement became apparent that the umbrella organization of the different popular fronts, the Unidad Revolucionaria Nacional Guatemalteca (UNRG) formed in 1982, appropriated ethnic identity as a central source of their demands (Jonas, 2000: 23–4).

The indigenous population, although obviously partial to the parties in the conflict, was often placed in the middle between the two sides, frequently being forced to affiliate with one side or the other (Schirmer, 1998: 35–80). If one did not actively and explicitly join the Civil Patrol Units (PACs) or the army (often under force), then the army would accuse them of supporting the guerillas, and either kill them or force them to inform on their '*compañeros*' (CEH, 1999; Martínez de Leon, 1994: 46; REMHI/ODHAG, 1999: 120–1; Schirmer, 1998:

45). General Gramajo (head of army operations in the Alteplano 1982–82, and important player in the military during the counter-insurgency war) stated in an interview regarding the indigenous population: 'They were between two fires ... and we made them choose sides' (Schirmer, 1998: 38).[5] Some also claim that the guerillas used similar tactics, although arguably less systematically and less violently (CEH, 1999; REMHI/ODHAG, 1999: xxxii, 9).[6]

Despite its relative inactivity in the organization of the guerilla movement, the 'counter-insurgency state' during the civil war years perceived the indigenous population as inherently subversive (Jonas, 1991: 128). The Guatemalan army/state and the ruling economic coalition subjected the indigenous peoples to genocidal aggression and economic, social, and cultural oppression.[7] The ruling elite of the Guatemalan state defined the indigenous population as inherent threats to the nation ostensibly because of their role as a popular base for the guerillas – and because their identification with their 'ethnic' group challenged national unity, if not militarily, then symbolically (Schirmer, 1998). The most recent, and perhaps, most directly violent attack on the indigenous people occurred during the late 1970s and early 1980s when the Guatemalan state conducted a major counter-insurgency campaign. Part of the counter-insurgency campaign involved homogenizing Guatemalan society and 'wiping out' those aspects of indigenous culture that threatened the need for a cohesive nation-state project (Jonas, 1991; 2000; Schirmer, 1998). The in/security discourse of the state identified the Mayan *pueblo* as *foreign*, as enemy of the state. *Ladino*ization included both the army's tactics during the most violent years (e.g. massacres, and the construction of 'model villages') and the more surreptitious destruction of the manifestations of Mayan culture (e.g. institutionalized discrimination, such as education policies).[8]

This campaign was aimed at destroying the Guerrilla's popular base. In actuality, this meant killing the peasantry – the large majority of which was indigenous – and destroying both their cultural and economic resources. Schirmer explains that 'Rios Mont [the president who came to power through military coup] in his weekly television sermon, called for the need to surgically excise evil from Guatemala, and 'dry up the human sea in which the guerilla fish swim' (Schirmer, 1998: 45). She explains that in the 'scorched-earth' campaigns:

> As in every counter-insurgency war, the primary objective of this scorched-earth campaign ... or '*La Pacification* (The Pacification) for short – was to separate and isolate the insurgents from the civilian populations ... The searing contradiction of the scorched earth warfare, though, is that in order to accomplish this 'separation' certain areas are targeted for massive killings: that is the military must treat the civilians they are to 'rescue' *as though they are combatants*, killing and burning all living things within the 'secured area'. No distinction is made between combatant and noncombatant; separation is purely rhetorical. Nor are killings accidental 'abuses' or

> 'excesses'; rather they represent a scientifically precise, sustained orchestration of a systemic, intentional massive campaign of extermination. (Schirmer, 1998: 45)

Since the 1980s, the army sustained sophisticated destabilization programs (with the help of the United States) through, for example, the installment of model village programs and forced PACs (Martínez de Leon, 1994: 46).

The developments in Guatemala must also be seen in light of a generalized politico-military crisis in Central America (and US Cold War-driven involvement) as a geopolitical region (Garcia, 1991). The 'threat' of communism (and ensuing economic consequences should communism 'win') led elites in Guatemala as well as their bedfellows in the US to support a hard-line counter-initiative against 'subversion'. As the regional military crises calmed in the early 1990s, the certainty of war, repression, and poverty in Central America was followed by the uncertainty of regional consequences of the North American Free Trade Agreement (NAFTA) and domestic political reform. The early 1990s therefore saw a continuation of the violence, although at a diminished level, as well as widespread poverty.[9]

'The central social characteristic of Guatemala during the 1980s (and into the 1990s) remained increasing concentration of wealth amid pervasive poverty' (Jonas, 2000: 27). By the end of the 1980s almost 90 percent of the people in Guatemala were living below the official poverty line and two-thirds were living in extreme poverty (unable to afford a basic minimum diet) (ibid.: 28). Jonas also established that the disparities between rich and poor rank among the third highest in Latin America. At the end of 1980s, it was estimated that 85 percent of women in the rural areas were illiterate, and that the largest 2 percent of Guatemala's farms covered 67 percent of usable land, while 80 percent of the farms only used 10 percent of the land (Jonas, 1991: 178). Jonas explains that these figures became even more exaggerated when applied to the indigenous population and to women. A 1998 UNDP study 'revealed that only 10.5 percent of the indigenous population lives above the poverty level, in contrast with 26 percent of the *Ladino* population' (ibid.: 183, cited in *Prensa Libre*, 13 October, 1998).

In sum, during the civil war, the Guatemalan government/military/economic elite – the 'ruling coalition' – claimed a monopoly over the definition of threat to the state, and over the meaning of *Guatemalidad* (Jonas, 1991: 92–4). According to nationalist in/security discourse, national security threats encompassed any subversive activity (Gramajo Morales, 1995: 99–106). This included seeking economic alternatives to feed oneself, organizing around demands for land to grow one's crops, and seeking the whereabouts of a loved-one's body who had been 'disappeared'.[10] Through naming, and attempting to eliminate these dangers, the Guatemalan state attempted to ensure its own agency and subject position. The state existed as a political subject, in part, through its monopoly over legitimate definitions of danger – and, of course, through the ability to protect this power through force (Campbell, 1992; Dillon, 1990–1).

Leaders of the Mayan *pueblo* sought to counter these nefarious forces, and wrote their own counter-narrative and in/security discourse. In this story, the *Ladino* society posed a threat to the Mayan *pueblo*. Safety to the *pueblo* lay in protecting its most significant currency: its culture. Ironically, however, in many cases the leaders had explicitly to recall the culture in order to preserve it. Many Mayan cultural activists sought to find the 'real history' of the Mayan *pueblo*, as well as its relation with colonialism, and more recently, the Guatemalan nation-state project. Attempts to 'rediscover the true Mayan roots' blossomed. Resisting meant preserving. The threat of 'losing' ones culture made preservation that much more politically loaded and important.

As part of the peace process, both the URNG (the umbrella Guerilla movement) and the government signed the Agreement on the Rights and Identity of the Indigenous Population (ARIIP). The ARIIP forged significant new paths in the history of Guatemala, and in indigenous-*Ladino* relations, reflecting the growing salience of the political identity of the Mayan *pueblo*. Furthermore, the accord provided the Mayan *pueblo* with an internationally recognized document that validated critical and highly charged *collective* demands on the Guatemalan state. Among those rights stipulated were access to land, educational reform, political regionalization and decentralization based on cultural and economic criteria, and *specific rights of indigenous women*.[11]

During the specific time of the interviews (June–October 1995), the insurgency war, although severely diminished in scope, continued, as did counter-insurgency tactics at all levels of society. Despite a civilian government, the military and the leaders of the private sector continued to share control of the country. Nevertheless, they themselves were also troubled with competing factions (Schirmer, 1998). The 'dirty' war no longer terrorized the majority of people who lived within (and were forced to flee) Guatemala's borders to the extent that it did in the late 1970s and early 1980s. This period at the final stages of the peace negotiations offered a unique moment in Guatemala's history, when there was a definite change in the political climate – a 'democratic opening'. Those who had suffered the heritage of over thirty years of armed conflict, counter-insurgency tactics, and unjust distributions of resources, saw the prospect of peace and substantial social transformation as a real possibility. Hence, people whose voices of resistance that had been (almost) successfully silenced during the bloodiest period of the civil war began to reformulate their demands and to tell their stories in light of their visions of a better future (Jonas, 2000: 232).

The Mayan movement: discourses of 'Mayanism'

> Our struggle is to recuperate and further develop our values, strengthen our identity, and to make people recognize our rights as Mayan people. (*Majawil Q'ij, El Nuevo Amanecer*, 1995)

Following the symbolically important political moment in 1992, a growing number of people who had previously been identified/identified themselves as indigenous (or even *indios*) adopted the identity 'Mayan' as a unifying identity.[12] Certainly, those who were considered/considered themselves to be indigenous did not placidly accept the violence and subordination of colonialism and racism since 1524. However, a pan-Mayan movement marked by a shared identification as Maya was a modern phenomenon closely linked to the context of the 1980s and early 1990s. Many began to celebrate the subject position Mayan as both a source of pride and a basis for political rights for a growing movement which included many sectors of civil society. Identifying oneself as Mayan provided a way to subvert the injurious racist discourses that included *Ladinos* as valid members of society, yet excluded *indios* (Nelson, 1999: 152). The 'recovery' of the ancient Mayan identity offered a counterweight to the destruction wreaked by colonialism, including contemporary racism (classism and sexism). This recovery of tradition was a central organizing theme in the dominant discourse of the Mayan movement (formulated by the leading 'elite', who were mostly men).

Although a recognition and articulation of cultural discrimination became increasingly widespread in the early 1990s, Mayan cultural organizations, leaders of popular movements and individual intellectuals were decisive in opening space for redefining indigeneity – and consequently for reassessing the identity, *Ladino*, as well as Mayan. The pan-Mayan movement was supported to some extent by non-indigenous intellectuals and non-governmental organizations (NGOs), as well as many in the international community. Certainly, these claims were not unique to indigenous peoples in Guatemala; they reflected similar processes throughout Latin America and elsewhere (Díaz-Polanco, 1997; Ivison et al., 2000). Increasing attention to indigenous demands globally were reflected in forums such as human rights NGOs, the United Nations, and the International Labour Organization (ILO) convention 169. There was a marked general shift away from the integrationist policies characteristic of earlier decades, to favor instead issues such as pluralism, autonomy and political representation. The prominent role of the international discourses on universal human and specific indigenous rights, in turn, influenced and strengthened local and national indigenous struggles. Increasingly, indigenous organizations related to an international community of similar concerns, where the agenda was globalized and communicated through new networks and media (Ivison et al., 2000).

While the Mayan movements articulated the pan-Mayan and pan-indigenous identities that emerged since the 1980s, these referred ultimately back to the local identities. Being Mayan was still primarily to be, for example, Chimalteco, the community with whom one shared life-world and cultural identity, yet also to connect oneself to a growing political project. These communities were no longer seen as homogenous and egalitarian, but as characterized by differences not only in class, but also in religious and political affiliation.[13] Nevertheless, the Mayan communities, situated in their specific landscape, were still recognized as the source and homestead of collective identity, social belonging and culture.

The narrators explained that people identified themselves primarily with a certain ethnic grouping, such as the Kakchiquel, and that they adopted the term 'Mayan' often as a political stance.[14] The identity, Kakchiquel for example, signified the organizing parameter in the people's lives. Being Kakchiquel was taken for granted, a self-identification, a 'natural' explanation for the ways people ordered and lived their lives (the ways that *tortillas* should be made, the colors of the *traje*,[15] the language they spoke, the customary ways one saluted elders, the connection to *their* land etc.). Kakchiquel became a conscious political site in the adoption of Mayan as an over-riding political identification in the particular historical context in 1995. However, being a Mayan woman was not a matter of simply adopting a political or ideological stance; instead, one's (gendered) identity was deeply ingrained in the rhythms of everyday life and memory – as well as the boundaries between the *Ladinos* and the Mayans.

The Mayan movement can be coarsely broken down into two main factions: first, Mayan socio/cultural movements made up of the cultural and educated elite; and second, the popular/political movements made up of both *Ladinos* and Mayans but driven by mostly Mayan peoples. The narrators all (with the exception of Elena) worked in the popular movement, as opposed to the cultural movement. The main differences between these two categories lay in the prominence of the 'cultural' aspects of the organizations' claims, and in the social/economic status of the movements' leaders.

The Mayan cultural movement placed the 'rescuing' of the ancient Mayan culture as its highest and most urgent priority. Through refinding and revaluing their culture, the problems that the Mayan *pueblos* faced would be solved. 'The politico-scholarly agenda of the Mayan cultural activists [was] based foremost on regaining at least partial control over scholarly and popular representations of the Mayan people. They sought "control over the representation of culture and history", which would enable change in the political and economic make-up of Guatemala' (Fischer and Brown, 1996: 3). Mayan cultural activists placed high on their agenda a revitalization of language as the crucial vector of Mayan identity. Language was essential to cultural resistance, and was the most important tool in combating the dominance of *Ladino* society in the context of a colonial state (Bastos and Camus, 1993).

The Mayan cultural movement was largely driven by Mayan academics, such as anthropologists and linguists. These leaders resented the representations of the

Mayan *pueblo* and the history of Guatemala that Western academics articulated. Most abhorrent was the view (presented also in the 'standard' book *La Patria del Criollo* (Martínez Peláez, 1994)) that Mayan (or even Indian) identity was a product of colonialism (Nelson, 1999: 130). Also repugnant was the 'constructivist' extreme, positing that Mayan identity represented a mirror image of *Ladino* identity, constructed solely in opposition and resistance and far removed (if linked at all) from the ancient Mayan civilization. Mayan cultural activists spoke of '*Ladino*ization' and 'assimilation' as lethal threats to the Mayan *pueblo* – threats that have existed in different forms since colonial times. Common understanding among Mayan cultural activist was that the Mayan *pueblo*, although certainly 'contaminated' by Spanish/*Ladino* influences, managed to maintain its 'roots' for 500 years. These roots nourished the modern struggle and, if cared for properly, the Mayan *pueblo* would rebloom into its former eminence. Identity, according to this view, was imbedded in a large process over time, not a construction in the present (Bastos and Camus, 1995).

The popular movement began articulating its demands and claims in terms of cultural (ethnic) identity in the late 1980s and early 1990s as the national and global discourse of identity politics, and specifically indigenous rights pervaded. (This also conjoined with the celebration of '500 years' of resistance.) Primarily made up of 'political' organizations aiming to combat socio-economic injustice and rooted in the experience of 'the Violence',[16] the organizations of the popular movement worked for human rights, the location of those 'disappeared', against impunity, torture, forced recruitment of PACs, and so on. Activists analyzed the Violence as deriving from a larger system that maintained socio-economic injustices. Mayan identity, although linked to the past, was also deeply imbedded in the Violence and experience of being poor peasants ('*campesinidad*'). Especially after 1992, the popular movement adopted much of the discourse of the Mayan cultural movement, although there remained tensions and divergent articulations of the focal point of the most urgent issues (Bastos and Camus, 1995; Jonas, 2000).

Despite a committed attention to the political and economic realities of the Mayan *pueblo* (and other disenfranchised groups, i.e. *campesinos*, refugees, victims of violence, widows, etc.), many organizations within the popular movement explicitly articulated their demands in terms of ethnicity. They repeated the discourse of the Mayan cultural elite, with slight alterations. Although a rescuing of the Mayan culture was paramount and would certainly lead to the re-establishment of the grandness of the ancient Mayan civilization and the complementarity of the Mayan cosmovision, salvaging the culture must occur within the context of the immediate political and economic situation of the *pueblo*. Therefore, for instance, leading *campesino* organizations represented the struggle for just land distribution as crucial to the existence of Mayan culture: the Mayan *pueblo*'s identity as 'people of corn', relations with nature, spirituality, and so on. However, the struggle for land was also situated in the subsistence needs of the people and the history of violence and oppression. Slogans for one of the most vocal and influential *campesino* organizations' national congress in 1995 read as follows: 'The salvaging of the Mayan culture and the struggle for land is the struggle for life and peace!' 'Our ancestors told us, "These lands are yours!" For the recuperation of Mother Earth, the struggle continues!'[17]

Despite the popular movement's alterations, the Mayan cultural elite still dominated in rewriting the dominant discourse of the umbrella Mayan movement. Demetri Cojti, perhaps one of the most prominent Mayan cultural leaders of the time, paints a picture of the Guatemalan state as one of 'internal colonialism', where *Ladinos* dominated and profited from the exploitation of Mayan culture by treating it as 'folklore'. Cojti countered the assumptions he believed guided the *Ladino* society's representations of Mayans. For Cojti, the Mayan *pueblo* must lift forward its unique cultural heritage as a counter to 'cultural mixing' and the homogenizing designs of the state – cultural genocide (Speech at '*Foro sobre Identidad Nacional*', Avancso, 1995; Fischer and Brown, 1996: 21). Salvaging, studying, and teaching in Mayan languages was the primary key to cultural vindication. Also crucial was political representation and autonomy, juridical reform, and Mayan-influenced development for a redefined Guatemala.

Nelson argues that Mayan cultural elite, like Cojti, advocated identity-with-a-difference. The Mayan discourse refuted, subverted, and reinscribed sites of subordination to become sites of pride and cultural promotion. She explains:

> It is precisely at the sites of enunciation of power that hybridity proliferates and where the Maya are working. Right where state-colonizer identity was most insistently repeated, the Maya repeat with a difference: what was meant to fix (ladinoize) is being used to fix or hold on to Mayan culture [...] I suggest that it is in the very sites meant to render indigenous people 'fit' (to fix them, or make them *Ladinos*, to 'fit in' to the homogenizing nation-state) that Mayan identity is partially produced, is being repaired. (Nelson, 1999: 143–4)

History, memory and tradition became resistance.

In 1994, both movements converged in working towards executing implementation of the ARIIP through the establishment of the Coordination of Organizations of the Maya People of Guatemala (*Copmagua*) (Jonas, 2000).[18] The leaders of *Copmagua* stated the following:

> We find ourselves in front of a new national political conjuncture, which enables a possibility to initiate national plans for the construction of conditions which will bring us to the conformation and direction of a pluricultural, plurilinguistic, multiethnic, democratic, state. To permit the full implementation of the decisions and participation, with identity, rights, and proposals of each one of the *pueblos* that live together in Guatemala. In this way, the state will stop being oppressive, dictatorial, racist, discriminatory, elitistic and, above all, monocultural and ethnocentric. (*Copmagua*, 1996)

Other organizations also bridged the divide between cultural emphasis and political goals. *Majawil Q'ij*, for example, was one organization at the forefront of the Mayan cultural-political conflux.[19] *Majawil Q'ij* also housed the *Defensoria Maya* and the *Defensoria de la Mujer Maya.*[20] Its leaders participated in the umbrella Mayan organization of the popular movement, *Instancia de Unidad y Consenso Maya* (IUCM) (Coordination of Mayan Unity and Consensus).[21] A pamphlet published by *Majawil Q'ij* can be seen as representative of the analysis of most Mayan/popular activists on the eve of the signing of the Peace Accords and the prospective implementation of the ARIIP. *Majawil Q'ij* drew connections between the 'blood' spilled by the Violence of the recent war and the Mayan *pueblo*'s history of suffering and resistance:

> It is a history that has already left a track of blood, suffering and death. However, in our vision for the future, we will follow the heroic example of our grandparents. Their fight and resistance, made in the midst of great adversity, created for us the space to build and develop our life as a *pueblo*, to rescue our culture, reinforce our identity, and assert our rights. (*Majawil Q'ij*, *El Nuevo Amanecer*, 1995)

The pamphlet provides the framework of an analysis and a program of action that comprehensively links the destruction of the Mayan culture with violence and discrimination against the Mayan people: 'The reason for resistance and fight is the Spanish invasion ... resulting in the death of our people and the destruction of our culture.' The *Ladino* society/state/Spanish have 'divided *pueblos* and land, changed [the Mayan's] respect to mother nature ... changed our values and way of thinking, changed our honesty, brotherhood, sense of community, life unity'. *Majawil Q'ij* calls for a program of action: 'To our Mayan brothers we invite you to walk together to build the unity of our Mayan *pueblo* and of our Guatemala ...'

In particular, the 'role of Mayan women in the transmission and development of Mayan culture' is underscored:

> For us, the Mayans, the woman does not just refer to a human being, but also to Nature is our mother, the earth is our mother ... The corn gives us life ... history comes from corn, culture, identity ... During the last 5000 years, Mayan women have been the principle defender of our identity, the Mayan culture ... Mayan women respect and care for Mother Nature. (Ibid.)

It concludes with a representation of the Mayan struggle as an effort to 'develop and reinforce our Mayan identity, educate our children to use, read, and write our languages, weave our culture, teach the history and the values of our Mayan *pueblo*'.

Mayan women's in/security narratives

The narratives analyzed in this book should be read in light of the overarching 'Mayanist' discourse depicted in the above paragraphs. More specifically, the eighteen narratives I consider in the next chapters could be read as representative of a (then) emerging marginalized discourse within the Mayan/popular movement in Guatemala – a discourse which was borne out of the 'dominant' one and yet one which was emerging from Mayan women themselves. These narratives are not, however, representative of all Mayan women's experiences of in/security. Furthermore, although much of the political claims and representations of identity which make up the main discourse resonate in the narratives of the Mayan women I interviewed, their testimonies are personal stories of the development of their political consciousness, how they made sense of their past and how they had come to be who they were at the time of the interview.[22] In the following paragraphs I will address these narratives – how I frame them, how they were constructed, and how I read them.

This book is based on partial life-history interviews with members of the most widely known and influential nationally based organizations, as well as internationally, (as in the case of Returnee organizations). During these interviews, I asked the narrators to tell me about their 'struggles as Mayan women', to tell me their partial life story around this theme.[23]

I read the narrators' texts as representations of in/security discourses through which the subject position, 'Mayan woman', is created. Mayan women's own accounts attest to how dominant discourses (such as those at work in the triple oppression they struggled to resist) attempted to 'hail' them, *as* 'Mayan women', into place – a place of multiple subjugation, vulnerability, and danger (Hall, 1996: 11). In more concrete terms, this means that many of the narrators attest to experiencing a host of dangers, discrimination, and limitations because of the meaning given to '*being*' 'Mayan women' in the various contexts of their lives. The violent in/security policies of the Guatemalan nation-state project (i.e. which, during certain periods, define 'Mayan women' as inherently subversive and dangerous) therefore emerge as signifiers in the narrators' text, as do discourses of racism (i.e. which name 'Mayan women' as being dirty, stupid, etc.) sexism (i.e. which define them as subservient to men) and classism (i.e. which name them as worthless laborers without rights to land). Crucially their accounts also refute these subjugated positions and instead craft a different 'place' – one of resistance, pride, and safety.

As representatives of the Mayan cultural movement warned, it would be a mistake to assume then that Mayan women's investment in, and politization of, their triple identity simply mimics the relations of power enacted by dominant discourses (or presents a subversion of them). They also reflect the narrators' individual attempts to invest in the subject position, 'Mayan women', which is, *in part*, produced by the Guatemalan national security discourse, and that of the emergent Mayan movement, as well as many others. The identity 'Mayan women' also clearly resonates with the lived experiences of the narrators' lives. The narratives that were inscribed in the interview process are therefore sites of 'performance' *as well as* negotiation and resistance (Butler 1990, 1993).

Given these framings, I have explored Mayan women's articulations of in/security by analyzing their narratives about their processes of politicization, about their coming-into-being as political subjects. Although certainly I am theoretically motivated (as I argued in the previous chapter), my focus on Mayan women's accounts of their processes of identification as a venue for studying their in/security is also largely borne out of listening to the ways they express their in/security and their struggles (*as* Mayan, as women, as poor). Focusing on political identity becomes especially salient when one takes into account that the narrators' struggles were explicitly articulated in terms of identity. The central role that the ARIIP played in the formulation of Mayan claims in the peace process attests to the centrality of identity in the dominant Mayan discourse and certainly resonates in the texts of the narrators.

As I discussed in chapter 2, politicized identification connotes a (temporary) fixing of a subject position in order for an individual/group to create a stable basis from which to make political claims. In the following chapters I analyze the narrators' specific attempts to 'pin down' their in/security in the story of their struggles as Mayan women. Such 'pinning down' (i.e. the spoken words transcribed into a legible text) can be seen as 'subjugated knowledges' of, among other things, relationships between in/security and identity (Milliken, 1999: 243). I argue that identities are formed through (among other mechanisms) the discursive naming of in/security, and can be seen as attempts to pin down a subject in order to secure it. Similarly the subject of security is named, called forth, or 'hailed into place' through the process of naming danger and threat, as well as safety and well-being. Hence I deem that the in/securities represented in these texts are intimately bound to the 'insertion' or 'articulation' of the identity 'Mayan woman'. I therefore focus on the ways in/security is invoked, as a discursive practice, in the subjugated discourses whereby people called Mayan women are 'sutured' to the subject position, 'Mayan woman'. My ambitions are therefore not to speak *for* Mayan women or to generalize from the discourses of identity-in/security, but to pose some questions around in/security-identity from reading their narratives as valid texts of global politics.

As this book is based on the life-history narratives of the Mayan women I interviewed, I will now turn to *how* I constructed a base 'narrative', or 'text' which could offer a representation of Mayan women's voices and which could be read as an in/security discourse.[24] Understanding the process of inscribing the in/security narratives is important for contextualizing my analysis of the narrators' words, as well as the conclusions I draw from reading their texts. The following section will therefore address my methodological tools, how I frame these texts, and briefly recount the process of conducting 'field work' during which I (co)created the in/security narratives.

Creating a security text

In preparing for the fieldwork, I conducted research on the popular movement in general and the women's and Mayan movement in specific during several initial trips to Guatemala. With this knowledge, I was then able to select key organizations (thirteen) that represented the immediate positions and interests of the Mayan women acting politically in the Guatemala civil society (excluding party politics) in Guatemala City. Primarily, I worked within the popular movement, and those cultural organizations that also considered themselves part of the popular movement, or that also bridged the divide between the popular/cultural movements.

The common denominator in all of the interviews was that the narrators explicitly identified themselves, and acted politically as, Mayan women. I attempted to include members of the most widely known and influential nationally based organizations. The organizations, considered collectively as making up the popular movement, could also be classified as human rights organizations, peasant organizations, Mayan cultural organizations, women's associations around specific issues, and women's returnee organizations. These organizations were not comprehensively representative of all the interests of Mayan women, or even politically active Mayan women. I focused on those organizations that represented the main interests articulated in the 'official' discourse of the Mayan popular movement. People who worked within the popular movement *explicitly* related their struggles in some way to the ramifications of the violence of the civil war, thus indicating that they would also address some of the issues 'traditionally' addressed by security studies in IR (thereby also enabling a comparison and challenge to conventional wisdom). This choice was clearly problematic, as it involved inevitable exclusions. Yet this book does not pretend to be representative. In light of this, I will make visible some of the choices I made.

The people I interviewed were leaders (some regional, some national) in the thirteen different organizations.[25] Few of the participants occupied the highest rung in the organization. Often, they were members of the National Board. Several were specifically responsible for women's issues within their organizations.

Each of the organizations had a base of some sort, even if the extent of the base varied greatly.[26] Initially I had planned to interview two women from each organization: one from the base and one leader, but after becoming more acquainted with the context, I realized that the differences between the two were enormous. My language limitations (most rural indigenous speak their local languages) made communication difficult. The women from the base were also much less explicitly politicized than those women in leadership positions, who were in a position to represent the most prevalent discourses of the Mayan women working in the Mayan popular movement. Furthermore, the research process itself (see below) demanded that those participants whom I interviewed twice could read the transcription of the first interview. Rarely could women from the base of the organizations read and write down their comments or corrections. This provided yet another limitation on the selection process, and certainly bears mentioning given my discussions on the silent voices unable to 'speak security'.[27]

As this study was not intended to be representative of the organizations' work, my focus was on the narratives of the people whom I interviewed, not on the organization itself. Of course, because I contacted them through their capacity as leaders in an organization and made it clear that I was interested in their struggles as Mayan women, much of their personal testimony was informed by their political involvement, as well as circumscribed by my questions. The collusion of political rhetoric with personal experiences became the subject matter of the narratives and the 'material' upon which my work rested.

The first interview

Once I had established contact, I met with the participants to explain to them in more detail what my project was about and what the interview process would involve. I gave each participant a brief written (in Spanish) project description and explanation of the research process. I then explained orally in more depth, also attempting to communicate who I was, where I came from, and what I was planning to do with the interviews.[28] I addressed any questions, doubts or fears, assuring the narrators that they would have complete veto right over their words.

I began each interview by asking the participant to tell me about her experiences and struggles as a Mayan woman. In most cases, the participant steered the narrative herself; my interjections (I tried to make as few as possible) were often requests for clarification. The first interview lasted between one to three hours. After the interview, I gave a copy of the transcribed document to the participant.[29]

Because my intention was to gain a better understanding of the multiplicity of Mayan women's in/security, I addressed the different in/securities the narrators evoked in relation to the different spheres and moments that structured their narratives. *I therefore read the narrative in terms of its main organizing spatio-temporal contexts*, such as the home/family, the Mayan community, the *Ladino* society, their organizations, the political economy, and the Guatemalan nation-state. I also noted the different power relations (mechanisms of inclusion-exclusion), which were articulated in the narratives (e.g. racism, nationalism, classism, sexism) in the different contexts, as well as how they seemed to inter-relate. My intention was to lay the groundwork for comprehending *how they articulated in/security in relation to different contexts, as well as in relation to different relations of power*. I also read the narratives in terms of their 'nodule points' identifying organizing oppositional relations that I found in the narratives, such as education-ignorance, sickness-health, childhood-adulthood (Doty, 1996).

The second interview[30]

After explaining my intentions for the second interview, I asked the narrator if the contexts I identified were accurate or if others were more or equally important. We read the document together and I raised questions. I often asked for the narrator's evaluation of an interpretation of mine, to elaborate, or to talk about a particular theme that may not have arisen. Frequently, I asked her to tell me a little more about the contexts in her text: i.e. things that harmed her, hurt her and things that made her feel good or gave her a sense of well-being.[31] Sometimes, I asked specific questions around these contexts, such as: 'Can you tell me a little more about what life was like inside the family ...?'

Finally, I asked her how she felt reading the testimony, how the things she talked about had influenced who she was at the time of the interview as well as her struggles. I concluded by asking if there were anything she would like to add and about restrictions on use of the document, change of name, places etc. and what she thought of the research process. The narrators received a copy of the transcribed second interview when possible. Thereafter I treated the text as if it were any other citable document. I did not consult the contributors in my citing (or translation) of their words.

In the above paragraphs I have recounted how I (co)created the texts upon which I base my analysis of the narrator's in/security. Yet what such a text *is* need not be clear-cut. How one views, and therewith analyzes, a text or a testimonial narrative depends upon ones ontology as well as epistemology. Is a text a description of, or a producer of, 'reality'? The answer to this question bears with it a host of implications, including, for example, how one views the insecurities/threats articulated in such a text. However, instead of delving into a detailed discussion on different ways of viewing a text, in the following paragraphs I will explain briefly how I perceive the security narratives which emerged form the interviews and upon which I base this book.

Narrative: 'storied lives'[32]

Like all narratives, I understand life-story narratives to be meaning-constructing activities, instead of meaning-preserving ones. When one constructs a story about ones life, events become meaningful through the act of narrating. Events certainly meant certain things when they were experienced; however, the process of making connections, of developing a plot (or many plots) in a narrative of one's life fashions new meanings to these events, meanings that make sense within that narrative and that 'make us feel coherent' (Stern, 2004: 6). Yet, importantly, since the meaning given to 'coherence' is culturally contingent, that which makes sense as a plot in one context might not in another.

The spoken story must also be seen as inscribing not only the narrative, but also the self/subject as character in the narrative, and the narrator. As work within psychology has suggested, we continuously construct mini-stories that interpret our actions, thoughts and that which occurs around us during the course of each day (Stern, 2004). The narratives that we tell ourselves (our interpretations) often occur even before we carry through an action. The continuous interactions between interpretation and event make it almost impossible to separate the two. Hence, living life and narrating life can be seen as integrally related and interdependent.

Furthermore, the act of narrating occurs in a particular political moment, which crucially informs the story told – as well as the subjectivity of the teller.[33] The stories the narrators tell are built around making sense of their personal lives and choices within the framework of a certain context. Their stories constitute a counter-hegemonic move – an act of resistance – against the violent totalitarianism of the Guatemalan state, racism, classism, as well as an act of resistance against sexism both within their communities and in society at large. They may also be an attempt to validate their struggles in a global context. Hence, the personal accounts of the narrators' process of politicization were written at the intersections of many competing discourses: i.e. those of Guatemalan National Security, the dominant Mayan movements; the emerging Mayan women's sections; the women's movement, etc.

For example, in instances where the narrative is about marginalized experiences and lives, it constitutes a political act that can challenge dominant and oppressive readings of these lives. The narrative, although partial and contingent, may serve to destabilize hegemonic and homogenizing discourses by calling attention to difference. In more concrete terms, this may mean that, for example, one narrative (e.g. Andrea in chapter 5), maps the politicization of an 'ancient' Mayan identity and discredits the Guatemalan military's assertions that the Mayan claims to political identity are dangerous subversive ploys, and thus effectively challenges the military/state's monopoly over 'reality' and over in/security. Her narrative challenges the notion that difference is only deviance, and celebrates 'difference' as a viable political alternative. Andrea's narrative, like many others, was also written in light of the discourses of power that framed the particular moment of the telling of her story; i.e. those that placed me as a white-North American-privileged-academic in the position of 'researcher' and the narrators in the position of 'researched'. These discourses also 'hailed the subject position' into place in different ways.

Yet, acknowledging the different discourses that circumscribe the narrators' stories does not foreclose that the Mayan women whom I interviewed were also the active authors of their stories. As noted above, they embraced particular and explicit political agendas. The texts were thus also motivated by specific political goals and the individual's investments in the subject position they articulated. Security concerns, personal trust, as well as political aims, were all significant factors in the construction of their stories – and crucially, 'the narrators' as textualized subjects of these stories. Furthermore, our different locations on matrices of power relations as well as our 'personal' rapport determined how they narrated their stories to me and what discursive moves they employed. What they included, excluded, as well as the structure of the narrative was decided (in part) by who they thought I was, what they wanted *me* to know, what they wanted me to tell *other people*, and who these other people are, in addition to what they *did not* want me to know. Because I provided each of the narrators the opportunity to censor their texts, they explicitly reflected over how they wanted to represent their stories. (One narrator even asked me not to cite or refer to her text – except in the manner I am doing here – after having read its transcription, out of fear for the repercussions for herself and her family.) I clearly stated that I was interested in their life stories in order to learn about the connections between security and identity through hearing about their struggles, and the stories they told me were directed by this guiding theme.

Moreover, those who narrate their life stories often speak to a specific audience besides the researcher. For example, one narrator, Delia, concluded our interview with the request that I sell in Sweden the handiwork that she and the women in her community produce. It appeared to me that she was preoccupied during most of her interview with the prospect of selling *huipiles* (blouses) to me. Her hopes of procuring a market for her work and therewith a possible livelihood strategy surely informed the story she told me. Furthermore, some wanted their names to be used, others not. Some wanted me to make their testimonies available in research archives in Guatemala, others did not.

Remembered stories

Life-history narratives, such as those relayed to me, necessarily rely on memory. In relaying a memory to another person, the narrator places the memory into a narrative schema, a framework for meaning that can make sense to the listener, as well as to one's self (Ricoeur, 1990; Stern, 2004). The form of narrative surely influences not only the structure of the memory, but also what is remembered. Furthermore, memory within the narratives is constructed in the moment, and thus, also subject to the power of discourse. Writing on memory and totalitarianism, Passerini explains that:

> Remembering has to be conceived as a highly inter-subjective relationship ... Memory is the tool we have in order to give meaning to our lives, if we understand it in the sense of an inter-subjective (or inter-human) word that connects different generations, times, and places. (Passerini, 1992: 2)

Hence memory (and thus remembered stories) are as much a part of the present as they are a part of the past. They are also shaped by expectations for the future (ibid.: 12). A (partial) life story is therefore not one story based on a string of memories that depict 'reality' as the individual experienced it at the time. The memory of these experiences is constantly reconstructed out of the context and the telling.[34]

Memories can also be embodied – both in the individual body, which experienced pain and in the body politic (Green, 1999; Nelson, 1999; Scarry, 1985; Zur, 1998). Understanding Mayan women's remembered stories therefore entailed studying the political moment in the particular interview situation, as well as in the larger context of peace negotiations after around thirty years of armed violence in Guatemala. As Edkins explains:

> Memory is not an object that we can abstract from social processes and that we can study, analyse or observe. The production of memory is a performative practice, and inevitably social ... individuals don't compose their memories, or at least they are not entirely in control of the compositions. Publics are not either. It is only the person as social being that can remember. Remembering is intensely political: part of the fight for political change is a struggle for memory. As Milan Kundera puts it, 'the struggle of man against power is the struggle of memory against forgetting'. (Edkins, 2004: 54)

In the same way it is difficult to draw exacting borders between one individual's life story and those of the collective, it is difficult to distinguish the individual's memory from those in her immediate surroundings, as well as those of the collectivity at large. Memories are circumscribed by dominant discourses; personal memory is part of public memory. Hence, the memories of the Mayan women I interviewed are enmeshed with the collective memory of the ethnic group, the Guatemalan national project, world history, in addition to the particular political context of the moment of the interview situation.

In studies of ethnicity and nationalism, scholars have underscored the importance of a common history for the fostering of feelings of group belonging and identity (e.g. Lindholm Shulz, 1999; Eriksen, 1993). Collective memory becomes a powerful tool in this process. As noted above, the common history of the Mayan peoples played a leading role in Mayan women's narratives, as well as in their memories. The political goals of re-enforcing their Mayan identities (which resonate with the claims recounted in the description of the Mayanist discourse above), and their identities as women cast a special light on the memories of their lives. Memories of the experiences of oppression, fear, and joy in the rituals of everyday life, for example, are placed into the very 'real' framework of the narrative context. They become, among other things, testimonies to a past of oppression and a hopeful future of justice for the Mayan *pueblo*.

Also addressing totalitarianism and memory, Sherbakova argues that as the wave of previously forbidden memories about a totalitarian era gains momentum, 'it begins to seem as if everything [the narrator] know[s] happened to them personally' (Sherbakova, 1992: 113). Intersubjectivity between 'personal' and 'collective' remembering can thus confuse an outside listener as to what belongs in one life story as opposed to another. However, notions of 'individual' subjectivity can include the 'subjectivity' of the collective; hence, the difference between one person's experience and the group's may lose significance (Salazar, 1991). The Guatemalan military, for example, may have physically tortured one person's mother, but in doing so they also tortured all of 'our' mothers.[35]

Memory can be seen also as a threat to the cohesiveness of both individual and collective identity. Memories of torture for instance, can serve as a powerful act of resistance against oppressive discourses – especially those as insidious and violent as those maintained by the Guatemalan military/state (REMHI/ODHAG, 1999; Rigby, 2001; Torres-Rivas and Arévalo de Leon, 1999). Such memories could pose a dangerous threat to the state if interpreted as a challenge to the idea of the state as a benevolent and inclusive project, or as fighting a just war against communist rebels. Similarly, memories that challenge the idea of a common history for the ethnic group may threaten the identity of its members and the political project(s) of the group as a whole (Arias, 2001).

The above discussions lead me to conclude that not only are there many 'subjects' in the texts of life histories, but there are also many co-authors of this text. In fact, it may even be difficult to neatly separate the subjects of the narrative from its authors. For instance, the narrating subject (i.e. Rosa) who spoke with me is necessarily a different subject than the textualized subject ('Rosa') of her narrative. Hence, it would have been impossible for me to be able to understand the person I was talking to as she lived her experiences. I was only privy to the interpretations, the meaning-giving narratives, of these experiences and feelings that she shared with me. A narrative recalling a memory is the closest one can come to being privy to another's experience. A memory may not be 'reality', but it can be considered a verisimilitude (Bruner, 1990, Stern, 2004). Furthermore, the frames delimiting the constructing of narrative and indeed lives, however, are not static and are subject to multiple readings.

However, a focus on the discursive, constructed character of stories, or lives, does not deny that people *really* live, experience threat and harm, or safety and well-being. We act, experience, and live, but the meaning we give to our actions is continually constructed within a web of different discourses. Similarly, we as subjects are continually reconstructed or reinscribed through narrative and representation. I suggest that the naming of security and insecurity is a crucial discursive move in this process. Importantly, however, a textual treatment of in/security is not intended to preclude attention to, or to call into question, the very real terror and danger that Mayan-women experience; instead it is intended as a means by which to claim Mayan women as also valid subjects of security.

Identifying and reading 'in/security' in the texts

Given the theoretical framework addressed in chapter 2, reading in/security in the narratives of Mayan women poses some tricky methodological challenges: viewing in/security as a textual practice which produces the subject of security through the naming of danger and threat implies that the 'definition' of in/security must be contingent and open, and can only make sense in relation to the text. How could I address in/security in Mayan women's texts without relying on an established definition of both security and insecurity? I argued in the previous chapter that dominant representations and practices of in/security close off terrains of meaning, obscuring from view the vulnerabilities and harms experienced by many people in precarious positions. Closure and definition can be seen as inherently violent. Since my intention is to unsettle such imperial moves through revealing disruptions and resistances in Mayan women's security narratives, basing my reading on a fixed or essentialized notion of in/security would defeat, or seriously impede, my intended purpose.

In order to be able to address in/security in these texts, surely, one needs a method for 'reading' in/security especially since the narrators do not talk about security *per se* except in a very narrow sense. For instance, the word 'security' (*seguridad*) means often freedom from threat from the state/military/death squads; that they 'leave us in peace'. The word 'threat' (*amenaza*) is often used to connote specific and physical danger having to do with life and death which has a definite source (e.g. the death squads). When I asked one narrator how/if she felt insecure, she responded: 'No, I have not received any threats this past month.'

Weldes et al. address this tricky problematique. On the one hand, scholars criticize the 'naturalization' or 'essentialization' of security as being almost exclusively tied to the state and crafted out of statist discourses. On the other hand, they may resist employing any definition at all to particular contexts, for fear of treating them as 'natural facts' instead of 'mutable social constructions' (Weldes et al., 1999: 20–1). They seem to be able to accept an *analytic* assumption of given-ness of actors for the purposes of a certain analysis, but refute the *ontological* assumption of given-ness of subjects or their insecurities.

I have addressed this dilemma by relying on an open-ended definition of security for the purposes of my analysis, and by resisting the tendency to reify either identities or their insecurities. When looking at other security discourses (i.e. the dominant and alternative ones in IR, as well as the Guatemalan state's), one can discern that *insecurity has to do with danger, threat, harm, and the peril involved with change and openness. The security of someone/thing refers to its safety, its well-being as well as to its limitation, its stability in order to assure its safety.* By adopting a working modality of security, I do not intend to create a new and improved model or definition that could be used universally; instead I reject the supposition that the referent objects, the sources and the specific content of in/security exist outside of specific discourses.

When reading the narrator's texts, I depend upon the loosely defined 'security modality' above with which to identify discourses of danger. In this sense, I have pinned down in/security in the broadest terms and left the assignment of referent objects, agents, recipients, etc. to be determined by the texts, to be formed within Mayan women's discourse. As Crawford and Lipchutz state: 'What does the term security mean? The answer quite clearly depends on the object to which the condition refers' (Krause and Williams, 1997: 151). For instance, many of the narrators talked of discrimination in the different contexts of their lives. I read their identification of discrimination as also a naming of threats and danger/harm – as a source of insecurity. This modality has been refined through learning from the narratives as well as looking closely at other discourses of in/security.[36] Furthermore, there is little point in talking about Mayan women's in/security if there is no common reference point between meanings of security. In assuming the language of security, I also place an analysis of the narrators' texts within the frames of reference that make up the study of security in global politics.

When reading the narratives, I organized them in terms of the common *spatio-temporal* contexts noted above. Explorations of in/security within these contexts later became the distinct chapters that follow. The nodule points I identified served as organizing themes throughout these chapters. Specifically, I focused on the following general questions in each context:

1 In what ways are definitions of in/security tied to identities in the text? Who/what connotes safety/danger and who/what needs safeguarding? How are self/Other relations articulated, and differences addressed?
2 How/where do the narrators name/locate their in/security? How do processes of interpellation and articulation of their identities converge with the naming of in/security through discourses of danger/safety?

These questions provide the basis for the reading of in/security and the attendant identity constellations in the narratives that make up the body of the subsequent chapters of this book.

Delimitations

Education was a theme that carried great weight in the majority of the narratives. The very magnitude of this theme implies that it should be addressed more fully than possible within the framework of this book. I will therefore not focus specifically on this theme in this book, but will, nonetheless, introduce it here as it runs through the different chapters in Part II.

Many of the narratives were organized around the narrators' studies. Education represented a passport out of a truncated life, and towards the possibility of participating in Guatemalan society on equal footing. Education promised access to power and knowledge – the tools with which to better ones life and to become 'somebody' in the eyes of the society in which the narrators were living. The mastery of Spanish, the language of power, allowed for a voice in society. Learning a trade enabled one, perhaps, to better one's economic situation and help provide for ones family. Education was the way to avoid fulfilling the stereotype of 'stupid *india*'.[37] Access to education therefore provided an opportunity for the narrators to attain a certain standard of well-being and status, which would perhaps protect them from the injuries that being a poor, uneducated, indigenous woman in Guatemala involved.

The official academic plan of the Guatemalan state was designed, in part, to create 'citizens' of Guatemala. These citizens were to belong to the Guatemalan national project and accede to the symbolic order of political identities imposed by the state, where a hegemonic view of national identity superceded all other possible subject positions (Avancso, 1995; Cojti Cuxil, 1991). This symbolic order also defined the sphere of threat, the realms of danger, and the enemies of the population at large. Learning the official history of Guatemala provided the narrators with an authorized story. Ironically, being Mayans forced to assimilate into a racist educational system, they also were provided a chance to challenge this story and reclaim history, language, culture and security through the rewriting of history, the wearing of *traje* in the school, and the writing down of languages.[38] Hence, being excluded from education was considered a strike of doom for the Mayan people in general and for the narrators; accessing appropriate education was named as a venue for safety.

Doing research in a post-colonial context

In doing research of any kind, and, in particular, research *on* others, there is always the problem of a starting point. Feminist literature emphasizes the importance of theorizing from women's lives, of not fitting women or other marginalized groups and their experiences into the already formed molds of theory. One can learn surprising things, and disrupt existing theories that purport to explain 'reality', from grounding an inquiry in an 'empirical' material that is otherwise silenced or expunged from the authorized subjects of research. If nothing else, such research prompts the recognition that alternative accounts may exist and that dominant discourse requires hard work to sustain a semblance of naturalness and closure. Mayan women's in/security constellations serve as reminders of the dangers involved and the harm implicated in dominant attempts at closure. The disruptions that their texts imply also offer apertures for resistance.

Yet, can I suppose that my very intention of conducting feminist research that aims to consider marginalized voices immunizes me from exploiting my research subjects? Many post-colonial scholars address central questions about power and discourse in their writings about colonialism and its implications for the construction of both the West and 'the rest'. In particular, feminist 'post-colonial' scholars have aided in bringing to the theoretical fore relations of power imbued in the representations of 'Third World women', and the exoticized, native, Other in Western/Northern discourses (even supposedly emancipatory ones – e.g. many feminisms).[40] Often even well-meaning representations of the 'South' repeat the power relations of colonialism through different, 'modern', yet insidious modes of violence and exploitation. Many attempts to 'give voice' to the oppressed of the world thus re-present the South as mere (inferior) reflections of the North and turn it into not much more than another self-reflective narcissistic look in the mirror (Clifford and Marcus, 1986: 13).

In research geared towards 'giving voice' to marginalized groups or even exploring marginalized discourses, the benefits of providing a space for people who are not able to 'speak for themselves' has been often mistaken for sufficient attention to power differences.[41] In the edited volume *Women's Words*, the authors raise crucial questions around whether ethical research is possible at all when Northern academics research 'Third World women'. They ask who gets to do research on whom, and critically discuss the implications of the very existence of privilege that allows the research to be undertaken (Gluck and Patai, 1991). Yet, perhaps in paying attention to power relations we (researchers) overestimate our power. As noted above, the people with whom we converse also wield power over *what*, *whether* and *how* they choose to narrate. They are certainly also agents in the forming of their own stories (Olsen and Shopes, 1991).

Although all of the narrators indicated that they accepted as theirs the testimonies that I later cite (with their permission), the ethical implications of using their stories for the purpose of a book about in/security-identity remain problematic. I will, therefore, briefly return to the role that I, as researcher, played in the co-authoring and analysis of Mayan women's security narratives.

Assessing the ethics of my research demands the posing of several critical questions. How do I treat the 'product' of the interview; what are my ethical obligations as researcher towards the people whose stories I am using, and towards the integrity of the texts themselves? These questions become increasingly salient given that I entertain a specific purpose besides 'publicizing' and 'giving voice' to otherwise marginalized voices. I have already decided the important areas of interest – and have superimposed my conceptualizations of in/security on the text and am therefore less open to the knowledge imbedded in the stories that lie 'outside' my area of interest. Furthermore, the narrators do not generally speak of 'security'; I interpret their words according to the modality of in/security I described above.

During the process of conducting my research, these ethical considerations have informed both my methodology and my methods. One way of dealing with the seemingly irresolvable puzzle of authority over the text is to acknowledge that I have co-authored the text, but not to belittle the sense of ownership that the narrators felt over their story.[42] Moreover, I shared the transcribed interviews with the narrators, giving them veto-right over the use of their words and honoring their requests for editorial changes and restrictions of usage or dissemination. I also encouraged them to revise the text if so desired, and engaged in discussion with them about the text – and some of my interpretations – in a second interview. Furthermore, by citing them, I have made clear which are their words, and which is my interpretation of their words in my analysis of the text. However, I have not consulted them over the use of certain quotes cited from their already authorized text. Nor will I restrict the dissemination of my work. This is inherently problematic and attests to the congenital exploitation of this type of research. Attention to these problematics – although uncomfortable and unsatisfactory in terms of the difficulty of resolving them – is crucial, I believe, to any responsible scholarship, feminist or otherwise.

The difficulties involved in navigating the rocky terrain of both solidarity with, and responsibility towards, the narrators, and the pursuit of the aims of this book – especially in terms of my analysis of the narrator's texts – certainly bears mentioning. Throughout this book, I strike a delicate (albeit imperfect) balance between representing the testimony of the narrators (which can be read as disruptions of the dominant discourses of security and thereby reifying the 'difference' they celebrate because of the very cohesiveness of their texts) and, 'deconstructing' the narrators' attempts at coherence and closure. Because this book is motivated largely by a dissatisfaction with the sense that in/security is narrowly written by a very few who purport to speak for all, I aim to disrupt dominant readings of both in/security and identity by locating spaces where, as Spivak suggests, the 'subaltern is already speaking' (Spivak, 1988). Yet, simultaneously, I act as trickster by disrupting the coherence of the narrators' texts through calling attention to contingencies, incoherencies, and anomalies in my attempts to reveal the workings of the dominant logic of security as present (and inherently leaky) even in marginalized sites. Plotting a course among both these trajectories – providing a space for marginalized voices, and disrupting the seeming coherence of these voices – and thereby 'challenging' the pictures of reality and subjectivity that are central to their struggles implies thorny choices.

For example, many of the narrators' texts can be read as attempts to constitute a stable and consistent political identity of the Mayan *pueblo* throughout history as a base of their current political struggle. In analyzing how they represent this identity as whole and cohesive in their narratives – both over time and space, I point to the discursive moves they employ to 'secure' this identity and thereby disclose how such representations require discursive work *because* of their very instability and leakiness. Yet, my disruptions need not diminish an explicit solidarity with the struggles of the people whose 'textualized selves' play a leading role in these narratives. That is to say: with the very real people whom one talks with during the interview process. Nor need one purport to replace one story, such as the one told by Guatemalan policy, with another more 'true' or 'pure' story, such as the narrators'. In this sense, the researcher can 'dislodge the ground from which persons and groups securely represent others', thus underscoring that 'cultural analysis [and the politics of everyday life are] always enmeshed in global movements of difference and power' (Clifford and Marcus, 1986: 22). Yet, she need not dislodge the political projects in which these people engage. Jabri and O'Gorman explain a similar approach in the introduction to their volume:

> The essays collected here challenge the ethnocentric tendencies of Western IR by asking how the other constructs him/herself. In so doing, they reveal that the categories of 'self' and 'Other' are not separate and pure categories of being but are implicated in the discursive strategies of subjects in the form of resisting, claiming and denying subject positions. More specifically, these critiques offer particular insights into the production of 'otherness', namely, the understandings of power and difference in self/other constructions and in self-understandings; how discourses of difference can emerge to oppress as well as to resist; and strategies to reclaim subjectivity through voice, agency and representation (Jabri and O'Gorman, 1999: 11)

It is to Mayan women's discursive strategies – strategies that both reproduce and simultaneously disrupt and unsettle in/security as it is written in dominant discourses – that I now turn.

Notes

1 During this period, I conducted eighteen interviews with eighteen different persons, nine of whom I interviewed twice.

2 'Ethnic groups: Mestizo (mixed Amerindian-Spanish or assimilated Amerindian – in local Spanish called *Ladino*), approximately 55 percent, Amerindian or predominantly Amerindian, approximately 43 percent, whites and others 2 percent' (Guatemalan Government Home Page, last updated March, 2001).

3 Some date the emergence of the identity as 'Mayan' to the violence of the late 1970s–early 80s; others date it to the 1992 'celebration' of 500 years of Resistance (and Rigoberta Menchú's winning of the Nobel Peace Prize), others to a combination of these factors, as well as the growing legitimacy warranted indigenous people by the international community because of Convention 169 of the United Nations. Many also posit that Mayan

identity, although 'new', is really a continuation of a dormant (and thus ever-present) identity inherited from the Mayan ancestors from the pre-colonial era. See e.g. Bastos and Camus (1993, 1995); Fischer and Brown (1996); Nelson (1999); Solares (1993); Wilson (1995); personal (informal) interviews with representatives of the popular movement and Mayan organizations 1993–95.

4 'The key word in this initial strategy was "participation" because the indigenous participated in the war effort' (Colonel Gramajo cited in Schirmer, 1998: 81): 'Nowhere in Latin America has an army managed to mobilize and divide an indigenous population against itself to such an extent – even to the point of forcing victims to become accomplices and kill one another. The creation and utilization of special companies of Indian soldiers and Civil Patrols by the army – linchpins for the 30/70 formula in which security was linked to the development as a way of controlling and separating the populations from the guerilla – did just that' (Schirmer, 1998: 81).

5 Colonel Gramajo cited by Chomsky: 'We have created a more humanitarian, less costly strategy (after 1982) to be more compatible with the democratic system. We instituted civil affairs [in 1982] which provides development for 70 percent of the population, while we kill 30 percent. Before, the strategy was to kill 100 percent' (Harbury, 1994: 20).

6 'The CEH report assigns blame for fully 93 percent of the atrocities to the government forces and their allied paramilitary bands, and only 3 percent to the guerillas' (REMHI/ODHAG, 1999:xvi).

7 In the narratives, the relationship between the army and the state is ambiguous; the narrators tend to refer to them as interchangeable institutions, separate from the soldiers that serve it/them. Hence, I use the term 'army/state'. See also Green (1999: 31); Jonas (1991); Schirmer (1998).

8 'Poles of Development with model villages are best understood as high-security areas built to serve as forms of population control – moving the displaced from camps into model programs – as well as to "integrate" the local indigenous populations into both the anti subversive fight and the "nationalist" security and development project ...' (Schirmer, 1998: 72). See also 'Guatemala: Acción cívica', 1985: 16.

9 For further discussion see Barry (1987); Brignoli (1985); Handy (1984); Jonas (1991); La Feber (1993).

10 Colonel Gramajo argued in an interview with Schirmer as follows: 'The destruction of villages went hand in hand with surveillance: For example, I was watching the widows from the destroyed villages: how many were there, how much they ate, who gave them food, and where the orphans were and who attended to them' (cited in Schirmer, 1998: 58).

11 The agreement was first drafted by the 'Sector of the Mayan *pueblo*' which was part of the 'Civil Assembly' formed in response to an attempted 'auto-coup' on the part of president Serrano in 1993. The Civil Assembly, representing different sectors of Guatemalan society, worked during the peace negotiations to present the officially conflicting parties with the 'society's suggestions for a viable peace agreement'. The conflicting parties accepted the Mayan pueblo's draft of the ARIIP as their own with minor changes (Inforpress Centroamericana, 1995, *Guatemala: 1986–1994: Compendio del Proceso de Paz, 1986–94; cronologias. análisis, documentos, acuerdos*).

12 In some instances this project is explicitly cited and adopted; in others, people have adopted the identity 'Mayan' with less explicit political motives, yet in relation to a larger political and cultural movement. Although far from widespread or wholly unified, this 'movement' became increasingly vocal and influential as democratic openings appeared in society.

13 The rise of evangelicalism in Guatemala drastically changed the constitution of the indigenous communities, both socially and in terms of political affiliations, as did the

spread of catchetism and Catholic-based liberation theology, such as 'Catholic Action'. The role of religion in identification processes as well as in the politics of the revolutionary movements and counter-insurgency strategies is indeed extremely important, although beyond the scope of this work. For further discussion see e.g. Green (1999), Melander (1999), Wilson (1996).

14 There are certainly many 'new' and 'old' tensions between the different ethnic groups that make up the Mayan population. The army/state also exploited 'traditional' conflicts within the Mayan *pueblo* for their own purposes – especially conflicts over land upon the 'return' to Guatemala from Mexico. For further discussion see Stepputat (1996, 1999).

15 *Traje* in Spanish means 'suit'. In the context of Guatemala it also means, specifically, the traditional clothes worn by Mayan peoples – especially women. Each village embroiders the clothing (especially women's blouses: *huipiles*) differently. Usually, a skirt – *corte* – is also worn.

16 I am referring to the specific violence intended to wipe out the Guerrilla movement and its base. This violence was inflicted on the indigenous and peasant populations (as well as all others considered subversive) during the late 1970s and early 80s in Guatemala. The narrators refer to 'the Violence' as an era.

17 I refrain from citing the organizations directly, in order to avoid any connections between the narrators and the specific organizations.

18 The Coordination of Organizations of the Maya People of Guatemala (*Copmagua*) was a coordinating group made up of five Maya umbrella organizations: the Council of Guatemalan Mayan Organizations (COMG), the Academy of Mayan Languages of Guatemala (ALMG), the Coordination of Mayan Unity and Consensus (IUCM), the Union of Mayan People, and the Mayan Council Tukum Umam. It was founded in late 1994.

19 *Majawil Q'ij* (New Dawn) was a Maya coordinating committee founded in 1990. It was a member of the Coordination of Mayan Unity and Consensus (IUCM).

20 *Defensoria Maya* (DM), the Mayan Defense Network, addressed questions of indigenous rights. The *Defensoria de la Mujer Maya* (The Mayan Women's Defense Network) concentrated on the specific rights of Mayan women.

21 IUCM was a broad-based coalition of more than eighty different Mayan organizations, formed in 1994 and a member of *Copmagua*.

22 The narratives consist of forty to sixty pages of text. The interviews were conducted in Spanish; I bear full responsibility for all translations from Spanish to English. It also bears mentioning that Spanish is neither my first language nor the first language of most of the narrators.

23 I took as my starting point that these people identified themselves as 'Mayan women' because all of the narrators made claims explicitly as 'Mayan woman' as their primary political self-definition.

24 See Arias (2001); Behar (1993); Clifford and Marcus (1986); Fonow and Cook (1991); Gluck and Patai (1991); Langness and Frank (1981); Ochberg and Rosenweld (1992); Sommer (1991).

25 Two participants ('Delia' and 'Leticia') were from the base of their organizations, although they also acted as leaders locally.

26 Only one organization did not boast a widespread base. However, I included it because the organization represented a specific and important cultural elite of educated Mayan women within the Mayan popular movement.

27 I also talked with additional women from the 'base' of the organizations, who greatly helped me to understand the situations from which the leaders came and the context of their daily work. On several occasions, I also participated in meetings held by the organizations.

28 I stated that I was writing a book about security and identity and wanted to hear about their struggles as Mayan women. Being forthcoming abut the purpose of the research is extremely important in a context where trust was difficult to earn, and psychological warfare promoted a culture of fear where people were afraid to confide in most others.

29 I then had the tapes transcribed by a trustworthy person, whose work I checked by comparing the recorded words with the transcription.

30 I conducted second interviews with only half of the participants for a variety of reasons, ranging from the limitations of logistics to the narrator's level of literacy.

31 These questions were guided by my 'working modality' of security, which I discuss below.

32 I am borrowing this phrase from Ochberg and Rosenwald (1992).

33 Literature on narratives (e.g. Whitebrook, 2001), resistance literature and testimonial literature (e.g. Arias 2001; Gugelberger, 1996) address the political and historically specific moment of telling as integral to both the story being told and the construction of the identity of narrator/narrated. See also Wibben (2002) on security narratives.

34 For further discussions on memory see Bruner (1990) and Stern (2004); on the politics of memory, see Edkins (2004) and Passerini (1992); and on identity and memory in narrative, see Lisch (2003) and Whitebrook (2001).

35 One particularly heinous memory which became imbedded in the collective memory was witnessing the military's brutal ripping open of Mayan women's pregnant bellies to murder the growing fetus and then rape and kill the mother. Many of the narrators spoke of this particular image.

36 This broad working definition arises out of reflection inspired from numerous texts on the concept of security (chapter 2). See also Stern (1991, 1993, 2001).

37 *India/o* is a derogatory term for indigenous or Mayan.

38 Crucial measures for those seeking to revindicate the Mayan culture through language included: redefining Mayan languages as equal to Spanish in their status, establishing them as written languages, and teaching children in their 'mother tongue'. See literature from *Academia de Lenguas Mayas* (ALMG), *Asociacion de Escritores Mayances de Guatemala* (CECMA). See also Bastos and Camus (1993, 1995); Cojti Cuxil (1991); Fischer and Brown (1996); Nelson (1999: 254).

39 There is a large and nuanced discussion within post-colonial studies which addresses issues relating to the 'imperialist/colonizing' gaze and the politics of 'writing back'. See e.g. Bhaba, (1994); Chow (1993); Mudimbe (1988, 1984); Said (1985, 1993); Spivak (1988); Trinh T. Min-ha (1987).

40 For further discussion see Appiah (1992); Chow (1993); Eriksson Baaz (2004); Marchand and Parpart (1995); Mohanty et al. (1991); Parker et al. (1992); Trinh, T. Minh-ha (1987, 1989).

41 For a critique, see Spivak (1988).

42 When discussing her interview outside of the interview situation, I remarked to one of the narrators (who had become a good friend) that I understood that her interview was only one representation of her life. She became quite angry with me, gestured towards the text, and said: 'This is my life, Maria!'

Part II

Reading Mayan women's narratives

4

Reading in/security in the family/community context

> I wish you could visit my house, because all I am talking about here is them, living, suffering, its sad [...] My family is the fundamental base of society. I'm part of the family, but in my family everything is bad. (Rosa, born 1956)

> My house, like the house of anybody from the area where I grew up, is not an island, so it received all the influence of this situation, of constant terror and permanent repression. So, I believe that a lot of our attitudes, men-women, inside my family resemble the attitudes that we were living outside ... The relations between patrollers and the civil population, between the army and the civil population, this type of power, also was reflected in my house ... On the positive side, we learned to fortify ourselves against what was on the outside, to unite ourselves, but on the negative side, we reproduced a lot of these relations [...] For example, the men wanted to order us around for the sole purpose of ordering us around ... This, I believe, had a lot to do with the ambiance outside, with all this control of the people, all this coercion which was maintained especially in the military or the paramilitary against the civil populations. (Manuela, born 1969)

FAMILY LIFE DOES NOT OCCUR IN A VACUUM. It is therefore impossible to talk about the family without also addressing the relations between the family, the community and the state. The home, like the community, both reflects and refracts national society. In many cases, Mayan communities and families were viewed by the government and the army not as the building blocks of the nation, but as its enemies. The family and the community therefore served as a point of resistance to the violent and homogenizing policies of the nation-state. However, these spheres were also deeply implicated in national discourses. The power relations that reigned in the family were informed by those in the community, as well as those that governed the relations between the community and the state and the community and the family. In short, all of these spheres were deeply implicated in each other. In this chapter I will explore some of these inter-relationships, instead of erecting solid boundaries between the familial sphere and those spheres in which the family also existed. Indeed, in the narratives, the family was so imbedded in the community that I refer to the family/community as one context. How did the narrators name in/security in this context? Primarily they focused on the ramifications of the Violence, as well as the gender discourses at play within the over-riding moment marked by violence and fear.

The narratives of the women I talked to all offered different understandings of the 'national security measures' briefly described in chapter 1. The narrators provided a counter-story to that of the nation-state: a story in which the army and the state were the enemies; and they, as Mayan women, its victims. They thus constructed their identity in resistance to the official version of national identity, expressed violently through national security policies.

Many of the narrators explained that the Violence or the Repression so drastically altered 'normal' relations and life that the basic site of security for both children and adults was obliterated. There was no safe haven, no space without danger, as expressed in Rosa's citation above. Similarly, Manuela explained: 'They killed many people here [...] Still in the walls of my house there are bullet holes. It was an epoch, which was very difficult [...] It was about survival' (Manuela).

Almost all of the narrators described scenes of terrible, bloody violence – violence that while experienced as a child, had been a major impetus for their struggles. They describe a period in their lives and in the history of Guatemala during which they lived in a 'culture of fear instilled by the army and the government' (Carmack, 1988/1992: 24; REMHI/ODHAG, 1999: 1–28). Recollections of the Violence had become a focal point for their lives, shaping their own sense of themselves, as well as the choices that they made. The Violence, all encompassing as it was (and for many continued to be), thus became a crucial reference point both in their personal reflections, and in the rhetoric of their political work. They located danger and threat in their experiences of the Violence at the hands of the army/state, recasting the state as enemy, and thus effectively subverted the discourses of danger employed by the state. In the texts, the Violence therefore appeared as a crucial moment, a catalyst to a 'reawakening' of their political identity and a *raison d'être* for their political struggles.

I have placed a discussion of the Violence in the context of the family/community because the narrators explained that they suffered violence often initially in their homes and in their communities. The intimate daily life of the people came under attack because the military and the PACs, the perpetrators of the violence, attempted to destroy the core of the indigenous and peasant societies. Hence, both by explicit design, and because of the reality of the circumstances, the family was deeply imbedded in the reality of the nation. For instance, Manuela drew connections between the violence pervading her home and the violence pervading the nation: '[It is] not necessary ... [to] talk to me about the national reality, because the national reality was around the corner from my house and in my own house' (Manuela).

Almost all eighteen of the people I interviewed related a different, yet nevertheless shared story of repression, division, persecution, torture, rape, death, separation, flight, and suffering at the hands of the army and the PACs. They also told of their (heroic) experiences of endurance and resistance.[1]

Additionally all of the narrators described their 'situation' as one of 'triple oppression'. Most emphasized the discrimination and suffering that they experienced because of their 'condition' (in the political conjuncture of the Violence) as women as particularly important in the story of their struggles. In each of the testimonies, the narrator addressed how gender ideologies, roles, and relations were formative in their lives. They emphasized how the context of the home and the community were especially important for the formation of their gender identity, and for their effort to give this identity new meaning through their struggles. Of course, gender played a part in all aspects of the texts, and cannot be extracted from each of the spatio-temporal contexts I address in this book. Yet, the power of gender was perhaps at its least hidden in the family/community context because it was such an obvious – and accepted – part of daily life.

Dividing families/communities

The family, in many cases, was the target of sophisticated methods that were designed to undermine an effective site of resistance. Families and communities were divided, for instance, by the installment of model villages, and the forced recruitment of PACs, as well as soldiers. One of the main objectives of these methods was to disrupt the building or maintenance of alliances that challenged the national project and thereby threatened national security.[2] Anyone who resisted these measures was considered subversive, an enemy of the state. The personal experiences – of threat, violence, and the torture, 'disappearances', and murder of fathers/husbands and sons – devastated families both psychologically and economically.

The army also used methods of terror in order to instill fear and to drive a psychological wedge between family members and between members of the community.[3] Trust within families and between community members was hard won and often betrayed (CEH, 1999; REMHI/ODHAG, 1999). Direct force and coercion instilled an overall sense of suspicion and fear. Instances of 'deviance' were rewarded with violence meant to teach a lesson to other possibly wayward citizens. Furthermore, the PACs and the army employed programs of indoctrination to foster national loyalty among the predominantly Mayan (male) 'recruits', and violently to discourage any identification with the Mayan *pueblo*, the boys' communities, or families.[4] Successful indoctrination was crucial especially when ulterior identification and subsequent loyalty could be interpreted as subversive. Much of this indoctrination rested on the creation of a violent form of racist, macho-nationalism which would ensure a unifying identification with, and obedience to, the interests of those in power. Through assuring that the bases of resistance to the state and its policies were divided and conquered, Guatemala seemingly guaranteed its national security.

The narrators dwelled on the theme of the intentional division of their families and communities as a policy of the army/state. In their narratives (and through their telling) the narrators' political identities emerged in relation to what the army was threatening: an 'I' and 'we' formed out of the descriptions of the valued life that was under attack. Images of a longed-for sphere that existed somehow apart from the state thus underscored the violence and harm inflicted by the army in relation to the harmony that would otherwise reign. Ironically, this harmonious vision of family/community life may also have been shared by the army – enough so that the communities were a threat to and therefore warranted attack by the state, not only in their status as 'water' for the guerillas (Carmack, 1992: 24).

One of the narrators' testimonies highlighted the weight of the blow against the family structure when a family member was killed or 'disappeared'. Susanna (born 1976) worked for a human rights organization that focused on making public demands for knowledge about the whereabouts of 'disappeared' family members. Susanna organized her testimony around, among other things, herself as daughter to her 'disappeared' father. She told of the pains she experienced as a young child when her father suddenly was gone; when she watched the army threaten her mother in their home; when her mother demanded to know where her husband was; how her mother and later she joined organizations to struggle against 'disappearances' and the presence of the army; and how her life as she knew it fell apart as a result of her father's disappearance and torture.

When talking about the effects of her father's disappearance, she explained: 'When he was sequestered, a vacuum was left in the home, because it's not the same. The family disintegrated' (Susanna). The army's act splintered a notion of family that she held dear and that she later worked to recapture through her political action in the organization and her involvement in a Mayan cultural group. In her narrative, she made clear how the forced separation/death of a family member effectively devastated a sense and place of well-being. This event reformed her from being a 'daughter' into being a 'daughter-of-a-disappeared-father' from the Mayan *pueblo*. She thus became a political subject in opposition to the state-army with specific and challenging political claims. She explained:

> I realized that if a group does not unite to struggle against the disappearances, of the violations of human rights, this will continue ... there is no pressure so that the

> government stops doing this, principally because the maximum violator of human rights is the state. In the years 1980 to 1982 it was the recruits of the army in the different communities who massacred, who sequestered. The women united, women whose husbands, children or relatives were sequestered, and began this struggle ... against impunity. I began to join, little by little, this group. (Susanna)

Many of her claims centered around making visible the disappearance/death of her father, and saving the values inherent in the Mayan culture (she practiced this by performing traditional dances). These values were all the more dear because of their imminent extinction, both at the hands of the state which worked directly to separate families, and through *Ladino*ization. Her political identity was fortified by references to the revalidation of the role of Mayan women in the Mayan culture and in the society as a whole. She focused on the reconstitution of herself as a Mayan woman – a member of the Mayan *pueblo* with specific value and roles that were rooted in the ancient history of her people.

Through reading this account (and others like it) it became evident that the family/community represented a dwelling for the narrators' intimate identities. When the state/army disrupted the flow of relations within the family, either by 'disappearing' a family member or otherwise dividing the family, they ruptured the context for the workings of these identities and thus catalyzed radical transformation. Susanna's sense of herself as a daughter, for instance, became devastated by the state but was then reproduced as a political identity in resistance.

The narrators also talked about the division of the family as a result of the state/army's tactics of 'divide and conquer'. They explained that ideological differences, forced cooperation and explicit collusion with the army ruptured a harmony that existed within the communities. The violence against the Mayan *pueblo* was thus redirected from the state to the 'internal' core of the family; trust and confidence was broken among family/community members, severely altering the safe space of the familiar by placing the enemy everywhere, and thus rendering this space foreign and dangerous (Green, 1999).

One narrator (Mercedes, born 1960), a leader for a peasant organization, illustrated the importance of resisting these tactics and maintaining trust within the family. She explained that her greatest fear was not of torture itself, but of betraying her father and family under torture. For Mercedes, such a betrayal would be worse than pain or death because it would eradicate the whole reason for struggling, and wipe away the base for her identity. The enemy would have effectively destroyed what was worth fighting for. She explained that she was afraid of returning to her hometown because she might be recognized:

> There could be people who knew me there. I was so afraid that I did not know what to do. If I went maybe I would not find a place to hide ... I was very frightened, because the first thing that they would ask me about if they recognized me was my father ... Yes I was afraid of what would happen if they were to take and torture me and I said where they [her family] were. This was the fear that I had. (Mercedes)

In additional to expressing her love and fear for her father, Mercedes also discursively underscored the necessity to maintain a unified front in the face of the enemy, the Other; if she allowed herself to be forced into collusion or betrayal, the lines between self (family) and the Other blurred and she was lost.

Another narrator, Lourdes (born 1978), a young leader for the regional chapters of a Mayan cultural/political organization, explained the difficulties she and her organization experienced in her community which was in a rural and heavily militarized area. (I attended a meeting of the organized women, which was held in her home; on the footpath to her house, we passed another small house with a little kiosk. Several men and boys gathered around the kiosk and stared at us in a hostile manner as we passed.) Lourdes explained:

> Others [in the community] are against that we [women] meet. Those who are in the store that we passed by on the way here, they are against the organization ... They said to one of [us]: if you are going to continue to organize, we are going to kill you ... because we are patrollers and the army helps us ... But we can not be ... humiliated by them because we know that what we are doing is the struggle of the future so we are not humiliated ... They commit a lot of sexual harassment ... towards the women in the community. If they continue [threatening us] ... we may ask for some collaboration with Minugua[5] ... to say in front of the community that they are the ones who rob the houses and commit sexual harassment.[6] (Lourdes)

Listening to her in the setting of this meeting (where, on the surface, one could see a pleasant, small community surrounded by lush woods and corn fields, and neighbors seemingly dependent on each other because of this closeness), the starkness and power of her words were striking. Lourdes talked about neighbors threatening and raping neighbors. The immediacy of this danger took form in the faces of the people we passed on the path. In her narrative, this potentially pleasant community was blighted by the presence of the patrollers, the army and those who colluded with them. Her community was thoroughly divided along both ideological and gendered lines. Her 'enemies' enjoyed immunity afforded by the state/army to invade and harm her family, organization and the harmony of the community. This immunity also allowed for the sexual harassment and rape (as was explained later in our conversation) of women.

However, Lourdes also said that she refused to concede to the patrollers because she knew that the organization was conducting the 'struggle of the future'. According to her account, the army/patrollers were attempting to silence the women in their efforts to form a political alternative to the rule in the community and in the state at large through threats and 'disciplining' measures. However, she was not swayed by these threats. She claimed that the knowledge of the righteousness and, perhaps most importantly, the ultimate success of her struggle gave them the strength to continue despite intimidation. She then suggested that her organization might appeal to a higher law than that of the state: to the UN organ, Minugua. Lourdes underscored her lack of identification with, and confidence in, the legal apparatus of the Guatemalan state. She thus undermined Guatemala's sovereignty, and therewith its definitions of in/security. In so doing, she also created the possibility for different definitions that located danger and identity in ulterior sites than those marked by the army/state.

Elsewhere in her narrative, she explained, for example: 'the head of the patrols is harassing the people who gather ... He is trying to kill the people ... but the people are meeting because of the projects [for clean water]' (Lourdes). Here, the people posed a threat to the army because they were organizing themselves into a collective that was outside of the army's immediate interests. They were articulating their own interests and making political claims from a shared collective subject position that challenged the national security discourse. The people located danger in the lack of potable water. It seems reasonable to conjecture that the danger posed by the people in this instance was not in their 'innocent' claims for clean water, but in the fact they, themselves, were identifying their own danger as well as safety. The state/army's sovereignty over the definitions of danger as described by Dillon were thus threatened (Dillon, 1990–91: 108).

Many of the narrators also referred to conflicts in the family that arose because families became split along ideological and political lines: some colluded with the state/army (either willingly or unwillingly), some resisted either openly or in private. Furthermore, many who did participate in the PACs or the army came home 'changed', even if they were originally opposed to the actions and ideology of the state/army. The conflicts that defined the national climate entered the walls of the home and hearth. Primal bonds holding families and communities together that provided the foundation for the constructions of identity, were thus severed. Sometimes, family members even killed each other. In other cases, they remained enemies on different sides of a violent war. In many of the narratives, it was clear that the turning of family members against each other was an exceptionally painful aspect of the government's policies (c.f. Green, 1999; REMHI/ODHAG 1999). Yet, for some, this tactic also prompted resistance. One narrator, Onelia (born 1972), who was a leader of a *campesino*-Maya organization, stated:

> We often experienced [the turning of family members against each other] because my father and my brothers were in the civil patrol. They were required to join; from 14 years on up, all were required to patrol. When the army arrived they obligated the patrol to ... 'kill your brother, kill your father, or kill your people'. Some did it to defend their own lives, because [the patrol] said [that if you don't] we are going to kill you as well. They did it to defend themselves. (Onelia)

She then explained:

> Others did not do it, but they died and this was one of the reasons that my father was sequestered as well. My brother too, because they did not want to receive arms. When

> [the army] arrived in the community to leave arms they demanded money from each family. My father [said] 'No. Why do I want arms if the arms that we are going to receive are for killing our own people?' ... Many people in the community had already died like this. (Onelia)

Onelia also elaborated about 'problems in the family'. She told the story of a close neighbor who did not want his children to organize. He said that he would kill them himself if they ever returned home but then finally forgave them. She then explained that her family was not like this because her own father felt the urge to continue struggling, emphasizing the special cohesion of her family as a fortress of resistance. The only one who opposed was her mother because of the fear of losing her children. This fear continued during the time of the interviews and had been the reason why she and some of her brothers questioned whether or not to openly resist the army/state. Nonetheless, they dedicated themselves to struggling 'for the Mayan *pueblo*' despite, and because of, the state/army's attempts to divide the core of this *pueblo*. According to Onelia, her family found strength and a meaning with their lives through their struggling. Indeed, her struggles comprised the basic organizing theme in her text.

The Violence hindered people's psychological well-being, both during its most violent moments and in its aftermath. Rosa explained that the Violence permeated the fabric of her family and completely unraveled it. Throughout her text, she referred often to sickness as a metaphor for the effects of the Violence in her and her family's life. The army, she explained, was 'making people sick'. Health, juxtaposed with tales of her bodily ailments, offered a promise of cleansing herself of the memories of the violence and repression of her childhood. She explained, for example, that her brother and sister suffered psychological traumas after the army razed her village and her family was forced to flee into the mountains. She, herself, suffered from such traumas, although not quite as severely as those of her siblings. However, she did not turn all of her pain inward. She was left with hate and fear towards her 'enemy', the army: 'It was part of the history of the Violence that one was not able to forget all that happened. A dread, a fear, a terrible hate against the army remained growing – the army which is the enemy of the Mayan *pueblo*' (Rosa).

In so naming the army, she clearly identified herself as a member of the Mayan *pueblo*. Her memory, fear, and hatred provided her with guidelines for her struggles, as well as for the way in which she defined herself. Furthermore, if one followed a reading of the metaphor of sickness one step further, connections emerged between the corporal bodies of Rosa and her siblings, 'people', and the political-cultural bodies of her family/community, as well as the Mayan *pueblo*. All of these bodies had been infected, made sick, violated by the enemy, the army. Yet, through identifying these violations and the struggles that arose out of these traumas, Rosa established these bodies as political subjects in resistance to the army.[7]

In relaying the division of the family in the citations above, the narrators depicted an undivided community that had come under siege both from the outside and from within. I was particularly surprised by the lack of conflict in the ways the narrators explained this phenomena. Upon closer reading, it became clear that, although individual members of their communities/families were indeed considered enemies, the blame for their collusion was clearly and neatly placed on the outsiders: the state/army. Indoctrination and the coercive policies of the state effectively divided their communities, yet, in the narratives, the core of the community remained intact, because it was still clear where the enemy *really* resided. Unity within the identity 'Mayan' remained ostensibly unchallenged. Furthermore, these acts of violence also bred resistance.

Sexism as divisive

The narrators also talked of the division of the family/community in a different way: namely through pervasive ('foreign') sexism which placed women in particularly vulnerable positions both *vis-à-vis* the army and the PACs and 'within' their homes. The devaluation of girls/women and the valuing of boys/men were themes that ran through many of the narratives, especially in terms of descriptions of family life. The narrators talked of the pain and suffering they felt as the victims of discrimination and unjust treatment. Yet, they (with a few exceptions) discursively placed the source of this 'internal' violence outside 'themselves' – outside the hearth of the Mayan *pueblo*. Often they related their particular experiences of sexism to the larger conflux of violent relations facing Mayan women in general, to a system of machismo perpetuated by the *Ladino* state through militarization.[8] The insidious workings of sexism could then be seen as yet another divisive tactic that was attendant to the Violence and its counterpart, racism. Ironically, speaking of sexism to me also posed a danger, as it revealed internal tension. Hence, the apertures in the narratives where 'internal' sexism was addressed were often quickly closed again through the overriding discourse of danger, which cast the state/army and *Ladino* society as the ultimate enemies (as we shall see in chapter 5).

In many of the discussions about danger and harm within the family in the narratives, men represented a physical threat. Leticia (born 1946) focused her story around her disastrous relations with men: first her father who constantly beat her, and then husbands who would beat her and then leave her with the responsibility of providing for their mutual children. The oppression that women/girls were subjected to at the hands of men was typified in the abuse that the men in Leticia's life inflicted through both action and words. She described, for example, her relationship with her latest husband:

> He'd leave and lock the door on Sundays. I would stay in the house like a dog. When he arrived, he was drunk. So I [asked] where he had been and why he had drunk and

> said that he should not do that. He said 'what does it matter to you? I am a man and I do what I like because I am free. You on the other hand are a woman, you should be in the house, you are going to care for the house and stay in the house.' [...] Every eighth day he would beat me after he had been drinking. (Leticia)

She explained that she finally decided to change her situation, to liberate herself from his oppression. She 'went to the mayor and said that [she] did not belong to him anymore and [she] left' (Leticia).

Leticia underscored that gender relations (epitomized by physical abuse) were a site of the danger and threat that punctuated her life and which, at a late date (49 years old), compelled her to join an organization to 'struggle'. She clarified that she aimed to reformulate her gender identity and those of her children in relation to the negative examples of her own experiences through her capacity as a mother, and by taking control over her own life. In the very framing and relaying of her story as one of victimization, epiphany, and then revindication through agency, she cast herself as protagonist and heroine. The plot was structured around a distinct 'discourse of danger' where men were the enemies, physical abuse and oppression their weapons, and where she, as a woman, was born as a conscious and indeed sovereign political subject.

Many of the narrators also focused on marriage (and the preparation for marriage) as a nodule moment of danger in how they represented the expectations made on them as girls. Maria (born 1966), for instance, explained: 'My mother and father did not get along well because my father always treated my mother very poorly. So, I realized that the man is more important ... and the woman is not worth hardly anything.' Her mother taught her that she must learn to suffer the fate of women and serve men, and even get beaten by her husband. She concluded: 'If it is like this, I will not marry!' (Elsewhere, Maria explained that her mother could not do anything without her father's permission, including 'having opinions'.)

Rosa relayed a similar account. However, she was careful to not alienate herself too much from the Mayan *pueblo*, as doing so might mean betrayal, and therewith, possible estrangement from a base of security. She explained that machismo was not the fault of her father and repeated several times in the text that machismo came with the colonial invasion, with the '500 years', a sentiment which Leticia also shared. She, like many other narrators, emphasized that both women and men needed to 'wake up' and recognize 'the *real* story', the Mayan story, which told of the complementarity between women and men and the value of women in the Mayan culture (Majawil Q'ij, 1995). Men and masculine power were not the 'real' problem; alluding to men as enemies risked creating a division between the Mayan peoples. Instead, women must recognize their own contribution to perpetuating (foreign) sexism and work towards recreating a gender identity/role that empowered both women and men, and therefore the community as a whole. The narrators thus explained the context of their gender relations as inseparably bound with the norms and customs of their ethnic culture and identification within the context of communities under siege. She thus tied her narrative back into a contained whole where the different discourses of danger fit under an over-riding one which served to secure the Mayan *pueblo* as cohesive.

Gender-specific violence

Sexual abuse

Guatemala's counter-insurgency tactics often involved a highly sexualized form of violent militarism. The state/army mobilized particular versions of idealized and violent masculinities (i.e. the macho soldier) in order to secure a (masculinized) national identity in the face of what they considered dangerous challenges to national unity (Schirmer, 1998: 189). The desirable type of masculinity celebrated violence, order, obedience, and domination. It served to form soldiers along a strictly disciplined code of behavior that viewed any deviance from the norm as inferior, 'feminine', and dangerous. Boys underwent a form of indoctrination, which included humiliation, and then the building up of the macho soldier. They were forced to follow orders which 'proved' their loyalty to the army; often these orders entailed acts which formed and cemented a self-identification as a macho soldier who was a part of the nation-state project. Potency needed constant renewal. In extreme cases orders included the rape/killing of young village girls, perhaps even in their own home towns. If the soldiers refused, they themselves were considered 'subversive' and killed (CEH, 1999; REMHI/ODHAG, 1999: 73–81; Schirmer, 1998: 189).

Hence, particular methods for also instilling a masculinized national unity on the 'civil' population as well as the soldiers included rape and sexualized torture of 'subversives'. During the most violent years of the 1980s, the Guatemalan military often 'rewarded' its soldiers with the gang rape of Mayan women before they massacred the women along with the men and children in the community (CEH, 1999; Garcia and Gomárez, 1989: 85; REMHI/ODHAG, 1999; Schirmer, 1998: 189). For instance, one narrator, Maria, a leader for a refugee/returnee organization, relayed her experiences of the Violence coming to her village; she explained the common occurrence of sexual torture and rape as an additional 'disciplining' tactic of the military:

> [The army] started to bomb and no one knew why they were bombing ... They massacred many people [...] [We] had to leave the house running [...] [We] climbed a tree to see to the next village. The army was burning everything. People were running ... [I] had to run [and] hide for fifteen days in the mountains [...] [There were] 300 people. The army found them and opened fire, killing the women. [They] took away women with their children. Four of the women were hurt. The army raped the hurt ones; they raped them a lot and then took them away. I ran and hid with some other

> women [One] woman was so afraid of the army hearing her crying baby that she suffocated it. (Maria)

Embedded in these tactics were strict definitions of what was and was not acceptable for men and women to do and be. Transgressions outside of these gendered roles became seen also as subversive acts against the state. Even seemingly innocuous daily activities (such as the purchase and preparation of food) which were included in broad definitions of appropriate women's work became political battlegrounds, as was witnessed in Gramajo's comments about watching the widows, noted above (Schirmer, 1998: 288). One narrator, Gloria (born 1964), explained how women's lives became particular sites for the repression of so-called subversive activity.

> The repression is manifested in the woman because they were looking at you if you bought much food … they would say, 'why do you want to buy so much, for whom do you want to buy so much?' So in this way the repression was manifested. (Gloria)

Women in the communities were monitored and even impeded from fulfilling the roles that they held in the community. Yet, these roles were not static. Because of the repression – and perhaps even the hindering of their 'traditional' duties – women began to seek venues to work towards countering the violence inflicted upon them, through, for example, organizations. However (as we shall see in chapter 6), their participation in organizations threatened both the men in their communities and, of course, the army/state. Stepping outside of the increasingly narrow space in which women were allowed to maneuver was dangerous, both in the home and *vis-à-vis* the state.

According to the narratives, women who formed opinions, expressed them, and even worked towards enacting their ideas were anomalies in the context of the Violence: a woman did not act politically in a 'public' space.[10] If she did, she must be under 'foreign' influence. As Carmen's (born 1955) following words explain, a 'real' woman could not have formed opinions on her own; she must have been influenced by someone (i.e. *male* guerrillas).

> One time when I went to organize some communities where there was a lot of repression, the heads of the civil patrols sat in the back of the [meeting] … and sharpened their machetes … I said, 'do not kill us because I feel that I what I am doing is good, its not bad.' […] When the meeting was over, the commander said that 'you say that we killed your children, fathers, husbands … but its because of you that your husbands were killed … they were looking for you because you have joined the guerrillas … [you] this Señora who is organizing women, where did she get her ideas? Clearly with the guerrillas she got her ideas.' But I felt that no, it was not the guerrillas who came to give us these ideas, it was all the problems that occurred which gave me the idea, all the suffering, the pain, the hunger. (Carmen)

Being a woman meant adhering to the norms of behavior and identity within the Mayan communities (often highly determined by either the Catholic or various

Protestant churches). This definition was curtailed by the demands of counter-insurgency surveillance, which depended upon narrow understandings of appropriate political activity. Gender identities were thus specifically and explicitly politicized. Moreover, even if one were to take caution and comply with these strict definitions, one was not safe. Merely being a Mayan (or indigenous) woman in the eyes of the state/army was considered subversive of the national project. Exerting this identity as an explicit challenge to the state was almost suicidal. Hence, danger existed as long as the political situation in the country remained relatively unchanged. As noted above, punishment for deviance, either implicit or explicit, often took the form of sexual violence. The army/state could thus demonstrate their 'potency' in the face of difference.

Often the majority of the men in the PACs and army were men from the Mayan communities. How then did the narrators reconcile the sense of threat and danger from these men with the knowledge that the very same men may also sometimes share their dinner or their beds, or at least their village fiestas? My even posing this question indicates that I approach this situation as if it involved an inherent contradiction. Yet in the telling of the narratives, the narrators did not express this situation as problematic in the sense that I surmised. Like in the above analysis, it became clear that the fault resided on the 'outside', in 'external' influences. Naming these experiences as ones filled with insecurity, while still clearly situating themselves within the ethnic collective identity, was an important discursive move. Loyalties remained intact, while specific instances of threat gave reason for their struggles and even fortified these loyalties. For example, when asked about instances of sexual abuse, Onelia replied:

> I believe that rape ... in my community comes more from the *Ladinos* and the *patrones* of the army. We saw this ourselves. The civil patrols in my community? Perhaps ... but they were more from the military commissioners, heads of the patrols ... Now, men of my own community, perhaps there is a very small percentage. They are men who have left the community [...] Almost all of the men in the community respect the women, but in knowing other places or cities where they see prostitutes, their mentality changes. They influence greatly the community. And the women can not denounce them ... Perhaps one will never know who was raped in a community. That which is very clear is that in the 1980s, the army raped many girls. (Onelia)

In the beginning of this citation, Onelia definitively distinguished between the enemy and 'the men of her community'. As she talked, however, this distinction became a bit blurrier, yet the message remained clear. Outside influences, e.g. *Ladino* influences, were at the root of the problem of 'disrespect' towards women. Sexual abuse was not a 'Mayan' problem, and therefore must be treated in the context of the 'larger' issue: namely the war against the Mayan *pueblo*.[11] She thus situated herself in this *pueblo* and refused to identify herself and other Mayan women as simply universal 'woman' and victims of state-sanctioned 'male' violence. Such an interpretation of sexual abuse risked deflecting attention away from the 'real' issue, which was the violence against the Mayans. Here it appears as if the very cohesiveness of her narrative was visibly haunted by parts of the story that 'did not fit' and therefore must be placed 'outside'. Sexism and violence within the family and community must be discursively rendered 'foreign'.

In her conversations with me, Onelia, a highly politicized and practiced leader, clearly and firmly established herself as a Mayan woman whose identity was closely interwoven with the unity of the organization and the Mayan/*campesino* movement as a whole. Her enemies were clear-cut: the army/state, the rich and racist *Ladinos* in general. Another narrator (Mercedes) handled the relaying of accounts of sexual abuse slightly differently: she (a less outspoken and stalwart advocate of Mayan rights) placed sexual violence in a separate category instead of considering it as one method in an overarching campaign of violence. She responded as follows when I inquired about sexual abuse on the part of the army and PACs:

> In the moments when the civil patrols were born, yes always there has been this. In the communities in 1978, people also said that the military commissioners raped the women ... But yes, this is always talked about since a long time back and now we see in the news that every day there are violations of women. Even deaths appear, but this violation is a violation against her dignity as a woman. (Mercedes)

Mercedes distinguished between a violation against a woman's 'dignity as a woman' and (what I read as) the unspoken, yet understood implication of her comparison: that the other violations are against the person as a peasant and/or member of the Mayan *pueblo*, or even human being. The sexualized crime was separate. In targeting women as victims of these crimes, the perpetrators were able to use sexual violence in both the punishment *and* establishment of identity, for example: that of 'damaged goods/soiled woman', or even 'traitor', and not as a viable political actor, of valid member of the nation-state. Remembering and narrating these experiences in various ways (or *not* remembering/narrating them) also established (or re-established) an identity: i.e. either a damaged and punished, or an indignant woman. Separating out one's gender identity as 'woman', like in the citation above, reflected how this tool of violence played upon deeply felt norms within a community, vastly expanding its effect beyond the physical violation to a multi-faceted religious, cultural, and psychological one. I presume, although it was never clearly stated to me, that not only were the women fearful of reproach at the hands of the army/state for talking about their abuse, but they were also ashamed and afraid of repercussions within their own family/community (El Jack, 2003; El Bushra, 2003; Rehn and Sirleaf, 2002).

Sexual abuse was therewith a taboo subject. The victims of the crimes often remained silent about what had happened to them publicly and even in their most intimate relations (CEH, 1999; REMHI/ODHAG, 1999). They often chose silence because of the many cultural and religious restrictions around women's sexuality within the family and the community, and because of the danger in publicly admitting that it occurred and thereby accusing the perpetrators of the crime. Silencing the women was therefore an effective aspect of this method of attack against a community. To repeat Onelia: 'Sometimes one doesn't realize, perhaps one will never know who was raped in a community. That which is very clear is that in the 1980s the army raped many girls' (Onelia).

This silence was reflected in many of the narratives. Often sexual abuse on the part of the military/PACs was not mentioned except, perhaps, as a part of a long list of violations against the Mayan *pueblo*, as demonstrated in the words of Carmen, cited above. Not until I asked the narrators specific questions about sexual violence did they broach the subject. When they did talk about it, one could surmise that its very absence in the initial narrative often was important in terms of their in/security. Safety resided in maintaining silence, both in terms of assuring their identification with the oppressed as a whole without being '*divisionistas*' (those who turn women against men and challenge the unity of group), and in terms of not becoming more exposed to the state/army. Indeed, many of the narrators explained that remembering experiences of sexual violence committed by the army or the PACs was a dangerous act – both for the woman herself, and in terms of the possible repercussions from her family or from those who committed the crime. Nonetheless, the act of remembering and recounting the experience could also serve as a powerful weapon against the perpetrators and against the injurious effects of their silencing tactics (CEH, 1999; REMHI/ODHAG, 1999; Edkins, 2004). As in Onelia's testimony, safety also resided in understanding the experiences of sexual violence as manifestations of the overall violence against the Mayan *pueblo*. The narrators thus linked their identities with the collective through naming these securities and insecurities.

Un-making Mayan men in the military

Another theme that arose in many of the narratives was the problems and divisions that occurred when boys returned from their military service or the civil patrols. They returned bearing the ideologies of the state/army – ideologies which placed them at odds with the 'civilian' members of the community, and often with their own family.[12] Joining the army then posed not only a threat to the boys, as they risked being killed, and to the community, because the army gained more manpower and robbed them of their male youths, but it also posed a threat to the community, because the boys became effectively 'brainwashed'. The 'enemy' entered their heads. They were forced to do terrible things, and soon they became terrible themselves, acting as the tools of the army/state's ambition to divide and destroy the Mayan *pueblo*. The boys – the future generation of the Mayan communities – were then lost to the community and to themselves.

One narrator, Gloria, expressed a fear of losing the boys who had been altered by their experiences in the army. She explained that they did not 'want to use a hoe or a machete', thus indicating that they had divested their connection with one of the most common and prevalent symbols of the Mayan male-peasant, the machete.[13] They had thus lost their identification with the community and with the Mayan *pueblo* at large. They came back 'delinquents' and 'damaged the community'. In 'their uniforms' they represented the enemy, and, in fact, had become the enemy. The defenders of the state became the destroyers of the community: the promise of safety was thus discursively moved from the space of the state to that of the community.

In many of the narratives, descriptions of this process revolved around the interface of sexism, racism, and violent nationalism. Onelia explained: 'I have some friends who were there in the army. They said to them: go there and take advantage of what you can, they left them the freedom to do all that they could, so an order, a mentality already formed and it was valued (Onelia). By 'freedom to do all that they could', Onelia alluded to the soldiers taking advantage of their powerful situation to rape the women in the communities. The soldiers 'learned' a mentality that was not originally theirs because it was encouraged (even forced) and valued within the context of the army. Another narrator (Lourdes) talked even more directly about how young boys from the community became vessels of (sexualized) violence through their experiences in the army and PACs:

> [The boys] are 12 or 14 years when they join the patrols ... There were massacres and then they began to discriminate against the woman for example. Now it does not make a man afraid to kill a woman, his wife or his daughter for the motives of this [his experiences in the army], for the motives of the arms in his hands. (Lourdes)

Lourdes' words resonate with the theme discussed above of the harmonious community with a cohesive identity that gets ruptured by the Violence. She explains how the violence pervaded the families and the homes of the Mayan peoples and violated the sacred, intimate relationships that bonded the family together. The boys/men lost respect for the women of the family/community – respect that served as glue for the maintenance and transmission of the Mayan identity. (Women's role as sources, defense lines, and transmitters of the Mayan identity was lauded in public articulations of Mayan identity, including the ARIIP.) 'Foreign' sexism coupled with racism therefore endangered the very identity and existence of the Mayan *pueblo*. The boys' political identity, crafted in the military institution, in many cases collided with the identities fostered in their homes (and often, in relation to the threatening political identity of the state/military). The boys became a threat not only against their mothers, but against the whole community.

Another narrator, Diana (born 1962), developed this theme one step further, specifically naming the identities that come under threat through the army's process of indoctrination:

> The army is [made up of] sons of the Mayas ... sons of the rich? No, our own brothers they gather up, they recruit and bring to service and there they give them an education which is contradictory to the ones which we have ... Brain washing and creating another mentality ... makes the youths believe that when they arrive at their community, they can devalue even their own people, their family ... It's a problem because it creates conflict in families ... to the point where [boys] are able to kill their own parents for being indigenous. If they do not not [kill them], they are ashamed when their poor mother walks behind them because she is seen as a woman who is not worth anything not only for being a woman, but also for being indigenous ... She is rejected by her own son ... This is what the government wants, to create a division between our own parents and children. (Diana)

In this description, Diana drew attention to the identity of the boys when they were 'gathered up' and recruited by referring to them as 'sons of the Mayas'. Her view of their identity after they had been 'brainwashed' became a bit more ambiguous. One could surmise from the tenor of her description that the boys lost their connection to their fathers and mothers (both figuratively and literally); they became disconnected from their 'roots'. They received a different education from *them* than from *us* and thus became Other. She also defined the ways in which the woman/mother was harmed by her returning sons: for her 'being a woman, but also for being indigenous'. Put in more theoretical terms: her gender-ethnic identity came under attack. Through defining the identities that are threatened and those that threaten, as well as the nature of the threats, Diana established the parameters of her political identity. She sculpted who she was, in part, out of naming danger and identifying these experiences of in/security.

The boys' indoctrination also resulted in the hindering of political protest to the army/state policies. As discussed above, these policies depended upon stringent definitions of gender roles as well as appropriate public (political) behavior. Many Mayan women, however, defied these controlling codes and organized around issues such as demanding an end to the forced recruitment of their sons. Yet, as Carmen, who was a member of a widow's group, recalled: 'there were youths [in the patrols] who did not let their mothers organize ...' Hence, the control of the state/army was once again instilled in the women's own families and communities. Nevertheless, these policies did not stop some women from organizing, despite the punishment they risked. Lourdes explained how she and the other members of her organization devised methods to punish those who attempted to 'punish' (through rape) them for organizing:

> What we are thinking in the groups now is that if one member of our group experiences this [sexual harassment/rape] ... one should say that she is having problems with this [publicly] ... perhaps we [will] see what we can do so that the ... men who do this ... are punished and also [forced to] support [any eventual offspring from their rapes] until the child is eighteen. (Lourdes)

These women were considering a radical move, which would subvert many of the intersecting mechanisms for the control and silencing of women. This move would refute the role of silent, ashamed, and tamed victim/criminal imposed by the state/army. It would also disrupt the understandings of accountability around gender, sexuality (and sexual violence) that previously reigned within the communities. No longer would the woman bear the sole burden of shame and responsibility for any children born; the rapist would also become a father with obligations. Lourdes thus employed a discursive move that denaturalized state-ordained representations of victim/perpetrator and enemy/ally. Even by considering such a radical rule – and by relaying her thoughts to me – Lourdes established herself as an empowered political subject capable of mighty resistance.

Silencing and memory

The army/state relied on a 'climate of fear' to silence dissidence among the people. Silencing the population also became a mechanism whereby control and even repression became internalized within individuals, and in the family/community. In talking of her experiences during the Violence, Elena (born 1962), a highly educated leader of a Mayan women's cultural organization, explained:

> One could not talk much. One must not say anything ... because it was dangerous. They would say that one was a guerrilla; the state would interpret one badly and say that they were going to kill us. So in this situation one had to remain quiet, one could not say what one felt, what one thought, like one was sleeping. One's conscience was sleeping [...] It was dangerous to speak for the security of ones own life ... It was a lot of moral repression. There was much questioning among ones own people about our capability. There was a lot of limitation as a woman in this sense. (Elena)

In addition to naming the dangers that one risked at the hands of the state through 'talking', she also named 'moral repression' and control by ones 'own people' as part of the effects of the army/state's climate of danger and fear. In addition to 'outside' control, ones own moral sense of what was acceptable was stifled. In her narrative, people were thus removed from the very basis of their own sense of self and those around them: through enforced silence, they became other than who they were, thus dissolving the base for a 'subject of security'. Furthermore, she concluded that there was 'limitation as a woman' which resulted from these restrictions. Hence, the army/state's silencing tactics served to squash resistance, to dissolve a basis of identity and community for this resistance, and rigidly to define the realm of potential behavior allowed. These behavioral codes followed strictly gendered lines of demarcation.

These silencing tactics were so very potent because their effect was long-lasting. Trust in communities took a long time to build up again, as did courage outwardly to challenge the army/state.[14] However, many of the narrators expressed that with the initiation of the peace process and the quelling of the direct violence, a certain 'democratic opening' occurred in society. The Truth Commission, as well as the presence of Minugua, UNHCR, and other 'internationals', led the people to feel as if the heavy cloak of silence was beginning to lift from their shoulders.[15] The narrators cited this lightening as an opportunity to reflect upon the harms caused because of the enforced silence. One narrator, Gloria, explained:

> There is now an opening of democracy. I have the opportunity to work, I continue, it is necessary to recuperate the lost time. This was what I always thought ... Here there was very strict control. Now afterwards with a democratic opening, one can participate. One can say in public what one thinks, and there is freedom of expression. Before, no. This was limited. Although you wanted to express it, you were afraid. (Gloria)

Hence, the narrators recounted how the memories of the onset of the Violence, its duration and its aftermath were laden with pain and suffering. In many cases, they drew attention to how memories continually threatened their wellbeing. For instance, Maria described how these experiences had become imbedded in her body: 'What happened ... Yes, I saw it in my body.'[16] She bore the Violence with her always; and she constantly relived it and infused it with new meaning.

Yet, breaking the band of silence also lead to healing. Johanna (born 1941), a leader of a returnee organization, explained both the therapeutic and the political benefits of 'remembering' and relaying what she remembered to others in her refugee community (and to people like me):

> Me, in the beginning, yes, I was also afraid [...] but now ... I am going to let out all of my feelings because I feel that if I say it, my heart remains open. But if I do not speak, I keep my heart guarded, as if my heart is tight and I am not relieved ... I like to open my heart. I remain calmer and others realize the sufferings we endured ... For this reason, it is better to explain all that hurts us.' For this reason, we are struggling to have a better life. (Johanna)

Memories were also a source of empowerment and resistance. Amara (born 1966) explained, for instance, how the memory of what had happened was imprinted on her forever: 'The only thing we know is [...] that the army destroys everything. Now they say it wasn't them, but in truth we have suffered much. We will never forget what the army did, they killed our relatives, our brothers' (Amara). The truth that she and Johanna espoused posed a constant challenge to the truths of the state, and therewith to its claims to sovereignty.

Recalled memories therefore became crucial fodder for the narrators' struggles, as well as the context out of which their political identities were reproduced. Rosa explained that her sibling's continual reliving of the trauma of the Violence impelled her to continue in her political work. As noted above, her hate and fear of the army continued growing inside of her. She then explained:

'That's why I don't want more violence, why I work for human rights. There is no government program to help victims of the Violence' (Rosa). In this sense, Rosa recalled memory as a continual threat to her well-being – and named it as an impetus to work towards change in her situation, towards security and as a resource for her political action.

Reconstructing 'Mayan women'

In the above quotation, Rosa also placed herself in relation to the 'Mayan *pueblo*'. She named the perpetrators of the threats against her and her 'people'. She thus constructed an identity for herself as a part of the Mayan *pueblo* in relation to those that threatened it and tied it to 500 years of power and ruling. In so doing, she defined who the Mayan people were: those threatened by the army (and in history, the Spanish), those who viewed the army as their enemy. She also built an image of the Other: those who threatened the Mayan *pueblo*. The relations between the two, as well as how they defined themselves in this relation, became clear. She named a political identity that resisted the victimized position imposed by the military/state. Both Andrea and Manuela also explained, perhaps even more explicitly, how their political identities had been constructed in relation to the experiences of the Violence and those who threatened them. Andrea clarified, 'my conscience began when my father was assassinated.' Manuela stated:

> [The Violence] leaves you with memories, fears. The people of my *pueblo* had to choose: leave all of this and try to change it or stay, more because of fear than because of conviction. The ability to leave my house, to work and to value myself for myself permitted me to construct in some way my own identity [...] The moment arrived when I said, 'well OK, I'll work for this, because I believe contributing to changing the conditions of life of the people.' (Manuela)

Manuela depicts how relations within her family both unsettled and reproduced dominant discourses. Gendered codes in the family/community were reinforced by national security discourses. Manuela explained that the men in her family internalized the violence in the community and directed their aggression and control against the women, augmenting the level of both machismo and racism in the home. Instead of accepting these relations of power as the plight of Mayan women, many of the narrators, like Manuela, fought against the identities imposed upon them through both the norms of the community and the dominant discourses of the state. She refused to be 'hailed into place' properly in either site.

On the whole, when talking of pervasive sexism 'within' the communities, the narrators did not simply relay the ethnic/gender roles and identifications in the narratives as examples of the inseparable interworkings of different systems of oppression, but they also represented them as sites of resistance. The narrators spoke of working towards recreating a gender identity/role that empowered both women *and* the Mayan *pueblo* as a unified community. Hence despite the violent forces which worked to tear the family and community apart, the cohesiveness of the collective identity remained (seemingly) intact and therewith securable.

Notes

1 It is important to reinstate that when I refer to 'constructions' of security and insecurity I do not intend to call into question the 'truthfulness' of the experiences of violence that these women describe. Indeed, many of the experiences described in their testimonies have been documented elsewhere and have even passed into the realm of common knowledge. See e.g. Carmack (1988); CEH (1999); Green (1999); Handy (1984); Harbury (1994); Hooks (1993); Ibarra (1991); Montejo (1994); REMHI/ODHAG (1999); Sanford (1997); Schirmer (1998); Solomon (1994).

2 CEH (1999); Martínez de León (1994: 45–53); REMHI/ODHAG (1999: 40–50); Schirmer (1998: 103–24).

3 These methods included instilling a 'culture of fear': family members were forced to spy on each together; men and boys were forced to patrol the rest of the community: family members were 'disappeared' in the middle of the night with no trace; the army came into the household to abduct men and rape women in front of children; houses and crops were burned, making tortillas became a suspect activity as women were accused of sustaining the guerrillas, etc. See Carmack (1988); CEH (1999); Green, (1999); Harbury (1994); Hooks (1993); Ibarra (1991); Montejo (1994); REMHI/ODHAG (1999); Sanford (1997); Schirmer (1998).

4 Schirmer exemplifies these tactics through excerpts from interviews with different members of the army. The army officers explain in detail the methods designed to destroy all sense of belonging to community/family/*pueblo* in (often forced) recruits (Schirmer, 1998).

5 On 19 September 1994, the United Nations General Assembly established the United Nations Mission for the Verification of Human Rights and of Compliance with the Commitments of the Comprehensive Agreement on Human Rights in Guatemala (MINUGUA) (A/RES/48/267).

6 Later in our conversation it became clear how my presence at the meeting also served as some protection for the members. My role was one of international observer and bodyguard.

7 For further reading of the embodiment of the violence, see Green (1999: Ch. 5); Nelson (1999); Zur (1998).

8 'Machismo' refers to an ideology which considers the male 'sex' superior to the female 'sex'. For a discussion of machismo in Latin America, see Schutte (1993).

9 For further discussion on the collusion of gender and militarization, see e.g. Cohn (1987, 1993); Enloe (1988, 1990, 1993, 2000); Goldstein (2001); Elshtain (1987); Kronsell (2005); Pin-Fat and Stern (2005); Peterson (1992); Peterson and Runyan (1993); Pettman (1996); Whitworth (1994); Zalewski and Parpart (1998).

10 See Youngs for a further discussion of 'public' spaces as 'political' (Youngs, 1999, 2000). See also Pin-Fat and Stern (2005).

11 Rape is often evoked in the Mayanist discourses as a threat to the culture; protection against the 'sexual abuse' of Mayan women is stipulated as a cultural issue in the ARIIP (ARIIP, 1995).

12 Any difference which challenged the national version of what being 'Guatemalan' meant (such as difference expressed in cultural articulations) was considered subversive. The military represented perhaps the highest form of *Ladino*izing institution. *Ladino*ization also referred to the process whereby an ethnic (indigenous) identity was (consciously or

unconsciously) rejected or 'lost' because of the demands of a racist modern society. See also Schirmer (1998) for a discussion of military tactics regarding *Ladino*ization.

13 The machete was a potent symbol of '*campesinidad*' (identification as a peasant) as well as of the Mayan *pueblo*. It symbolized the Mayan *pueblo*'s connection to the earth, to corn, etc. Pictures of men holding a machete were figured in much of the literature from *campesino*/Mayan organizations. See also discussion on 'People of Corn' in chapter 7.

14 REMHI/ODHAG (1999); Rigby (2001); Torres-Rivas and Arévalo de León (1999); Zartman, William and Rasmussen (1997).

15 One of the accords called for the establishment of Guatemala's 'Truth Commission' under UN auspices, to function after the final signing of the peace accord. (Jonas, 2000); CEH: Guatemala: Memory of Silence, 1999).

16 See Green (1999); Scarry (1985); Zur (1998).

5

Constructing security-identity in Ladino–*Mayan relations*

> I always say, since I began to reason, began to use my own thinking, I always say that I am from such and such ethnia, in this sense I am from the ethnia Quiche, my name is Mercedes. I say this because it's mine; It does not shame me to say it because this is who I am. So, in this sense, I identify myself in this way, as a Mayan woman. I have always maintained this presentation. [...] I was born Mayan and I can never not be Mayan. (Mercedes)

> The fact of being a Maya woman or belonging to the Mayans, to be their descendents ... is a motive of pride. (Susanna)

PERHAPS THE MOST STRIKING ASPECT of popular resistance to the structural and direct violence during the later periods of armed conflict in Guatemala can be found in the rise of 'ethnic' political identity among the indigenous populations. State violence was increasingly understood and articulated in terms of culture. Class as a basis of analysis no longer sufficed to mobilize resistance or to explain the pervasiveness of the repression. Supported by global recognition of indigenous rights, the local Mayan movements increasingly claimed their space in opposing repression and in redefining the place and role of indigenous peoples in relation to the *Ladino*-dominated society at large.

The exclusion of indigenous peoples from the Guatemalan society was a long-standing characteristic also before the armed conflict. This exclusion was articulated in various ways. For instance, both political and institutional authorities, including the judiciary system, were almost exclusively *Ladino*. On regional levels in Guatemala, there was often also a strong and nepotistic liaison between official authorities (including the army) and land-holding families (Jonas, 2000). Thus, Mayan peasants had little expectation of just treatment in turning to these institutions and therefore often avoided any contact. Furthermore, many Mayans did not speak the language of power and public spaces: Spanish.

At the time of the interviews, *Ladino* interests continued to define 'public' sites in Guatemala. Moreover, the dominant society (with much of the power and resources) identified itself as overwhelmingly *Ladino* (or *Meztiza*). Hence, the 'Mayan' struggle occurred in direct relationship to the *Ladino* society. I address *Ladino*-Mayan relations in this chapter because the narrators situated themselves, their struggles, and the solutions to their in/security in the context of *Ladino*-Mayan relations within a racist society that was a legacy of colonialism. Many of the claims made by the Mayan movement in general and Mayan women in particular addressed experiences of exclusion and exploitation on the part of the state/military, but also on the part of the *Ladino* society at large. In the narrators' texts, these claims were punctuated by stories of discrimination and insecurity, as well as resistance around such symbols.

The narrators focused on the construction of their political identities as Mayan women in the face of this discrimination, often placing their personal struggles in the context of the struggles of their *pueblo* since the '500 years'. They thus tied their political identity to a collective self that spanned centuries. In their texts, the narrators attempted to revindicate the meaning of being Mayan – an identity that was rooted in a glorious past – in relation to the *Ladino* society, which had discriminated against their people throughout history. Revindication and salvaging of the culture were intended to refute the negative and discriminatory identities defined for them throughout Guatemala's modern history and the policies of ethnocide and *Ladino*ization that were integral to the counter-insurgency tactics during the Violence. The political identity 'Mayan' thus became not only an identity in resistance, but a positive norm, rooted in a mythical history, which represented all that was grand and pure – a model for the future.

The narrators identified racism as the overarching power dynamic that produced these types of experiences of discrimination. In naming the harm that befell them, they also identified the dangers and threats that they feared. They thus wrote an in/security discourse based on the particular articulation of their identity in the context of Mayan-*Ladino* relations. The Mayan *pueblo* emerged as a political subject in resistance.

Exclusion

The narrators spoke of marginalization and discrimination as continual themes which set the context for the representations of their lives in Guatemalan society. In this society, they were insecure, inferior, 'outside', powerless. They were different from the norm, because they were represented as inferior beings in relation to *Ladino/Ladinas*. However, it was also within this context that they envisioned subverting these hierarchical relations, and therewith the meaning of being Mayan.

In all of the texts, racist discrimination had direct and concrete consequences for the quality of life that many Mayan women led. Carmen explained:

> When we as indigenous ... arrive in the offices of some authorities, they hardly speak to us ... They hardly consider us ...When one is a *Ladino*, they come rapidly. We sit there, enduring hunger ... What we want is to be [treated as] ... equal. We encounter discrimination in the hospital, the municipal, the town, and with authorities ... As indigenous, we have all received discrimination. (Carmen)

These experiences revolved around a sense of oppression, which was most prominent in stories about discrimination in school and in the work place. Specifically, the narrators emphasized difficulty with speaking Spanish, and discrimination because of their *traje*. Rosa, for example, explained that one of the distinguishing differences between *Ladinos* and Mayas was their agility with the language (for men) and their *traje* (for women). She explained that she had found it difficult to navigate through the necessities of life, such as going to health care centers, because her knowledge of Spanish was limited. (It is important to remember that the theme of health was crucial in Rosa's text.) She explained, '[because of the language] they don't take us into account ... [we are] always seen as if we are animals.'[1] Both Rosa and Manuela, for example, explained that they had experienced discrimination in school because they were '*indias*'. Rosa also told of her experiences as a domestic worker, where she was discriminated against for being stupid, indigenous, uneducated, speaking Spanish poorly and wearing *traje*. The man in the household tried to rape her and she was forced to flee. Rosa clarified that this was a common occurrence for Mayan women: 'Mayan women are discriminated against because of their *traje* ... They are ashamed if the worker wears *traje*.' In the texts, the markers (*traje* and language) were sites of oppression and threat; they also became explicit tools of resistance and therefore vehicles for the promise of safety.

Many of the narrators located the recognition of difference between *Ladinos* and Mayas in the experiences of exclusion and discrimination. The cognitive forming of a *we* and a *them* was precipitated by the experience of hierarchical difference and marginalization. When I asked many of the narrators when they first realized that there were differences between Mayans and *Ladinos*, they recounted their first conscious experiences of feeling discriminated against, of being harmed. Often this occurred in school when they had left the safe space of their homes and communities and entered into '*Ladino* society', thus further activating an inside/outside dichotomy which produced the excluded and ultimately resistant self. Onelia explained:

> When I lived in my house or in the community, we did not suffer discrimination because we were ... all from the *pueblo* Maya, there were no *Ladinos*. But, then when I went out of my community, I encountered discrimination ... I saw that the very same nuns ... gave more opportunities to a Ladina than an indigenous [...] There arose in me

> certain concerns ... I asked [the teacher] why there were *Ladinos* and indigenous, why there were two cultures. (Onelia)

Onelia, who had been taught to view the world in terms of class analysis by her parents and her brothers, began to see the world in terms of 'two cultures', situated in history. From the perspective of placing herself among the Mayans, she refuted the discrimination she faced: 'What we did not like was that in school they prohibited us from speaking *our* language.' She emphasized the difference between *Ladinas* and Mayans, thus defining who *they* were in relation to the *Other* who threatened *them* and naming a *we* that could be secured.

All these differences depicted a hierarchical relationship where *Ladinos* enjoyed access to resources, power, opportunities to better their situation, and Mayans were excluded, handicapped, discriminated against, underdeveloped, unsafe. For instance, Onelia's text also restated the (perceived) view of the Mayans as inferior and *foreign*, held by the *Ladinos*. The narrators thus defined the Other (*Ladinos*) as well as the imposed or ascribed identity of the Mayans in the dominant discourses of racism employed by 'The *Ladinos*'.

The narrators also emphasized that marginalization from *Ladino* society was not gender-neutral; Mayan women experienced racism differently than Mayan men. Through their texts, they established that Mayan women occupied a particularly debased and vulnerable site at the confluence of many different systems of power relations.[2] For example, Mercedes explained how Mayan women received much worse treatment in the workplace than Mayan men did, although both women and men suffered discrimination.

> Work ... is worse for the woman, because they still don't pay her an equal salary; they pay half, or less of the man's salary [...] The boss is always *Ladino* ... There is a perception that women are always less. (Mercedes)

When talking about this triple oppression, the narrators indicated that their oppressors were the *Ladinos*, and not members of their own community. They thus drew a clear boundary between the way *they* treated Mayan women and the way *we* treated them. Hence, they identified Mayan woman in one way at the face of oppression from the *Ladino* society and then in other ways in terms of the women's role within their communities, thus distinguishing between her community and society at large in terms of sexism and the acceptance of women. While Mayan women were beginning to receive their due in their own community, *Ladino* society did not accept them; it remained an unsafe place.

Re-constructing identity

Redefining 'Mayan'

> To have ones culture, language, *traje*, and to feel a part of this culture is to be Mayan because we have our own identity which is expressed through our culture, our traje and language, our rights. (Mercedes)

Being Mayan not only implied an identity that contrasted the Ladina identity, or common experiences of discrimination, but it intimated a shared 'positive identity', a cleaving together around a common experience. Many of the narrators explained that experiences of discrimination led them to begin to value what was theirs, instead of being cowed by shame and injustice. They articulated a sense of pride in their Mayan identity, and placed new political meaning in being Mayan. Andrea (born 197?), for example, attempted to overthrow the imposed meaning of being 'Mayan'.

> We are discriminated because of our *traje* ... We have suffered without education or development. This is the difference between Mayans and *Ladinos* ...We haven't had the right to vote, to elect our own authorities ... The majority of us are illiterate, we have no 'development' ... yes, we have the same rights ... as a *Ladina* woman ... but we've never been given an opportunity. (Andrea)

In this citation, Andrea dwelled in dynamic relations of subjugation and resistance and played with Janus-faced meaning of difference. She refuted the imposed negative differences, the marks of subordination, and celebrated the differences when they placed her in a position of superiority. She thus took a resistant stance. She began by alluding to differences between Mayans and Ladinas as simple (differences that she later in the text claimed as heirlooms from a noble and grand heritage). Most tangibly, Mayan women wore *traje*, spoke a Mayan language, and were therefore different. She then placed the blame for Mayan women's position of subordination on the *Ladinos* (through their Spanish ancestors). Next, she shifted the meaning she gave to 'difference' and rejected the idea that there were differences at all – differences, in this sense meaning aspects that rendered Mayan women inferior to *Ladinas*. '[When the] Spanish came ... [they thought Mayan] women were only good for being in the house, yet what are the differences? What capacity does *Ladina* have and not a Mayan? Nothing, there are no differences' (Andrea).

The narrators chose to resist the imbued meaning of the identity placed on them through *Ladino* society. They were not 'hailed' into the place allotted them by racist discourse. Instead, they recreated their own political identity, partly in response to the insecurity they experienced when dwelling in their assigned roles. Manuela, in particular, disclosed this discursive move:

> One of the most frequent insults was: 'You are an Indian!' ... I believe that from very early I began to have consciousness that in my house, being a woman implied obligations, attitudes, a whole lot of things that were different from men. ... From there I [recognized that there was a difference.] But it was in school since first grade, that I began to realize that being indigenous implied that I was treated differently and often in a way that I didn't like, but I did not understand why ... and I stopped using my *traje*. [Her mother didn't use *traje* either] [...] She did not want them to treat me as they treated her ... and when she told us about this, I didn't understand what this discrimination was. Now it has a name for me. I learned as a little girl how to respond ... being a woman, being indigenous ... implied for me to make even more of an effort to demonstrate that I am capable, that I can. And *now, I am reconstructing these situations, these responses that I would give in these situations, and I [realize that I] felt threatened, I did not understand why, but I felt different, excluded from certain circles* [...] I am a rebel against the stereotypes. The stereotype of being a woman, the stereotype of being indigenous ... I think I am not the stereotype of the indigenous woman either but I am an indigenous woman and absolutely no one has the right to tell me otherwise. (Manuela) [*My emphasis*]

Manuela, in particular, consciously and specifically named the process of the reconstruction of identity in relationship to feelings of threat. Unlike most of the narrators who constructed a relatively stable identity from which a specific valuation of Mayan women emerged, Manuela articulated how she struggled against 'stereotypes' – a stance that placed her at odds with many other highly politicized Mayan women. Although all of the narrators lauded their Mayan identity as a source of pride, Manuela's representations of her subjectivity were more fluid than most.

The narrators, overall, talked of their use of the term 'Mayan' as a conscious choice in adopting a political stance. Elena explained, for example, that she began using the term 'Mayan' as a means to alleviate the pain that the term '*india*' evoked.

> [Before] I used the term 'indigenous' more. The *Ladinos*, they treated us ... as '*indios*', and for us. Well before, for me, they said 'India'; it was a derogatory term, a term that offended me, made me feel bad. [...] They used the term always to offend one, to hurt one ... But since then ... the correct term, [for me to] feel better ... is 'Maya'. (Elena)

Nonetheless, despite the clearly novel political usage of the term, the narrators emphasized that, although the term 'Mayan' may have been new, its referent existed before: The Mayan culture survived throughout history. Furthermore, Mayan political activism (albeit in a different form) preceded the early 1990s. Many members of the Mayan *pueblo* identified themselves in similar ways as those developed through the celebration of 500 years of resistance. Diana explained:

> The word Mayan ... came from [the 500-year celebration], but in many communities, they were already managing some of these things ... We knew that we had a culture, we had differences between indigenous and *Ladinos* but yes, we ... knew that '*el indio*'

> was imposed on us, but in practice it is what we used. But yes, we knew that we came from the Mayas because ... in school they taught us that there were the Mayas and I don't know what and then all the Mayans died out, so ... the word was [not] new in the 500-year [celebration]. (Diana)

Although Diana reified the Mayan culture (e.g. 'we knew that we had a culture') and the differences between *Ladinos* and Mayas, she revealed her sense of the Mayan *pueblo* as a political construction. Diana referred to the term 'Mayan' as a political posturing in the way she stated that there were many who were already 'managing the terms before.' Yet, in her citation, and elsewhere in her testimony, she clarified that being Mayan connoted a cultural reality, rooted in history, which required defense. Diana disclosed a common *double entendre* of Mayan culture as fixed and static at the same time as being a novel political construction. She seems to have claimed that the political construction served to protect the Mayan essence from the dangers of ethnocide, from those who wanted to destroy it, as well as from the advancement of history.

Remarking difference

In the texts, the narrators corresponded overwhelmingly in calling forth language, and the use of (feminine) *traje* as critical identity markers between Mayans and *Ladinos*.[3] The gendered markers of marginalized ethnic difference denoted racism and oppression, and symbolized the power held over these groups; these markers ensured the difference of the marginal group as a 'constitutive outside' to the identity of those in power. However, they also served as a site of struggle and resistance. The narrators represented these markers as primordial – a natural, given aspect of being Mayan. However, they also assigned certain social/political meaning to them within the particular historical context.

Language

Speaking a Mayan language (be it Kakchikel, Quiche, or Kekchi) symbolized a critical marker of belonging and security to the pan-Mayan *pueblo*, and difference *vis-à-vis* the *Ladinos*. Diana, for instance, made a distinction between how members of specific language groups shared the same trunk (of the tree, which symbolized the Mayan *pueblo*) while the different language groups together shared the same roots. The tree signified the unity of the *pueblo* in its rootedness in history – the *pueblo* as the protecting, safe shelter for the Mayan people:

> I come from the ethnia Mam: it's my language first, and second, my *traje*. I feel proud to still speak my language ... It has a significance very deep inside of me. When one learns something from the breast of one's mother, it is never forgotten. The significance is, in the first place, the language, which makes me identify that I am indigenous. I may not be able to say to you that I am of pure blood ... Maybe there has been a mixture, but within this mixture I have conserved my language. So, because of

> this, it is important for me to be able to communicate with other people who are Mam, to relate to them, feel as brothers, as if we are united, like we belong to the same trunk. I also feel it with the Quiches, Pocomchis, because we belong to the same roots. For this reason, I say that the significance for me is unity, to maintain the relations, to feel indigenous ... When I was a child, we did not distinguish because we only spoke Mam. (Diana)

Diana explained that her language held 'a significance very deep inside' of her. She located the source of her indigenous identity in her language which, metaphorically, she received as milk from her mother's breast. If one understands culture in terms of gendered symbolism, then her mother can be read as the source of culture, which is rooted in biology (nature). Cultural identity resides in the breast milk of language. Once it has nourished the child, the power of this milk supercedes any impurities in blood. Because other members of the Mam ethnic group also partook of the milk of language, they were united as 'brothers', and could 'relate' to each other. This connection or relatedness extended to other language groups, i.e. the Quiches, who, like cousins, shared the same roots, the same identity as indigenous, and the same history. Language, for her, was the critical external symbol of belonging (or difference); it was also the crucial internal sign of attachment and inclusion, marking the subject 'Mayan' which could then be secured.

Hence, in the narrators' discourses, that which was a mark of difference from the dominant culture also marked the binding of familial bands, and the inscribing of a defense line against the Others. Understandings of gendered roles and relations underpinned the ways in which identity markers were internalized within the individuals and the group, as well as how they were mobilized in the meeting with the Other. Seen in this light, the metaphor of language as mother's milk sheds light on how centrally the 'mothers' of the culture bore the weight of its continuance. Furthermore, if women 'mothered' the culture, then likening language with the sustaining force of life (mother's breast milk) revealed how language played a critical role as a life-sustaining and securing force of identity in the texts.

Traje

Traje was perhaps the most immediately prominent marker of identity and difference in the texts. Being indigenous, for a woman, meant wearing *traje*. The colors and patterns of the individual *huipiles* and *cortes* linked one to history, the Mayan *pueblo*, Mayan spirituality, an ethnic identity, a region, a village, a family, and a home. *Traje* signified belonging. Onelia explained: 'Wearing my *traje* makes me remember my *pueblo*, my house and my family and I feel that I carry them with me ...' Similarly, Diana stated:

> *Traje* is what identifies an indigenous woman by the cosmovision and the figures that the *huipile* presents. [...] The drawings have meaning. The colors too. So for me ... if I

> change my clothes, I would lose part of my identity. At least I would not feel good ... *Traje* contains the identification as indigenous. (Diana)

Similarly, Laura (born 1963) explained (below) how her *traje* symbolized connection to family and community. A sense of community and belonging grounded her and made her feel safe; she knew from whence she came and to whom she belonged. Replacing one's *traje* with Western clothes would imply a devaluation of who she was, and would open up her identity for questioning, rendering it unstable and therefore that much more difficult to secure. She would be without the familiar landmarks that guided her way home. By adopting foreign clothes she would deny the relations that existed and insult her family, her heritage, and a sense of unity among her people. It was therefore crucial that this connection remain intact.

> In the family, I was taught to value myself and my culture ... This is important ... My grandparents, ancestors valued it [*traje*] a lot because it is what the indigenous woman identifies herself with. In addition, it would be uncomfortable in the family if one were visiting one's indigenous family and one appeared wearing other clothes, as if there did not exist any relations, any *confianza*, any communication. This would be broken. This is what we don't want, that we maintain ourselves with distance, no, instead we have always been a very unified family. (Laura)

Women's *traje* not only bonded them with their *pueblo* and their history; it also symbolized the whole of Mayan culture. Laura's worries about devaluing herself and alienating her family bore the weight of a culture bolstering itself under siege. In the texts, as well as in the dominant discourses within the Mayan movement, women were charged with ensuring that this symbol remained strong and powerful, while men traversed the dividing line between the Mayan *pueblo* and *Ladino* society. Mayan men could (partially) adopt the dress, language, and values of the dominant *Ladino* culture without severely threatening the continuation of 'tradition', according to the dominant understandings. The narrators reflected the gendered slipperiness of *Ladino*ization in their accounts. Many explained that rurally based men who worked in the cities assumed an identity as *Ladinos*; when they returned to their villages, they resumed their Mayan identity. They expressed that if a Mayan woman became *Ladino*ized in any significant way (such as not wearing *traje*), she had 'lost her roots'.

When reflecting on the dominant Mayan discourse, the narrators activated gender differences in their texts. As we saw in terms of the discussion of nation-building in chapter 2, they discursively affirmed a gendered division that allowed their 'unified' cultural identity to look both backwards and forward, to embrace 'tradition' while meeting 'modernity'. Men were the agents of progress in the public, political life; women maintained and reproduced the communal practices and symbols of the timeless culture in the 'private' apolitical life. Elena, for example, illuminated why women wore *traje*, while men seldom did:

> Because of ... the same depreciation of men [by *Ladino* society], men had to stop wearing *traje*, while women were much more strong in their resistance. Much of the culture is owed to the woman who has conserved it, as much the language as the *traje*, and the moral values ... The woman is the one who transmits this. But the man, he lost this. A long time ago in school, when the man got involved in activities ... they divested him of his *traje*. (Elena)

In the narratives, the wearing of *traje* symbolically bonded women to their mothers, and the 'mothers of the culture', providing them with a stable identity marker throughout time. *Traje* also connected the Mayan *pueblo* to nature through the antiquity of the tradition surrounding its making and wearing.

The reflections of nature in the symbols of the design and the cloth itself, as well as in its association with a femininity 'born from the earth' symbolized Mayan women's symbiosis with the land. Ironically, the obvious fact that *traje* itself had undergone changes in light of modernity reinforced the apparent importance of *traje*'s symbolic value in Mayan identification. Most contemporary Mayan women embroidered and wove *huipiles* with synthetic thread because natural fibers were too expensive. Many made huipiles expressly to be sold to tourists. Despite the evident impact of modernity on this cultural artifact, *traje*'s symbolic value lay in its tenacity throughout time and therefore its anchoring of the Mayan culture, and spirituality in the rich sea of history. Through the wearing of their *traje*, the narrators established their place after their mothers in the ancient line of the Mayan family. Elena, for instance, explained why wearing *traje* was so important to her:

> My mother was dressed like this. My whole family has dressed like this ... In our *traje* we reflect a lot of our way of living, of our spirituality, There is our symbolism, for example, yellow represent s women's fertility. (Elena)

Codes of behavior

The narrators also represented distinct social mores that were integral to the Mayan traditions and culture, and that governed the behavior of Mayan girls. Elena, for example, identified a gendered code of moral behavior that circumscribed what being Mayan meant for girls. She linked the wearing of *traje* with standards of decency for girls. She juxtaposed these standards with the supposed lack of such standards for *Ladinas*:

> I went to lodge at a school where there were only *senoritas* and indigenous. One of our problems ... is that one has to stop using the *traje*, to put on a uniform, skirt, and practically, one is not accustomed to this ... One is not used to showing ones legs. (Elena)

What is unspoken, yet apparent, in her text, is that *Ladinas* were used to showing their legs, and therefore lacked the superior moral standards upheld by the Mayan culture.

In her narrative, Susanna maintained a system of differentiation which lent itself to strict dictates of how a Mayan should think, act, and identify oneself. This system was in direct relation to an (imagined) assessment of how *Ladinas* thought, acted, and identified themselves. When I asked Susanna how she could tell if someone was Mayan or *Ladina*, she responded:

> [One can tell if someone is Mayan through] the customs which they have. Because when I studied in X, the *compañeras* who were not Mayans did not look like Mayans and did not have the same thoughts as Mayans. They think differently. For example, we do not have the same customs as the women or men who are not Mayans. If there is a party ... or a disco: 'Let's go', [they say] and they go. Among the Mayans, this can not be done. Yes it can be done, but it should not be done ... We do not identify very much with ... disco music or with going to parties. We identify more with making Mayan ceremonies or fiestas, like marimba ... Also it looks bad for our parents or our grandparents if we go out in the case of girls/women. Women should not go out to parties. One has to be careful that one's girl does not go out and get a bad reputation or, that is, stain the honor of her father more than anyone else. So this is the difference. (Susanna)

Here one can read how gendered-ethnic ideologies determined how a girl should *be* Mayan, (also in relation to how boys were to be Mayan). Clearly, in this statement, gender ideologies became discursively important in determining the differences between us and them, as well as female and male. Gender also inscribed the discourse of danger underlying Susanna's statement: the threat of indecency would impair the dividing lines between an immoral them and a pure us. The representation of we, as a morally superior community, fundamentally unblemished by the evils of Western modernization would lose its salience as a call for unity and resistance. The decline of the Mayan culture (as well as gender-specific honor) would be at risk.

Susanna also acknowledged the politicization of these systems of differences. She underscored how they were necessary to maintain in theory and as a cornerstone to the rhetoric of Mayan revindication. However, life was more complicated and the dividing lines between Mayans and *Ladinas* blurred much more fluidly. She thus revealed – through her efforts at obscuring – the anomalies and contradictions in the cohesiveness of her representations of the identity: Mayan woman. When I pressed her and asked if she (then seventeen years old) liked to attend discos, she smiled and laughed, saying 'Oh Yes!' Then she explained:

> I grew up in an ambiance in which my parents and my grandparents were not so radical in the Mayan culture. One is Maya and one does not stop being Maya because of the act of going to a party with others. One is always Maya and one will continue being Maya even if one doesn't want to. So, if there is some party, I go. (Susanna)

Susanna deemed that she was so grounded in, *aware* of, and secure in her Mayan-ness, that she need not uphold the exterior signs of Maya-ness with the same rigidity as she prescribed for Mayan girls in general. She was neither in danger of changing her way of thinking, nor losing her culture (as many of the *Ladinas* had). She therefore need not limit her activities to those which solely reproduced/repreformed the Mayan culture and the gender roles and ideologies that sustained it.

Hence, customs, norms of behavior, dress, etc., as well as a shared marginalized position in *Ladino* society became the distinguishing material of Mayan-ness in the narratives. The narrators defined *Ladinos* in direct relation to their self-definitions: 'They are what we are not.' The narrators identified the history, knowledge of, and access to, culture as one of the largest areas of distinction between *Ladinos* and Mayans: Mayans *had* culture (though they might have temporarily lost it), while *Ladinos* did not.

Losing culture – finding culture

'Paradise lost'

Mayan activists, I propose, did not politicize an existing – reified – timeless culture (as it may appear on the surface), they recreated a culture of resistance. Certain cultural artifacts were invested with new, political meanings. The markers discussed above were only the most apparent of these cultural expressions. The preparation and eating of *tortillas*, for instance, also came to mean a revindication of the ancient Mayan culture and all of its values in the face of modernity and in confronting *Ladino* society. Laura, for instance, explained that her mother warned her not to emigrate to the capital because she would 'lose a part of [her] culture ... because in the community, one eats *tortillas* and ... in Guatemala [City], one eats bread. So, a part of [one's] culture gets lost'(cf. Nelson, 1999: 130). Surely, the making and eating of *tortillas* carried symbolic weight in the organizing of daily life for centuries in indigenous populations. However, in the narratives, *tortillas* also came to represent the ancient and good Mayan culture that was lost and must be discovered anew.

Much of Mayan spirituality (as it was relayed to me) referred to the Mayan *pueblo*'s relation to nature and land: how Mayans were 'men of corn' who lived in balance and harmony with Mother Earth (chapter 7). The land signified a 'Paradise lost' and defiled by colonization and the economy of capitalist modernization (Lindholm Schulz, 2003). Many of the narrators explained how the degradation of the land mirrored the degradation of the Mayan culture. The connections between the Mayan people and the Earth could be evidenced in how the machete represented the essence of Mayan peasantry and its integrality to the land. When young men returned from the army to their villages, 'they [brought] with them another ideology. They no longer accept[ed] what they were doing in the community [...] They [did] not want to *use a hoe or a machete*' (Gloria). Gloria implied that the boys rejected who they were, their origins, and their land/homestead. The narrators thus evoked culture as a being 'rooted' in history and the land. They established how the Mayan struggle was, in part, to find the way back to the 'roots' (or core essence) of Mayan-ness.

Onelia explained why it was important to salvage the Mayan culture:

> In our culture, the things that we have lost have a lot to do with the situation that we are living. If we see this from the issue of the harvest ... now sometimes the corn grows, sometimes it does not ... Why does the corn not grow? ... Our grandparents said 'You have lost the respect for nature. It does not give you what you want anymore because you do not ask it anymore, you do not thank it, and you do not have the respect that you should have.' (Onelia)

She then held forth the ancient culture of her ancestors as the solution to the problems of both subsistence and large-scale agriculture in modern-day Guatemala. The message seemed to be: 'If we could only return to our roots, all of our problems would disappear.' She also implied that the predicament represented a form of punishment for Mayans who had lost their way. Security and safety then resided in refinding a lost and mythic culture.

> [We need to] maintain the culture and rescue what we have lost. I know that there are many things that we do not practice anymore ... natural medicine ... respect ... the culture ... religion ... nature. [...] But ...we have lived it and we have seen that we have lost it ... and this is what we ... want to rescue. The parents, they know, the grandparents, they know. (Onelia)

The past

> To be Mayan means to preserve our customs, traditions, rituals, language ... *traje*. This is being Mayan. (Mercedes)

The culture was not just lost, it was also found. Many of the narrators talked of the lost culture, yet *already* belonging to this absent culture was implied in their longings. True Mayan-ness still lay dormant and even had begun to 'resurface' in the current struggle. One leader of a Mayan organization reflected on the policies of ethnocide during the Violence: 'The Mayan *pueblo* has not lost its roots, although its branches may have been cut down' (my paraphrasing). The culture lay buried somehow in the soul/roots of the Mayan *pueblo*, and through rediscovering and revaluing their identity, the Mayans would revive their ancient and majestic culture. Culture became essential, tangible, yet still out of reach; it lay in waiting. In this sense, the culture remained a *thing* of the past that could be repossessed. Susanna explained:

> To be Mayan for me is to be a part of ... a very old culture. To be a descendent of this is very important; of a very old race which had many advances in technology, medicine and which is even living but has lost all, and it is necessary to recuperate it. (Susanna)

The clarity with which the narrators connected themselves to a certain past also distinguished Mayans from *Ladinos*. Rosa explained:

> *Ladinos* are looking for their identity, but they are not going to find it ... We can identify ourselves as Mayans ... *Ladinos* still haven't found their identity. But, we have made forums and meetings to identify ourselves because we don't want confusion about our being Mayans. (Rosa)

Furthermore, a clear distinction between us and them resonated with the locating of threat and danger: *we* have been hurt by *them* for 500 years. The nature of the threat had remained essentially the same, as had the struggle.

Additionally, the past provided the narrators with a discursive strategy to resist and subvert the harmful stereotypes which inscribed their subjugated positions *vis-à-vis* the *Ladino* world. They placed the themes of discrimination and marginalization into the context of the struggle of their *pueblo*, in myths of 500 years of suffering and resistance. They thus made sense of their own personal struggles and joined their suffering with those of their ancestors. Rosa explained: 'When I learned the history of the invasion it hurt.' Her personal painful experiences were seen as examples of a collective phenomenon and therewith became further fuel for the larger political project. She constructed a political identity linked with that of the collective. Like in most resistance or testimonial literature, in the narrators' texts, individual experience was explained as collective experience, as part of much wider power dynamics which defied the borders that contained both time and space.

Andrea, for example, talked about her process of politicization as a turning point, a gaining of 'clarity', and a connecting of her experiences to those of the collective. Andrea described in detail the injustices against Mayan women, as well as the reasons why Mayan women should be revindicated, drawing upon the myths surrounding the history of the Mayan *pueblo*. She reinterpreted her experiences and placed them in the context of Mayan women throughout history, as ever-sacrificing and resisting. In so doing, she also defined who she was in relation to those who threatened her at the time of the interview, such as the military, the state, and men, as well as her enemies of the past, the Spanish (who were discursively interchanged with their descendants, the *Ladinos*).

> My consciousness was born there [in the jungle and the CPRs.] It is not correct when they tell us today that we are not worth anything, that we don't have any participation in the society, in the development of Guatemala ... The same situation that I have experienced since I was a child up until today has made me have this consciousness to rise up as women to guard our heritage, to guard our sacrifices ... Always the female elders said that ... when the Spanish came here to Guatemala,

> when they came to invade, our grandparents were burned, tortured, burned alive. All the books where they had their scriptures were burned ... In this sense I understood ... the situation that they talked about when I had to live it. So I came to appreciate the elders because it is they who know more of the culture, how we have been for 500 years ... For me it is painful that we have not [only] been suffering for ten, fifteen years, but we have resisted for 500 years. (Andrea)

In mapping an uninterrupted lineage from the Spanish invasion to the counter-insurgency war of the 1980s, Andrea defined herself as re-experiencing the past struggles of her people. Although, the Mayan *pueblo* had been forced to change strategies to confront new threats, it drew upon its rootedness in history, struggle and resistance. The Mayan *pueblo*, according to Andrea, remained the same character in the unfolding of an ancient narrative about danger and threat. It is this history, which also decided the form of the present struggle and gave direction to the future struggle.

Andrea thus established her political identity, placed it in the context of her past and fixed it as a timeless given, thereby creating a stable base for resistance that rested upon the heritage of over 500 years. A 'we' of the past was created and resurfaced in the present, such as in Leticia's following words:

> With the knowledge of our ancestors, the history of them ... it was very beautiful when I grew up. My mother, my father said that I had to obey the elders; *we* obey elders ... Our ancestors left us to obey a great heritage. (Leticia) [*My emphasis*]

Nonetheless, the narrators' need to maintain cohesion in the face of external threat seems to involve circumscribing the identity categories upon which claims for change were being made. Security/safety involved cautiously defining and limiting who they were in the many different power relations which affected their lives, as well as carefully weaving a direct lifeline to a certain and linear history to which they belonged.

Safe-guarding identity

Much of the literature on gender and ethnicity and nationalism posits that as both custodians and transmitters of a particular identity, women (and their behavior) become highly political and decisive in cultural boundary making.[4] Correspondingly, Mayan women's role as 'guardians of the culture' was written into the ARIIP and in the 'official' discourses of the Mayan movement. The narrators also continually re-emphasized how women were ascribed the role of reproducers and guardians of the culture: in giving birth to children; providing for the needs of daily subsistence; care-taking of the young, elderly, and sick; and maintaining tradition through clothing, religion, ritual, customs, etc. They also lauded their unique relationship with the land. Women were the symbolic bearers of 'who they were'.

The narrators reinforced that their safety required a stable representation of Mayan women that could be identified throughout history, the present, and also, in the future. The stability of this subject demanded specific safeguarding; hence, the narrators paid much attention to establishing the continuity of their political identities throughout history. Their struggle and suffering mirrored that of their grandmothers; their identity was better articulated through their grandparents' lives. They therefore must reclaim the identity of the past. Hence, rescuing the culture entailed ensuring its meaning, as well as the borders that determined it from the Other. Women, the narrators explained, played a particular role in such archeology and 'excavation' of identity demarcation. Resistance, for women, meant preservation, revindication, reproduction and reconstruction.

Because the Mayan *pueblo* was threatened, the role of 'social reproducer' therefore became crucial in terms of cultural survival, and took on augmented significance in the politicization of Mayan identity.[5] Gloria explained: 'My mother always gave us this ideology: we are from here, you need to use your *corte*, and have to carry with you the customs that we do because tomorrow ... you will have to teach your children' (Gloria). The proud wearing of *traje* also symbolized a conscious act of resistance. Being Mayan, specifically a Mayan woman, meant resisting the dominant *Ladino* culture. Mercedes explained:

> Our *traje* is part of our identity, identification. Because our clothes are of us and we make it ourselves, so it is something very much our own. Somebody can't appear and tell us that we have to change to something else. As people, we have the right to choose our own clothes. But its not only that we ... like the clothes it's that they are part of our grandparents' heritage, therefore ... this is part of resistance that we – the Mayas – maintain. (Mercedes)

These roles were not just imposed upon women by the dominant cultural articulations, or the men in their communities. Many Mayan women recognized and esteemed their particular roles as 'defenders of the Mayan culture:' they ensured the reproduction of the culture – the language, the traditions, the cosmovision, against the barrage of both *Ladino*ization and ethnocide on the part of the Guatemalan military-state. Wearing *traje* in the face of a system of racist discrimination and marginalization that devalued or outright prohibited its place in the national culture was a central moment in many of the narratives. Many cited this moment of consciousness and opposition as the beginning of their active struggle. The Mayan *pueblo* did not necessarily succeed in transmitting the value – and the political significance – of Mayan women's roles as learned from the ancient Mayan cosmovision. Mayan women's crucial charge of maintaining and preserving the culture must therefore be *taught*. To achieve this, for instance, young girls who were members of a cultural organization clamored to speak into my tape recorder when I attended a congress organized by their organization. They had a message they wanted me to spread in the North:

> We ask for a call to consciousness of the grandparents that they know the heritage that they have and that they tell their children more and to teach them so that they are not ashamed and that they continue forward because the future is with the children. Also a call to consciousness to all the youths to integrate into the organizations because they are the future. All the grandparents and all of the organizations should teach them to use their *traje* and to speak their language ... I want to say this to all the people and this is what we are doing in the name of God. (Girl, fourteen years old)

The 'grandmothers', many narrators explained, could guide the way to the 'real' role of Mayan woman, and to their 'true' identity. Any deviations from this path were a result of the Spanish invasion and the resulting colonization/imperialism. The 'Spanish' and their descendents caused the degradation of Mayan women's standing and dignity. Mayan women, therefore, needed to find their original connection to the life-giving forces of the earth in order to regain their importance and respect. They could thereby re-establish the balance between men and women, people and their natural environment – and the stature of the Mayan *pueblo*. The past as seen through 'historical memory' therefore offered Mayan women a way to navigate back to their identity and culture and 'true' value. The past thus also promised security and safety. Onelia explained the salvaging pledge of a 'return' to the past as follows:

> The woman is the educator, even the generator of this world ... The woman has a lot of importance ... We are starting to see, as part of the history, as Mayan women in Guatemala. The grandparents have told us that before the Spanish invasion the woman was respected ... and her opinions were taken into account, because ... women shared much with Mother Earth. Mother Earth gives life; also, women give life ... Women lost all of this importance after the Spanish invasion ...[which made] women's importance be lost. From that point on they began to rape the women, our grandmothers. They would look for beautiful women and rape them. There was no more respect; this respect began to be lost. (Onelia)

Onelia underscored the importance of claiming the knowledge that the grandmothers enjoyed as a source of resistance and safety. The influence of the colonial powers, and, modernity led both men and women astray from their 'true' selves. Men had been 'forced' to adapt to colonial ways of dressing, working, and being in order to assimilate into *Ladino* culture and thus earn a living wage. Given the agricultural demographics of the country, traditional farming was no longer an option for the majority of Mayan men. They were thus already once removed from the land, which was seen as their spiritual and cultural origin. Women, and their connection to nature, therefore gained in symbolic currency. However, they too were eclipsed from their 'true' roles because of the insidious degradation of the Mayan *pueblo* in general and Mayan women in particular.

The narrators agreed that the notion that women should occupy subordinated positions in Mayan communities had been implanted by the sexist

Ladino society. Many explained, however, that Mayan men and women had succumbed to compliance with the colonial system. It was therefore crucial that they recognized their mistaken paths and re-connected with their heritage. This included revaluing Mayan women. Elena, for example, explained how she turned to the *Popol Vuh* to learn about the role of women and understood that women had also been partly responsible for allowing their positions in society to be limited, although, of course, the basic fault lay in the 'invasion'.[6] According to Elena, the key to re-establishing women's value and ultimate safety was through consciousness-raising about the mythological heroines who knew the way Mayan women should be, as well as the source of fortifying nucleus of Mayan women's worthiness:

> The woman contributed to assuming [her role]. It was the role that was imposed on the woman. I understood after ... I began to read the *Pop Vuh*. ... I took into account the grandmother Ixmucane.[7] She had much to do with the creation of the world ... The woman had an important role, now its cut short, limited ... One [reason] is that the same woman accepts it too, because it was the role imposed on women since the invasion, a thing which is not ours. So this was a failure for me ... It [required] ... consciousness-raising ... to understand that women are very capable, and it has been a challenge for me to continue raising people's consciousness. Historical memory is to recuperate all that is our culture. [...] In recuperating our historical memory we are going to really know what our role is, what our role was before in history, what our role is now today, how to interpret and understand the situations. (Elena)

Revalorizing Mayan-ness

The main thrust of the Mayan movement was directed towards 'rescuing' and revaluing Mayan-ness. The Mayan *pueblo* therefore specifically worked towards countering the definition of the victim and the Other in the oppressors' eyes with a subverted, valorized identity. It replenished the denotation of being indigenous with positive associations of national (ethnic) pride and belonging, culled from the past. These new meanings provided a sense of security, belonging, purpose, as well as (it was hoped) a means for attaining a more advantageous political position in Guatemala in terms of the divisions of resources, knowledge, and power.[8] At the precipitous time on the eve of 'Peace', being Mayan bore with it not only a history of racist repression and violence, but also one of greatness and splendor. It is this latter sense of being Mayan that offered the narrators a safe and nourishing space, pregnant with future possibilities and still glimmering with the glory of the past. Onelia succinctly explained how identifying herself as Mayan – naming her identity – gave her pride and made her 'feel good:'

> I feel that I am part of a *pueblo* ... with a grand culture that was very strong ... The *Ladinos* say that if a person ... is indigenous she ... feels inferior. I do not agree ... We are exploited ... but there is honor [which comes from] saying 'I am from the Mayan *pueblo*' and I feel good saying it. (Onelia)

Many of the narrators emphasized that because of the violence and extremity of the marginalization of Mayans throughout history, it was paramount that the *pueblo* counter the harms caused by the nation-state and the *Ladino* society by rescuing and reclaiming the culture. Only through an excavation of the culture could the Mayan *pueblo* find the tools to create a future which would honor the grandness of their heritage and religion, and which would deflect the power of the forces of modernization, militarization and *Ladino*ization.

Being Mayan thus carried with it not only a history of suffering, but also a fledgling notion of privilege. It is this privilege that the narrators sought to recognize and feel in their depictions of what it meant to be Mayan and ultimately, safe. When I asked Gloria if she had recently begun to identify herself as Mayan, she explained:

> Before we worked to have our consciousness, but we did not see. There was a certain division between the classes, but we did not identify ourselves as Mayas. We always said ... 'this one is *Ladino*, and that one is indigenous' ... Now we have succeeded ... to revive the name 'Maya' [...] There is a song that one of my nieces sings: 'I am Maya, I come from Mayan blood and that is why I speak my Mayan language' ... It is very beautiful ... I believe that many *compañeros* ... have sacrificed much to succeed all this, because we now have the privilege to say that we are Mayans. (Gloria)

Gloria also touched on an aspect of the Mayan movement that has confounded many researchers and critics alike: namely how did the politicization of class and ethnic identity coalesce? Why did political claims that previously were articulated as class based (such as those for land reform) become articulated as elements of cultural survival and revival? Gloria seemed to say that political, cultural awareness arose in the Mayan *pueblo* through time and through political work around class issues. Although always aware of the differences between indigenous and *Ladinos*, many did not 'see' the 'true' value – both in terms of cultural worth, and political power – of being 'Mayan'. Only recently did they understand that their political identity resided in their historical cultural memory, in their Mayan-ness, as it also related to their *campesina* identity. The material basis of their class-based identity also underpinned the spiritual and cultural connection to the land described above. To argue that an 'ethnicization' of what was previously a class struggle arose for purely 'instrumental' purposes, neglects the deep and long-standing import of the cultural meanings informing the way people think and act.

As the narrators relayed in their stories, their class identities (often as *campesinas*) and their ethnic identities (Mayan) informed each other. Any attempt at separating Mayan-ness from *campesina*-ness resulted in parceling a dynamic whole that was constantly changing form and constitution into separate components for analytical or strategic purposes. Similarly, the in/security configuration that was formed in tandem with these identity constellations could neither be partitioned off into separate 'security' needs, nor for that matter, specific threats. The threats involved with land issues could not be solely tied to a *campesina* identity; the narrators named them as threats from the complex and even contradictory subject positions they occupied in different contexts. Hence, Gloria did not thoroughly resolve the queries noted above. However, perhaps they are simply not resolvable in a tidy way; indeed their very untidiness might offer surprising venues for constructive resistance – such as the rejection of a parsing of ones identity into separate components.

Crossing traitorous borders

In sum, the fear of losing the connection to history, as well as 'losing the culture' ran as an underlying theme in the majority of the texts. The threat of cultural dearth loomed over the promise of posterity, as well as the connection to history. Belonging to an anchored identity category assured a stable base of security and a platform from which to look ahead towards the future. And it allowed the narrators a clear and irrefutable sense of who they were in the midst of a seeming morass of historical and present-day subjugation and danger. Knowing who they, their ancestors, as well as their children were, offered a safe space, a space where uncertainty was thwarted and belonging brought both support and immortality – as well as the establishment of a political identity from which to make claims of protection, for security. The Mayan heroes and heroines of history lived on and enjoyed a particular site in the human community, despite the enemy's attempts to destroy them. Thus, many of the narrators indicated that their safety was contingent upon securing and strengthening the identity category, 'Mayan woman', through cultural revival and historical remembering. It was dangerous to 'forget'.

Elena, a highly politicized cultural activist, warned of the dangers of allowing the culture to decay. She chastised those who strove towards acceptance in the 'other' society, either out of necessity or choice. The markers of *Ladino*ization usually included not wearing *traje*, as well as the speaking of Spanish and 'forgetting' one's Mayan language. Abandoning one's culture also involved espousing the gendered norms of behavior that prevailed in *Ladino* society. She explained that it was dangerous to participate in allowing the culture to decay and to contribute to the devaluation of Mayan women:

> Many Mayas have stopped wearing their traditional clothes so that the other society ... the *Ladinos* will accept them ... The group doesn't view them anymore as Mayas, because they do not speak the language, don't wear the clothes, as if they devalue themselves, devalue the culture. But they can't be *Ladinos*: they are forming another group without identity, without culture. ... There are women who have done this ... and it is dangerous, dangerous to devalue [us]. The majority of women are [already] devalued ... The Mayan culture is starting to decay ... and we women are those who supported it the most ... It is not necessary to arrive at this ... losing being Mayan. In [such a] case, she loses everything, it is dangerous because she is decaying the culture.

> ... Instead, she needs to be sure of herself, valorize herself and be conscious of her role as a woman. (Elena)

I have found it most challenging to try to follow the reasoning of this type of statement; once again my difficulties might hint at possible lacunae and gaps in the cohesiveness of the narratives.

On the one hand, Elena said that it was possible to lose one's culture and consequently contribute to the overall decay of the Mayan culture. On the other hand, she explained that it was impossible to become *Ladina* (although this seems to remain the inherent threat). Instead, those who tried formed a group without culture. Thus, it seems that according to Elena, *Ladino*ization could not fully occur; instead, attempts at 'crossing over' created a lost and identityless group of aspiring '*Ladinos*' who did not fit in anywhere, yet nonetheless degraded their origins. The threat of 'decaying the culture' thus came from the racist *Ladino* society, and the seduction (constructed via racism) of 'becoming' *Ladino* – which was necessarily unsuccessful.

Mayan women needed to focus on their own participation in the degradation of the culture and themselves, as well as on their own room for maneuvering and resistance within these confines. Where the threshold of being able to maintain one's culture lay – and therewith the sphere of danger and the assignment of threat – seemed to shift in different settings. Diana, for instance, explained that if Mayan women stopped wearing their *traje* because they were refugees or because of economic necessity (*traje* was expensive), then they remained Mayan. Hence, their culture might have been dormant or underprioritized because of material and situational necessity, but it was not lost or destroyed. If, however, they moved to the capital to find work and consequently started wearing Western dress and adopting Western 'ideologies', they lost their identity: 'Although they do not lose their being indigenous, they lose a part of their culture' (Diana). Here, Diana seems to have distinguished between being indigenous, which was inescapable and presumably carried a negative connotation, and being Mayan, which was a privilege that could be squandered. The threat, as she identified it, resided most clearly in the unaware or even conscious neglect of Mayan women's inherent value, which in turn threatened the political identity: 'Mayan'.

Diana placed herself above those who were unable to withstand abandoning one's traditions and therefore, culture. Mayans (indigenous) thus fell into at least two different categories: those who threatened the culture through their neglect, and those who actively worked at cultural preservation and revivification and were therefore superior. Without conscious effort, the risk of cultural betrayal was enormous.

Although apparent in these statements, the gray areas in between these categories remained as an aside to the narrators' main point: namely, one became dangerous and threatening (to the *pueblo*) when one contributed to the decay of the Mayan culture. Mayans who lived and worked in the rural areas and were somewhat separated from the more *Ladino*ized cities, however, seemed generally to be an exception to this critique. Nonetheless, their role in the maintenance and the revalorization of the culture was neither simple nor clear. On the one hand they were lauded and held forward as the foundation of the Mayan *pueblo*, and on the other they were treated as if they were ignorant children who did not yet realize the historical or political significance of, for example, their *traje* or their language. They needed to be taught about their identity as Mayans. Indeed, the Mayan popular movement commonly criticized the more elite 'cultural movements' for a patronizing attitude that neither fully respected nor reflected the daily lives and political problems of the majority of Mayan peasants (Bastos and Camus, 1993, 1995). There was a grand effort to raise political consciousness about their identity as Mayans among the *pueblo*.

Lourdes, whom I interviewed at a meeting for women in her community, held at her house and organized by a cultural organization, explained: 'Some people have said that we have lost our culture. This is what they [in the organization] are saying. So clearly we are not going to lose it if we reclaim it' (Lourdes). She then explained that it could be reclaimed by going on courses and learning about rights and their culture. For me, it was quite surprising to watch the meeting as it took place. Many women were gathered in a small room and were looking at the pictures in a consciousness-raising booklet about rights of Mayan women. In the first half of this booklet, there were pictures of a Mayan woman experiencing discrimination in many different settings, including the home, marketplace, school, etc. Its purpose, as it was explained to me, was to highlight how Mayan women had been devalued, and to indicate that such discrimination need not occur. The second half of the booklet was devoted to depicting how Mayan women were respected in the ancient Mayan traditions (hence, blaming *Ladino*ization for sexism and racism) and what constituted the rights of Mayan women, as stated in the ARIIP. The organization that called this meeting presented the booklet as an 'effort ... to give knowledge about, and promote the rights that we enjoy as Mayans [in Guatemala]. This is to impel activities geared towards succeeding in rescuing the thinking and values of [the] Mayan culture.'

The women seated around the room could understand neither Spanish, nor the Mayan language spoken by the meeting's facilitator. The meeting was therefore falteringly translated from Spanish into their language by one of the women's husbands. Although the booklet was geared towards identifying and rectifying instances of discrimination, the meeting was almost solely focused on reciting an oft-told narrative of political rhetoric about the ancient Mayan *pueblo* and the importance of calling oneself 'Mayan'.

Envisioning the future

While explaining their efforts to rescue the culture, the narrators identified a vision of a safer, better future for the Mayan *pueblo*, rooted in the remembering of the past. In working towards this future, and in rejecting the subject position allotted them in the current situation, they reformed what being a Mayan woman meant to them, both in the present and as an ideal for the future (as it was conjured in relation to the imagined past.) Carmen described her sense of the larger scope of her struggle:

> We have to struggle ... although we are threatened ... because we feel it is good what we have accomplished now. These are our ideas. We want them to respect us as women ... with our languages ... with our *traje*. ... We do not say that only we as indigenous have to be respected, no [we want to] make it equal, a unity [irrespective or whether they are] poor *Ladinas*, or indigenous. (Carmen)

Although her very struggle placed her in a position of danger, and she continued to endure many difficulties and harms because she was a Mayan woman, Carmen confirmed the value of her struggle and sacrifice. She was even able to extend her vision for the future to include equality and unity with *Ladinos*.

This statement at first may appear surprising, considering the ardor of her struggle for Mayan cultural revival, and her condemning of *Ladino* dominance and discrimination throughout history. However, Carmen's statement also shed light on the subtle, yet foundational discursive interdependence of the subject positions: 'Mayan' and 'Ladina'. Elena's and other's texts clarified that being Mayan connoted a subaltern position as well as a struggle to refute that position. Similarly, 'Ladina' connoted a superior position in relation to 'Mayan' and mediated a history of colonialism and racism. If the Mayan *pueblo* were to 'rescue its culture' and succeed in recreating a *pueblo* that mirrored the grandeur of it's past, its relation with *Ladino* society would necessarily transform. The interrelated and continually co-constructed categories of self and Other would form new (yet perhaps still binary) constellations. The meaning of both 'Mayan' and '*Ladina*' would change dramatically, as would the tenure of the power relations between these subject positions. Furthermore, the embracing of both identities would rely on different assignments of threat and danger, as well as safety and well-being.

Notes

1 Being treated as 'animals' is a common theme in the texts and reappears in different contexts throughout the narratives.

2 One narrator even altered this standard triple identity to include a forth subject position of 'illiterate' (Gloria). According to figures available in the early 1990s, 85 percent of the women in the rural areas were illiterate (Jonas, 1991: 178).

3 Language and the use of *traje* were prominently important markers in many different articulations of the Mayan discourse. They warranted special protection under the

stipulations of the ARIIP. See also Fischer and Brown (1996), as well as Green (1999: chapter 6).

4 See e.g. Anthias and Yuval-Davis (1989); Anzaldúa (1987); Jayawardena (1986); Kandiyoti (1991); Moghadam (1994); Peterson (1994); Radcliffe and Westwood (1993, 1996); Trinh, T. Minh-ha (1989); Wilson (1992); Yuval-Davis (1997).

5 Ibid.

6 The *Popol Vuh*, is considered the 'post conquest Mayan bible' (Nelson, 1999: 161). It is one of the earliest and most reliable sources of history that describes the Mayan cosmovision. It has also become a political marker of identity and of the Mayan *pueblo*'s links to pre-Colombian Mayan civilization (English edition: Saravia, 1980).

7 Ixmucane is the Mayan Goddess of Creation.

8 Paraphrased from interviews conducted with leaders of *Copmagua*, in October 1995.

6

Organizations/movements: building a collective self

When someone kills your family, the more you are going to organize, the more consciousness you will have, and the better you will work for your *pueblo*. (Onelia)

IN ADDITION TO THE UNRG (the umbrella guerrilla organization), many political and social organizations (including unions, human rights organizations, church study groups etc. devoted to ending the counter-insurgency and oppression) blossomed during the armed conflict. These arose during the 1970s and 80s and became rooted in the Guatemalan peasantry and the indigenous population. While the guerilla movement primarily articulated a discourse of class struggle, demands based in Mayan identity and experiences of exclusion burgeoned among the peasant populations and the indigenous intellectuals (Le Bot, 1995; Warren, 1998). The experiences from state structures of control and abuse were intensified during the conflict, which lead to an even further indigenous alienation and distrust of state and government, while also intensifying demands for societal change. The articulated public concern was not only to establish a sustainable peace, but also to redress the long-term repression and discrimination of indigenous peoples and peasants.

Although severely diminished in scope, the insurgency war continued during the time of the interviews (1995), as did counter-insurgency tactics at all levels of society. Despite their endorsement of a civilian government, the military and the leaders of the private sector continued to share control of the country (although they were also troubled with competing factions.) A 'democratic opening' had indeed occurred with the failing of the auto-coup in 1993. Nevertheless, the state/army still perceived those who organized as threats to the nation. This was evidenced in continued human rights abuses and death threats directed at leaders and members of the Popular Movement (CEH, 1999; REMHI/ODHAG, 1999).

In 1995, those organizations working for indigenous rights formed a coalition, with a leading co-ordinator, *Copmagua*. *Copmagua* was intended to lead the popular movements in demanding indigenous rights and the government's fulfillment of the ARIIP (Jonas, 1999). It was also a bridge between the Mayan cultural movements (made up mostly of academics and linguists) and Mayans working in the 'popular' organizations (i.e. in *campesino*, widows, human rights, organizations etc.).

Because of their common over-riding goal of 'salvaging the Mayan *pueblo*', I use the term Mayan movement in my discussion to refer both to the Mayan cultural movement and to the popular organizations that also articulated their demands in terms of rights/identity of the Mayan *pueblo*. Despite their differences, the organizations for which the narrators worked all provided a forum from which they could participate politically *as Mayan women*, although they imbued its meaning differently. I have therefore treated the organization/political movement as a spatio-temporal context. I address how the narrators situated themselves discursively within these movements, and within the broader site of their political projects.

Reasons for organizing

At the time of the interviews, organizing or belonging to a political movement that could be considered critical of the state was treated as a subversive act in Guatemala. Nonetheless, many people chose to join such organizations. Why? Several of the narrators explained that they became politically active out of necessity; they were left with no other options. For some, such as Andrea and Susanna, the circumstances created out of the violence left them little room to maneuver. Andrea explained, for instance, that she and others organized in order to survive in the jungle after fleeing the assault of the army on her village. Susanna joined others along with her mother in search of her 'disappeared' father. Both described their lives as being without options; organizing became a means by which they could perhaps attain basic goals, such as food, water, and the knowledge about the whereabouts or death of a loved one. For them, it was not initially an explicit political act or even choice. It was the only alternative.

Others organized for concrete and immediate needs, such as clean water, money, and material to build a house, and land to plant some subsistence crops. Carmen, for instance, organized a group of widowed women so that, together, they could make claims on the government for land and assistance. The act of joining together as a collective and demanding to be heard and regarded by the state placed them immediately in an explicit political site. Through their experiences as newly configured political subjects, they identified themselves as actors in resistance to the racist and violent strategies of the state. When I asked Carmen how she became involved in the widows' organization, she replied:

> I myself organized it. It turned out right because now it is growing with people ... not only for the food, but because of threats, the sequestering, the patrols, the youths ... In all the areas women are organizing. (Carmen)

What at first was an effort at gaining some material benefits turned later into a larger more comprehensive movement for justice for the Mayan *pueblo*, an end to the repression, as well as an end to the forced recruitment of Mayan youths into the army and the civil patrols. She continued to organize the women because: 'the *Señores* who were making lists were bothering people in their houses.' The already-formed widows' organization provided a venue for the larger political platform.[1]

Others did not talk about their engagement in the organizations as a conscious choice. Instead, they became involved with working with their organizations through a series of circumstances apparently beyond their control. They spoke about their life as if it were a path that they tread out of necessity. Some, like Mercedes, Onelia, and Lourdes, became involved with the organizations as children. They established in their texts that working with the organization was part of their family heritage and was a 'natural' choice in the context of their families, although in most cases it was far from uncomplicated.[2] Mercedes explained, for instance, how her linkage with her father and the rest of her family determined her analysis of 'the problems'. She talked in terms of the 'discrimination' of the 'workers'. She thus situated her analysis of the causes of the conflict and her situation in the ideological legacy from her father, thus soldering a link to her family and community. This link guided her to choose to travel with other members of her father's organization when the repression closed the option of studying. She stated:

> It is the one thing that joins us ... Since I was little, from my father, I began to know the problems ideologically, and understand the roots of the problems ... In the Costa Sur, the people discriminate against the workers ... You abandon your house, you lose everything, lose your studies. What is left? For me, there was nothing left but to integrate myself in [my organization].
>
> Q: Were you afraid?
>
> A: Yes! Afraid, yes!. [...] There was nothing left for me to do ... If I am here, I may die. If I am there, I may die. So it is better I go to die if I am ready to die here ... [So] I accompanied the *compañeros* to different areas. Yes, we encountered difficult moments. (Mercedes)

Most narrators concurred that, given the horrors that the alternatives promised, there was nothing left but to join an organization and resist. Similarly, Carmen stated that she 'organized because of the repression ... As widows, we are left with many children.' Carmen asserted the necessity of caring for children as a catalyst to organizing, clearly expressing that she/they were left no alternative. Many narrators also indicated that their sense of justice did not allow them any alternative but to struggle. Delia explained, for example, 'We are struggling for land and [against] sickness, my husband struggles for the land and I [against] sickness ... I am going to work with medicine, and to meet with the people. This is my duty' (Delia). Here, Delia clearly articulated her sense of duty as a driving force in her choices. Nonetheless, I believe that it would be a mistake to interpret these words as expressing a passivity or lack of agency in joining the popular struggle against the repression in all of its forms. There were many who did not choose to address their situations through organizing. Indeed, organizing clearly bore with it intense immediate danger.

Dangers of organizing

According to the narrators, being an explicitly politically active person (perhaps especially a woman) in Guatemala was dangerous.[3] For instance, many of the people whom I interviewed explained that they were under constant surveillance; several told me that they had received death threats, as recently as a few weeks before our conversation. They conveyed to me a distrust of their own personal future: their death might arrive at any moment. Rosa feared leaving the organization at night, walking alone during the day, and even attending social gatherings, because 'the enemy might be there.' Mercedes explained that she knew that she was alive by providence: 'this work was dangerous; we knew that we escaped from many things.' She then recounted for me some of the experiences that were most terrifying for her. However, upon reading the transcribed copy of our first interview, she asked me to refrain from retelling these instances in my writing for fear that the army might become aware of the tactics she and her *compañeras* used to avoid detection and abduction.

Through representing an ever-present and looming threat, the army exercised a potent mechanism of control over the population. Although in many instances they did not succeed in fully silencing the narrators, the army instilled a fear of repercussions, which propelled them to act cautiously and often covertly. For instance, after reading her narrative, one narrator decided that she did not want me to use any of her testimony in my work. She feared that the information she had given me was too sensitive and might enable the army to identify her. After consultation with her family, she then requested that I dispose of all copies of her text and not refer to her story (except in the manner in which I am doing here.) Her potent absence spoke in some ways louder than her text might have. Thus, the narrators censored what they said to me. In the case where they did divulge sensitive information to me, they asked me to censor myself in the rewriting of their stories. A new circle of silencing and secrets including me was then added to the already intricate relationships of distrust and confidence that organized their existence.

Gloria, for example, told me two very different stories in the two times we met. The first time, I foolishly chose a well-frequented *gringo* restaurant for our meeting. She gave me a general account of her 'struggles', with little detail or emotional content. The next time we met in private. When I asked her if she would like to add anything to the interview that we had begun the night before, she explained that what she had said was censored and careful because she did not know who was sitting around us and behind us. She did not know who was listening to our conversation. She then explained that she had experienced much 'control' recently and was afraid to speak openly. She explained that despite the so-called 'democratic opening', danger and fear still organized her life and the difficult choices that she made every day. She concluded: 'Because of this I think that the repression will continue always here in Guatemala; I do not think that this will end. Truly, I am a little afraid. Sometimes one intends to struggle for the good of all and it is a very strong sacrifice'(Gloria). Organizing openly therefore implied committing oneself to live life in a state (both literally and figuratively) of constant insecurity.

According to Gloria, part of the military's tactics was to be ever present. One never knew when they would appear or when they were listening, or where the *orejas* ('ears', informants) were. The menacing figures of the military were a constant reminder of the dangers of trespassing the dictates of national security. Gloria's testimony mirrors the experiences Carmen described in chapter 4, when the military commissioners and heads of the PACs sat at the back of the meeting 'sharpening their machetes', and threatening the women who were organizing with, among other things, sexual abuse. Gloria explained that 'always there is military presence' around those who are organizing on behalf of the Mayan *pueblo*. She explained, however, that she refused to admit that she was afraid of them because 'if she does, they will continue with the same methods.' However, during one period, the threats became so intense that she stopped working for the organizations in order to protect herself. It is 'a pure miracle that nothing has happened to me!' she reflected (Gloria).

In addition, Gloria commented that the constant threat of the military also created a climate where time for reflection was scarce, and where intricate systems of 'covert' activity and communication developed to counteract the ramifications for the movement of leaders being killed or 'disappeared'. She explained:

> There are *compañeras* who think and think. But I say to them, 'Look the time slips away from us while we think about if we should do it or not.' [...] I rapidly tell the information that I hear [to someone] because we do not know, perhaps tomorrow I will not exist anymore and my *compañeras* will not have any information. (Gloria)

Gloria explained how the members of the organization must hold in mind their own mortality and perhaps even the imminence of their own death in order for their work to continue despite their demise. This necessity required that they define themselves as members of a community whose individual role could not be separated from the collective. Sharing knowledge assured the security of others in the struggle as well as the overall work of the organization.

As one can surmise from the tenor of Gloria's statement above, although present, fear for one's own life did not punctuate the narratives in the same magnitude as fear for other's lives did. In this sense, the army/state capitalized on the solidarity felt among the Mayan *pueblo* to hinder politically active people from openly organizing others, and thereby endangering them. Maria explained, for example, 'It does not bother me to die ... if I am going to die it is for something ... there is a reason. What hurts me is for the people, that they will kill them.' Additionally, Mercedes explained that one time when she was in the rural areas the army persecuted her. (She then told me the story of that persecution, but asked me to extract it from my work.) She commented, however, that her main concern was the position her presence created for the people she was attempting to organize: 'The fear that we had was that they would capture us. What would they then do with the people there?'

Mercedes explained that the army had told the people that if they were in the organization they were members of the guerilla and would therefore be killed. She expressed that hers was a difficult position because on the one hand, she wanted to provide security for the people by getting them to join forces against the army and the large landowners, while, on the other hand, she was endangering them by her presence and by encouraging them to join the organization. The locus of security for the people, according to Mercedes, therefore, was tentative and ambiguous.

Silencing through generating fear thus hindered people from challenging the dominant discourse of the nation-state and the army. Because of their fear, many did not join organizations that were seen as subversive by the military. Amara explained that it was 'hard to organize people because the army manipulates how they think. I will never tire of mentioning the army' (Amara). Gloria also echoed similar concerns:

> Due to the same discrimination that gave rise to the organizations, if a group is organized, they qualify it as subversive. So all organization became undone ... For example, there are leaders of organizations who had to go into exile because of the repression (or) ... received death threats, were sequestered, tortured, forced into exile ... So, the people in some communities still do not like to organize ... [They say] 'We are afraid ... because we do not know what consequences we will suffer ... Still this fear exists. It has been a mark that has been left ... It is very alive, because still the people have not forgotten it. This is a limit that we encounter ... [the danger] still exists, we can not say that we are already free, no, there is still control, still this fear. (Gloria)

Becoming involved in an organization and thus explicitly contesting the hegemony of the state required that the narrators place their individual bodies in greater risk in the hopes of 'rescuing' the cultural/political body of the people, the *pueblo*. The narrators thus named an 'existential' threat against the survival of their (imagined) community in complying with the violent policies of the state which transgressed – and even placed into question – their individual existence.

Gendering participation

Participating in an organization involved placing oneself in a precarious position in sites other than those directly determined by the hegemony of national security. Many narrators explained that the constellation of gender relations in the family, the community, and within the organization made participation difficult, if not impossible for many Mayan women. Onelia depicted a situation whereby women's obligations in the family in terms of housework and social reproductive work (i.e. caring for children, the sick, and the elderly) made their participation practically laborious. Their subordinate position to their husbands rendered them subject to their will and wrath if they 'disobeyed' them. Women belonged in the realm of the household and the family; 'political' work outside of the family sphere was inappropriate for them. Furthermore, the narrators explained that generally, within the Mayan communities, girls and women were socialized to believe that they should not form and express opinions, especially if speaking their mind implied challenging the men's authority. Their low self-esteem in terms of presenting themselves in public with opinions and capability impeded their full participation.

> We thought in the beginning that it was easy to say that one should participate. Yet, we were met with difficulties ... Often the woman said, 'well, I cannot. I am not going to go' even if the husband said that she could participate in the meeting. 'I cannot. I do not have the courage to speak. It is better if I do not go.' Other times the woman has the desire to participate, but the man says, 'No, you are not going to go because you have to remain in the house, because if you go, who will do the cleaning? Who will care for the children, who will make the food?' (Onelia)

Hence, in addition to the momentous endeavor of establishing themselves as political subjects in opposition to the nation-state, Mayan women must also overcome many deeply ingrained and obdurate ways of being and relating to others in order to construct themselves as political subjects. These modes of being were axial in their gender identities, and, of course, informed all other identities.

When I asked Johanna to elaborate on the obstacles that she encountered in her work with women in their organizations, she talked about how the *Señores* capitalized upon the power of these discourses. She explained as follows:

> More than anything [the obstacles we encounter are] the men. They speak about us and say that we go out and do things that we should not do, they accuse us badly to our *compañeros*. They say, 'Ah, these women are giving themselves to other men, doing things that they should not do and you are stupid and remain in the house.'

> Many *compañeras* do not want to accept the duties they are assigned [in the organization] because their *compañeros* are those who pressure them. 'I do not want to bring problems on myself' they say 'because my *compañero* will not let me. If I go to a meeting, he is going to say that I am making problems ...' They think that they have their women only to keep her inside, they think that the women do not have rights to work or anything, this is the big ignorance of these people. This is what limits us most. (Johanna)

Through questioning the men's 'masculinity' (as measured by his ability to control his wife and assure her sexual fidelity), the men harnessed the gendered regulatory practices within the family and the community to impede the people (women) from organizing. The mutually reinforcing economies of sexism and national security policies thus doubly silenced the women and delimited their ability to be active political subjects. Johanna explained that in defying these codes, the women placed themselves in danger in both the family/community context and in the context of the national political climate.

Organizing a safe haven

Despite the often dramatic insecurity which openly protesting the state (and others in power, such as the plantation owners) entailed, many of the narrators expressed that they felt better organizing than remaining quiet. Rosa explained: 'If you organize, you are considered bad, if you don't, the same. It's better to organize'(Rosa). She explained that the benefits of organizing and struggling for one's rights outweighed the risks of placing one's life and those around one in danger. The narrators argued that they were at risk anyway; that the government/army might kill them no matter what they did, so it was better to at least try to change the political and economic conditions that made this omnipresent threat possible than complacently to accept oppression and violence.

> A *Señora* told me that she would not organize because they come and kill you if you do ... So, I explained the importance [of organizing]. Now there is persecution, there is much pressure. And, now we should have more organizations to not let them win. [...] Several *compañeros* were afraid and retired from the organization [...] We have seen cases where they have sequestered families and then they turn up dead, but ... our slogan is: 'the more the repression, the more organization', because we do not want the bad to overcome us. We have to work to combat these wrongs.
>
> There arrived a moment when people who are from the intelligence of the army were following me and made threats. So, faced with this situation, one has to take care, because one does not know at what moment they will get you ... But this does not discourage me ... Oh no, on the contrary ... It gives me more courage that it is necessary to continue in the struggle ... to not give up hope that we'll arrive at living in a more just society. (Onelia)

Onelia explained that the army could never overpower the Mayan *pueblo*, because the more they attempted to extinguish the efforts of opposition, the more the people would struggle to find ways to counter them.

When I asked Carmen if she were afraid to organize, she explained that she was not truly afraid because she was organizing for a just cause. The righteousness of her struggle provided the fulfillment that she needed to continue working, despite the accusations from the authorities. Her belief that her work did 'good' alleviated the fear of repercussions because they would be based on erroneous claims. They might occur, but because of their bogus character, they could not harm her soul and her work, her *self*, although they might harm her body. She stated:

> No, I am not afraid ... No, we want good ideas ... We already have force. We are enough...I am not afraid. Sometimes it pains me, but it only pains me a little ... If my day arrives, I will fall, if God [wills] I will have a little of life [left], I will be given a little [time left] to work. Yes, so it is. (Carmen)

It seems as if Carmen located her subjectivity somewhere beyond her body, although, of course, she recognized the constraints of her physical self (as witnessed in her statement 'If my day arrives, I will fall'.) Nevertheless, who she was in relation to her struggle was crafted both in resistance and in her 'good ideas'. These ideas indicated that she was working towards a different future than the one promised by the national policies. Her 'work' towards these goals then delineated her identity.

Indeed, it appears that the narrators' 'subjectivity' (as they defined it) transcended their physical selves. For instance, many of the narrators explained that they would prefer to die struggling against oppression than to accept living under the control of the military and therewith the demise, as they seem to have seen it, of their *pueblo*. Diana explained, for example, that despite the danger, she had 'no other choice' but to struggle, because there were many more who were suffering beside her. When I asked her if she were afraid, she replied:

> [It is] not only me who is suffering; there are thousands of children, youths, women, elderly. So if I die, so what? There is no other choice for me. One needs to search for ways to take care ... I do not want to die yet; I still have some small things to do. (Diana)

Yet, despite her apparent acceptance of possibly being killed because of her political involvement, Diana indicated that she certainly did not wish for martyrdom – if only to be able to keep resisting. When I asked Onelia if she were afraid, she replied:

> No, If I were afraid, I would not be here ... If one is afraid, it does not help one to continue struggling ... it is certain that one is afraid of death ... because if one is already dead, what can one do? I could not help; I could not do anything. We try to protect our lives ... because what we want is to struggle, to help the people to organize. But, if one day we fall, what is left? ... If the enemy kills us, what can we do? The important thing is that there are others who are struggling. (Onelia)

The narrators also explained that the organization provided safety both in sheer numbers, as well as in offering a community of resistance. Mercedes stated that despite an increased occurrence of threat, she felt safeguarded by the fact that other people were aware of the danger she faced and would monitor any incidents. 'Now I feel again the pressure from the patrols, but I believe there are more eyes, more hands, and laws, which are going to aid us, to protect us.' Furthermore, an international community made up of NGOs, Minugua, and researchers like me (to name a few), lent their protection through their presence and awareness of the political situation.

Organizations also provided a collective counter-force to the brutality of the hegemonic forces of those in power. Rosa told of how because she was ensconced in her organization, she did not allow the military to intimidate her.

> When I received death threats, I did not go backwards. On the contrary, I said I'll have to find a way to solve this, and I counted on the organization and the *compañeros*. [I asked them] 'What ideas do you give me, because if I continue with my struggles, I will always be persecuted, if not the enemies will always bother me ... so it's better to keep struggling.' (Rosa)

The organization bolstered Rosa with moral support and ideas of how to resist the persecution of the army. It also provided her with a vocation, shelter, and a community – the backing that she needed in order to withstand the army's pressure and threats. Together she and her *compañeras* fought back with tools soldered in the experience of collective marginality and resistance.

For many of the narrators, the organization also offered a forum for the writing of a counter-narrative to that of the nation-state. Carmen explained how the shelter of the organization allowed people to begin to speak. She explained that her conversations with me, for instance, gave her the opportunity for her voice 'to be heard'.

> Before we did not talk to people like you because of fear and because we did not have the ideas, or the experience. But now, well, I am not going to say that now that we are organized, we are not afraid to speak. Yes, we are afraid. But now we can discuss our situation ... The change now is that we are in the public light, in every country, the voice of X can be heard ... [to let people know] that we are in this situation in Guatemala... The government says that in Guatemala, the people are well, are content, [that they] are giving aid to the communities ... My god! Not one time have we collaborated ... with the government. Yes, we have assistance, but it is result of our own efforts. (Carmen)

Through the venue of the organization, Carmen not only spoke, but she directly challenged the 'Truth' as stated by the state and thereby named her in/security and its attendant identity, Mayan woman. Her organization offered a different account of reality both nationally and internationally which disrupted the official story. The organization provided a ground from which countering the government/army – and being heard – was possible, although still dangerous.

Additionally, Manuela explained how the organization countered the hegemony of the nation-state by creating an enclave of community and trust in the rule of terror established by national security policies. Manuela talked of the safety she found in her first experience with a church-based organization. 'The message was not to confide in anyone, because you never know ... [It gave me] much security to be in a group of people where no one would say what you said to anyone else' (Manuela). According to many of the narrators' experiences, belonging to an organization offered a united front against the oppressor, and a forum for the sharing of confidences. These offered security and safety. Furthermore, this sense of community undermined the 'divide and conquer' strategy of the military; instead, it constituted a forum for strengthened resistance.

Hence, in addition to 'safety in numbers', the organizations, and the Mayan/women/*campesina* movement represented comradeship, and a sense of belonging to a group with a common history and a common goal. Onelia, for instance, explained that the organization had been imbedded in her since childhood. It gave her a purpose and a place to fit in; it became an important component of the identity of her family as 'those who resist' (and have suffered). Similarly, Susanna explained that she was 'happy because there [was] "*companerismo*".' She explained that 'there are no conflicts' and that everyone in the organization 'supports each other'. Delia juxtaposed the organization directly with the army, and openly identified herself with the organization, refuting all that the army stood for and did. She stated:

> The army does not like the organization ... I am not afraid. I prefer the organization [to the army] ... I am not afraid here. Yes it is good because there is support; there is advice ... The army, on the other hand, only kills ... All the women like the organization; they talk about good things. (Delia)

The majority of the narrators thus demonstrated that belonging to an organization and a larger political movement could provide security through the very feeling of belonging. The narrators relayed that they belonged to a larger project, a collective with a particular history. They located themselves and their trials in this history, thus finding solace and inspiration for struggling to change the situation of their people. Through this project, they found a voice that articulated an alternative challenging narrative to the one that harmed them. If they were to die in this process, there would be many more to carry on the work, hence their immortality was, in some sense, guaranteed.

The self therefore was sculpted by its connection with, and belonging to, the collective. Mercedes, for instance, spoke of her political consciousness extending beyond the 'personal level' onto that of the *pueblo*:

> I feel ... that the vision and the consciousness of one opens a bit more and this pain that one has suffered is no longer kept at the personal level ... It is certain that it is painful; these experiences are ugly. The saddest is that a whole pueblo ... all that we as a family have had to live, continues to suffer at this very moment ... I am participating in an organization, I think of the life of the organization, not of my immediate family [who] at this moment are my *compañeros* in the organization. (Mercedes)

Mercedes explained that the organization had become her 'immediate family' – a family that defined the contours of her political consciousness, as well as that which was at risk and must be protected. The survival of resistance superceded all.

Additionally, the linking of suffering and the fate of the *pueblo* resounded as a common theme throughout all of the narratives. When Carmen concluded her story, I asked if there were anything she would like to add: She then restated the connection of her story with that of her *compañeras*: 'It is not only my situation. Not only I am affected. All the widowed women are. Yes, we feel happy when we are together' (Carmen). Elena adjoined herself and her 'awakening' as an aware political subject to a collective subject, 'Mayan women', that spanned history: 'So to know our history, to give it to other women so that they strengthen themselves as women. These values are important as women and as a culture because ... we are very devalued. So, it is for this reason that I participate in the organization' (Elena). Elena linked her struggle (and her identity) with the struggle of Mayan women throughout history and expressed her political calling as one of imparting the knowledge of history and culture to other Mayan women. Her goal was to strengthen them *as women* in order to resist the devaluation and discrimination that they suffered. The organization provided the venue for working towards these goals as well as a locus for the collective identity from which these goals were determined.

Building self-esteem

Overwhelmingly, the narrators all seemed to speak of the context of the organization as being one where they had found a sense of community and a vehicle for the betterment of their lives and self-esteem. They appeared to have grounded their process of politicization through the gaining of knowledge, the sharing of experiences, and the encouragement that comes from working together for a common goal. When I asked Mercedes about her life in the organization, she replied:

> I feel good ... in analyzing the total situation from my history until now, I feel good in the sense that I have new ideas; [...] I feel that I have a base. (Mercedes)

Gloria expressed similar sentiments:

> [Through] the participation of the woman, the woman's actual situation, her level of education, we contribute to her self-esteem. We also talk about self-esteem and the human rights of women ... about the global accords ... And, we give them education about identity. (Gloria)

Carmen, in particular, was explicit in showing her happiness and emotional attachment to their organization. When telling me of how happy she was about belonging to the organization she was moved to tears.

The narrators talked about the context of their organizations and political movements primarily as spaces for the canalization of their struggles. In this sense, this context offered a place where they could fashion (within the reality of their positions in intersecting power discourses) who they were and who they wanted to be – individually and collectively. In her text, Rosa established the organization as the stage for her politics. She learned to co-direct (together with the collective) the construction of her political identity within the relatively narrow maneuvering room provided by the limitations of the organization:

> Little by little I was developing. Now I have clarity about why I am struggling: How, for whom and against whom. I see the reality ... If we do not know why we are organizing, we are lost. (Rosa)

From her position of clarity, she could place her and other's experiences in a relational and historical context. She defined her struggle, enemy, allies, and goals. She thus also determined who she was in all of these relations, in the narrative moment, and in the historical moment of the telling. This process of self-identification became, in part, an aware act of will, as she reconstructed her political identity as a Mayan woman.

Gloria also explained how she was becoming increasingly aware of her own capabilities, and identity (as well as Mayan women's potential in general) through her work in the organization. She discursively located the organization as a laboratory for the reconstituting of her self, and for the redefining of the Other (*Ladinas*). She explained:

> Little by little I was raising my own consciousness that, yes, I could do something with the women, that the women need much support ... I identify more with [Mayan women], and I have recognized sincerely who I am, I have spent the most time working with them ... I feel that the *Ladina* people do not have the same need that we, the Mayan women, have. (Gloria)

Elena told me that her involvement in the organization gave her the opportunity to gain experience, 'better consciousness', as well as 'fortification in the practice of her spirituality' as a Mayan priestess. When I asked her if her sense of herself as Mayan had changed over time, she answered that her development as a 'Mayan' was a process that occurred, in part, under her own direction: ' Before the very same society isolated us from each other, the Mayans, but we are finding ourselves through our analysis, through our organization' (Elena).

Similarly, Amara worked with a women's refugee organization which had its base in the refugee communities in southern Mexico. She also spoke about how the women in her organization became agents in their own lives while living in the camps. She likened the gaining of agency, or 'voice' to 'waking up from a sleep' which was induced by fear:

> The problem was that they felt that they could not speak ... that they did not have education, the women could not read or write. This ... is what cost us so much. But, little by little there were women who got rid of their fear. Sometimes the fear dominates one; and the women, it was as if they woke up from a sleep. So, little by little, the women began to analyze [their situation] ... One of the Grand Women spoke ... that it was necessary to do something, it could not be that all our lives we were going to continue ... under the orders of the *Ladinos*, the rich, and always all these men ... There were many ideas that surfaced from the Grand *Señoras*. (Amara)

Amara evoked the triple oppression in her identification of those who ruled: '*Ladinos*, the rich, and always all these men.' She explained how the 'Grand Women' inspired the others to gain command over their lives and to refuse the subordinate position 'below the orders' of those who oppressed them. Once awoken, the women would redirect their lives in order to resist that which previously immobilized them with fear and a sense of victimization.

Making sense of suffering

In addition to providing a community of belonging and collective experience, many of the narrators explained that the organization and popular movement provided them with a therapeutic forum for exploring and making sense of their suffering. Mercedes explained how before and during the repression, she was not able to comprehend her situation, or that of her *pueblo*:

> Before the repression: at that age, one does not succeed in analyzing all the things ... Now ... being in the organization, one realizes why one suffered. ... that which I lived in my family, in my childhood, did not only happen to my family, no this happened to all the *campesino* families.' (Mercedes)

Understanding that many others have shared one's experience and that one belongs to a community that, in part, is defined by those experiences gave the narrators tools with which to place their lives in an historical, sociopolitical, as well as cultural context. As religion often provides solace in accepting and overcoming hardship, the analytical framework that the organization provided apparently gave the narrators comfort in dealing with their pain. Placing their experiences in a comprehensive context also seemed to aid the narrators in gaining a perspective from which to write their own historical accounts, as well as in building a base for resistance and healing. Building such a base involved defining who she/the collective was in the face of those who were responsible for her suffering, as well as those who might provide her with a safe community.

Suffering was obviously a grievous result of the Violence, as well as of the socioeconomic situation in the country. The narrators drew upon their experiences of suffering to define who they were, as well as to guide the way towards their future. In fact, suffering seems to have become a passport into the communities of the organizations (Lindholm Schulz, 1999: 123–4). Almost every person with whom I conversed in the popular and cultural movements emphasized their personal suffering, as well as that of their *pueblo* and community. To have suffered was a signifier for belonging, a marker of identity, and an important organizing theme in the narratives. Diana, for instance, concluded her narrative by saying: 'During my thirty-three years of life, this is the suffering that I have lived and which I continue to live. Exactly' (Diana).

Becoming Mayan (women)

Many of the narrators joined the organization for specific purposes, such as the wish to discover the whereabouts of a 'disappeared' loved one. Many also joined in order to find place in a community of people/women who had had the same experiences and who were struggling for the same goals, such as land, money to build a house, or a decent wage. However, emphasis on the revival of the Mayan cultural and spiritual identity was reflected in the narrators' accounts of how they became politically 'aware' of their cultural identity through their contact with and work in the organization. For instance, I asked Lourdes when she realized that reclaiming the culture was important to her, she responded: 'All the organizations said this, that it is important, so this compelled me to think to see if it was right and I realized that, yes, it was important' (Lourdes).

Diana explained, for example, how she saw the 'politicization' of her Mayan identity:

> Now I identify myself more as Mayan than before ... I did not know about many things. I did not give being Mayan importance. For me, the language was not worth anything. But the experiences within the organization have made me see many things, including the Mayan faith. Before I did not believe in this, now it is becoming clear ... I have my identity as indigenous, Mam, so there have been changes ... [When I was a child] I did not identify as a *campesina* or as a Maya ... But now, I have encouraged it, not only for myself, but also inside my family. (Diana)

Diana recognized the symbolic and political importance of being Mayan, *campesina*, and speaking her maternal language through her 'experience with the organization'. She then imparted her political awareness on her family in the hopes of 'raising their consciousness'. It bears making note of how she talked about this process of politicization: before she was in the dark, and she was then 'enlightened' through the organization. As I discussed in chapter 5, the narrators constructed their identity as Mayan women through both defining the other in relation to the self, and in locating experiences of insecurity. Diana explained how this semi-conscious process also occurred within the context of the organization. She set up oppositional pairs, between, for instance: the Mayan faith and Catholicism (although a silent presence in this citation); indigenous languages and Spanish; and knowledge (given by the organization) and ignorance of her cultural heritage. She indicated that those mentioned on the left side of the dichotomies had gained in value, while those on the right had decreased. The organization was the catalyst for these 'changes'. The organization was therefore also critical to the forming of the collective and individual identities to which she referred.

Becoming (Mayan) women

Of course, it is impossible to speak about the organization as if it were isolated from the other contexts in the narrators' lives. However, by concentrating on how the narrators experience the shaping and expression of their gender identity in their identification with, and work in, the organization, different aspects of the connections between political identity and in/security emerge. Who/what, for example, did they identify as threats in this context; who/what offered safety and well-being?

It is clear that, like in the family/community context, the army/state severely threatened the narrators because of their connections with the organization. Many explained, for instance, that their impetus for joining the organization arose out of their sense of insecurity and danger *as women vis-à-vis* the army. Amara told me the story of a legendary old woman who reclaimed her rights to land and was killed by the army in 1978 because women were not expected to make any political claims whatsoever; if they did, they must be acting as spokespeople for subversives. She explained:

> Before there was not a woman who reclaimed her rights, women do not know, the army said. 'Why this woman? Where does she come from? Where did she get this idea? Because she never spoke before and now, why? So therefore, someone must be putting ideas in her head.' So, the army killed this *Señora*. (Amara)

Amara further explained that this legend was the genesis story of her organization of returnee women. She exclaimed that she and other *compañeras* reasoned: 'If she could do it why not us? Why only men? Why can't we do something'(Amara)? Together, they then formed an organization and reconstructed themselves as protégés of this 'grandmother'. Amara represented this heroine as The Model for Women. She lauded the myths surrounding her bravery in opposing the army and in constructing herself as a political subject by demanding her right to land, and by becoming a political martyr. These articulations of gender identity depended upon the denotation of the army as enemy warranting resistance and defensive measures.

Amara established that through the venue of the organization, the women found the space to begin to analyze the context of their lives and to reconstruct themselves out of this context. Through the grandmother's story, it became possible that women, too, could explicitly participate in fighting repression, and in resisting the enemy.

Onelia also recast women as heroines in her narrative. She explained how she and her *compañeras* began to recognize and value the ways in which women *already* participated in the struggle:

> We began to analyze ... that it is true that the woman is incorporated in the struggle; it is not that she does not participate. So, we began to see the experience of many *compañeras* ... of all of a community. We began to see how we could confront the very strong repression that occurred. Many women would say, 'If my husband dies, if my children die, what could I do now? It is better if I kill myself as well.' But, she had to confront this whole situation in the middle of solitude ... At this time, [name of organization] arose. And we saw that it was possible. We even said that the woman's participation was necessary because she has many very valid experiences that have not been incorporated into or given value in the struggle. (Onelia)

Onelia reformulated the roles of wife and mother, recasting these roles as those which fortified women's ability to resist. She connoted that the strength of women's connection to their family enabled them to risk 'sacrificing' themselves in order to protect their husbands or their children. Onelia seems to have been establishing that women's lives, without their families, lost meaning (and they thus might as well kill themselves.) Hence, they could find meaning in resisting their enemies to protect their families or, in the case where their families had already been killed, in working together with other women to protect families like theirs. A woman found 'community' in the midst of solitude and meaning in the midst of senseless violence.

Yet, Onelia's focus on the gendered performances of wife-mother also opened up room for renegotiating the roles women could play. A recognition of women's rights challenged the rigid definition of Us-Them that was set up through the counter move against the state and those in power (i.e. the state/army.) Struggling 'as a woman' began to take on a different meaning than engaging in the already-defined struggle against the army/state. I asked Maria why it was important for her to struggle as a woman. She responded:

> For me it is very important because I want to help the women. There are many women who do not understand the reality ... My idea is to support them ... with what I can [so that] ... the women understand that these things [should not] continue – all this discrimination, all this inequality. The woman is always the servant ... the maid. The woman is the one who is not worth anything. The woman is not valued in her work.

> Well, these are the things that I'd like to help them with so that they too can defend their own rights. (Maria)

Maria explained that it is important to struggle as a woman in order 'to defend her own rights'. She also offered a fledgling definition of these rights and redefined herself as a citizen through using the language of 'rights' (thus redefining the enemy and the struggle and themselves in that struggle).[4] Laura also clarified that she struggled to value herself and her work through the organization. 'To defend herself as a woman' and to 'not permit others to insult her or discriminate against her' became important goals. Both narrators emphasized themselves *as women* in a dialectic relation to men, where men became the Other in the binary pair, men–women. Men, as a group with a collective identity, became a potential threat against 'women' as a group.

Diana also implied that, via her work in the organization, she acquired a clearer sense of herself *as a woman*. She needed actively to protect herself from the dangers that *being* a woman incurred. In Diana's narrative, stories of sexual abuse in the *finca* (plantation, see chapter 7) and as a domestic worker served as impetus for much of her convictions regarding education and the rights of her *pueblo*. While relaying to me her need to study and to work for the organization to escape the tyranny of discrimination she had experienced, she switched into a discussion about machismo within the organization:

> Perhaps these very same experiences that I have had have made me think and mature ... even now *compañeros* yell at me because I have not married ... 'You have not married, the train has left you behind ...' 'No' I say, to live the history that I have lived, I do not want to return to that. If I marry someday, I will marry a man who really gives me freedom, where I can work in the organization. I do not want to live in slavery. It is for this that we are working in the organizations with groups of women. (Diana)

In this citation, Diana appears to be discursively likening her situation of discrimination and sexual abuse as a Mayan domestic worker in *Ladina* homes and in the *finca* to the conventional condition of marriage. She thus linked different systems of oppression and ended her story, summing up: 'and up until today, I remain struggling.'

Mercedes mirrored Diana's account of the 'traditional' gender regimes that dominated life in the community. However, she made a distinction between those who had become 'organized' and those who had not. She therefore located the threat against women as residing outside the organization. Men who were 'organized' had been enlightened to the effect of *Ladino* influence, and were therefore not dangerous in the same way as men who had not joined the popular/*campesino*/Mayan movement. She explained:

> The majority of the women have to make the food, clean the clothes, do everything ... This is seen principally in the people who are not organized. The people who are

> organized ... in some manner, they collaborate in the kitchen, do something with their children. Already this is common among the male *compañeros*. (Mercedes)

For some, like Mercedes, the organization potentially dissolved the enmity between allies in the 'larger' struggle between the Mayan *pueblo/campesinos* and the *Ladino* society/state. The organization provided a safe space where women and men could feasibly re-establish the balance and respect that existed in the mythological ancient Mayan *pueblo*.

Housing hybridity: linking struggles in the organization

> When we speak, for example, about identity, we speak about the culture, the customs, traditions, medicines, religion, everything, everything. Every aspect is linked to various different aspects. So, this has aided us, I would say, a lot to better the participation of the woman. (Gloria)

As Gloria remarked, the organization provided a forum through which she could make sense of the ways in which different aspects of her identity and realms of her daily life conjoined. The organization's official analysis of the links, for example, between the discrimination of women, *Ladino*/colonial dominance, and the division between rich and poor (landowners and peasants) united what could be diverging (even competing) struggles into one main struggle. Similarly, the common and often-repeated claim to Mayan women's triple identity (Mayan, women, and poor) named and resonated (perhaps) with different identifications and experiences in the narrators' lives. Each organization wrote a different narrative constructing this triple identity.[6] They linked struggles in different ways, depending on the profile and specific history of the organizations and those who directed them. For example, Diana equated working in a peasant organization with struggling for women. She wrote this story out of her own derivative of a Grand Narrative of Oppression. She analyzed various manifestations of oppression as being rooted to the invasion and the loss of land. Mayan land was the central protagonist in her story:

> [There are] three parts of my main struggle: 1) Struggle for more just society: no discrimination between *Ladinos* and indigenous. 2) The revindication of women: her rights, her values (to not consider women as objects only to serve others, but to value her and give her space to make her own decisions. 3) Land Rights. The lack of land generates a series of needs: we do not have education, health, food, home. Because we do not have land to cultivate ... These lands belong to our grandparents ... When the Spanish invasion came we lost the sentiments [for the land] because for us the land has its significance. [...] We appreciate women like the land. Before, our grandparents would beg the pardon of Mother Earth before harming her ... Now there is deforestation. (Diana)

Furthermore, for many, the organization helped them make sense out of the numerous realms in their lives in which they felt victimized and insecure. Within the organization, they acquired tools to relate the different ways in which they experienced discrimination and violence to each other. Comprehensive understanding provided a cohesive framework that delineated the lines of struggle and the women's place in these trajectories. The leaders of the organization rewrote a grand narrative that gave its members a central and active role in the plot. Leticia explained how she saw the organization's role in helping her recognize her rights and constructing herself as an agent in her own life:

> They gather up our children and send them to the army. This is what they do here. Our very children kill us because the army wants [this] ... If we do something in the struggle, they send the soldiers to kill us ... The women ... we are abandoned. No one remembers us. If one makes her struggle, no one supports her. Thanks to [name of organization], they unite the people ... The [leader of the organization] told us that we all have rights, not only men, not only the *Ladinos* but [those who violate them] are not going to say that it means you. (Leticia)

It bears remembering that Leticia was a not a veteran of the organization; my interview with her took place at the first national meeting she attended. It is therefore interesting to note how Leticia drew on the rhetoric of the organization's leaders to write the story of her situation. She mirrored the 'discourses of danger' as stipulated by the organization's elite. She named the dangers, the perpetrators as well as the heroes/heroines that she learned about in the workshops at the organization and made them hers. She thus also aligned herself with the 'Grand *Señoras*' of the organization, designing her own personal story – and identity – within the script of their narrative.

Who is welcome? Inclusion and exclusion within the organization/movement

In the large majority of the texts, the narrators underscored the importance of the unity of the Mayan *pueblo*. Unity, they explained, was especially salient when the community experienced itself as under attack from the 'dominant' culture. The narrators emphasized that the struggle against the *Ladino* society and army/state overshadowed all other possible conflicts within the community. Conflicts between, for example, different classes, language groups, or between men and women became subordinate to that which threatened the *pueblo* as a whole from the 'outside'. It appeared that for some, unity denoted the 'life blood' of the group and its culture, both in terms of sense of self and in terms of survival tactics. We can gain some perspective on these dynamics by referring to Frederick Barth's words:

> If a person is dependent for his [*sic*] security on the voluntary and spontaneous support of his own community, self-identification as a member of this community needs to be explicitly expressed and confirmed: and any behavior which is deviant

> from the standard may be interpreted as a weakening of the identity and thereby of the bases of security. (Barth, 1969: 226)

Any division can be read as a plot by the enemy to 'divide and conquer', not as an expression of differences within a marginalized and struggling group. Onelia stated:

> We need to struggle together; we have to have a unity to arrive at our goals. Because, alone, I am not going to be able to succeed because I do not have the force and the support of the other party, and it is the same for him. So simply a division is created and it suits the state to make this division to divide the forces of the struggle. (Onelia)

Onelia's argument underscored that the need to protect the sovereign cohesiveness of the Mayan *pueblo* might therefore preclude the developing of other, challenging loyalty bands. Many narrators alluded, for example, to instances of sexism in their organizations and within the Mayan communities. Manuela and Rosa, for instance, stated explicitly that sexism in their organizations and the movement in general was a problem that they confronted. Andrea, on the other hand, talked about sexism in general, but did not mention it in the context of her organization or the Mayan movement. (Perhaps their responses would have been different if I were not such an outsider, and if their testimonies were not crafted with the purpose of recounting their political struggles.) Manuela explained the conflicts that arose when Mayan women located oppression within their own communities and organizations.

> We talked before about the necessity to present a common front, cohesive, before a situation of discrimination and exploitation of more than 500 years. But I personally believe that it is a risk not to recognize the differences and it is a risk not to take a stand as Mayan women, because at least in my daily life and in the processes which I have had, seen, and lived, discrimination [occurs] even by Mayan men towards Mayan women. And I believe that it is almost taboo to talk about these things ... but it's like moving the floor because it's a delicate theme. (Manuela)

Similarly, Rosa explained (after I asked her about conflicts in her struggles as Mayan and as a woman:)

> There are conflicts between groups. The oppression comes from the same system. There is paternalism, homogenization. Some *compañeros* did not want me to (organize for women). The organization is mostly for men. It was difficult for me to work for the participation of women. (Rosa)

As discussed in chapter 2, the perceived need to mark the boundaries of that which was excluded from that which was included may therefore have defined the parameters of what it meant to be a member of the collective identity. Hence, the narrators employed a discursive strategy whereby instances of disharmony within the organizations could easily become attributed to 'outside' influences. This need for an over-riding and defining identity with the community may have made it difficult for women engaged in multiple and related struggles to pursue avenues of feminism, for instance, which directly threatened the (perceived) cohesiveness of the group. For example, although Rosa mentioned sexism in the context of her organization, both she and Andrea seemingly resolved the conflicts of divided loyalties by explaining sexism as really an external influence and threat. Rosa established that the oppression of sexism came from the same system (the racist, nationalist, capitalist system). Similarly, as cited above, sexism according to both of them, stemmed from the invasion and Colonialism.

Despite their insistence that the Mayan identity was deeply rooted in history, the political identities constructed by the narrators were fragile and contingent. Because these identities were considered so crucial to a political project, they were perhaps especially precarious. They demanded constant reinforcement and a system for knowing who belonged and who did not. For example, when I asked Rosa what the difference was between Mayans and *Ladinas*, she described an elaborate system whereby, based on the use (or non-use) of *traje*, she could tell who was Mayan, who was not, who was denying that they were Mayan, who had lost their identity, and who hadn't lost their identity although they did not wear *traje*. She thus stipulated rather explicit criterion to determine who belonged in the identity category, Mayan woman, and who did not. Similarly, Andrea explained that she was very happy that 'women [were] taking their place in the struggle ... [that] Mayan women [were] demanding their own voice.' She also explained that: '*Ladinos* come to manipulate our struggles, [but] we have to [struggle] *as* Mayan women' (Andrea). In this statement, she made an important distinction between those who were allowed into the struggle of Mayan women, and those who should remain outside. It was crucial to her that the category was closed and protected – secure; and that her discourses remain cohesive.

Yet, Manuela's reaction to experiences when she felt herself being forced into a stereotype or excluded from an identity category indicated that delimiting identity categories and establishing strict criterion for who belonged and who did not risked erecting exclusionary and harmful boundaries that homogenized and controlled the inside, while excluding those outside. People might have been rendered insecure as result of this process. Manuela, for example, expressed the frustration and pain she felt as a victim of such boundary construction and maintenance.

> I assume the triple identity, even if I don't look like one thing or another for many people. They even question me about it. ... They say: 'You are not Kaqchikel, you speak like a *Ladina*, you think like a *Ladina*. So I said: 'Damn, we are making stereotypes amongst our own selves, so if I don't appear [to be Kaqchikel], I am not? So what ... are we constructing? So what does it mean to be indigenous?' (Manuela)

She further explained that in a discussion she had with a Mayan woman who questioned whether or not she was indigenous, she argued: 'You are pushing me out of a space, without any right, out of a space that I consider mine, as well ... And what preoccupies me is where we are going to end up with these types of positions' (Manuela). She explicitly talked about this exclusion as something which frightened her: 'It [the criteria of wearing *traje* and *corte* as necessary in order to be a Mayan woman] makes me afraid ... because it has to do with how we are making claims for ourselves and in front of others' (Manuela).

For Manuela, the Mayan movement's tendency strictly to define Mayan identity delimited what for her was a highly personal and fluid identity.

> Identity is more [than an expression of resistance.] It is the values we received, that my mother transmitted to us ... Identity is very difficult to express in words, that is, it is almost like it is reduced each time you try to describe it. For this reason, I also have a lot of conflicts with these visions [in the Mayan movement] which say that identity is like this, or like that, or as if its a fixed thing, prefabricated which is there. I conceive of it, at least in my life, as a movement, as a development, as subjective values. (Manuela)

She explained that constructing a unifying identity as 'Mayan' (instead of a 'local' identity) might be necessary as a political strategy. She feared that by fulfilling the need to create a political identity in resistance, the Mayan movement might reproduce some of the harmful and unsafe mechanisms of homogenization, control and exclusion that the nation-state exercised to the harm of the indigenous and poor people in Guatemala.

> If you go and ask any woman in any community what she is, she'll tell you: 'I am Mam, Pocomam, Tzutuil, I am Canjobal' whatever it is. I believe that in many circles they use the word, the name, or the denomination of 'Maya-Kaqchikel, Maya-Pocomchi, Maya-quiche, Maya-I-don't-know-what. It has to do with political questions, that is to say with the necessity to construct themselves as a nation, as a *pueblo* with the necessity to take a stand as social subjects with sufficient force and thrust to really obtain some change, some benefits. In this sense, I am in accordance that this denomination is used, but now the question is that we can not generalize ... There is a tendency to homogenize to say 'we are all Mayas ...' and if I am not in agreement [with the definition]? ... There are different visions from the different Mayan *pueblos* in Guatemala ... [The movement's definition] is converted into a dogma, like the religious dogmas. (Manuela)

Manuela dealt with her feelings of exclusion and hurt by finding alternatives for her struggles.

> How are we going to construct (build something) on the basis of exclusions and auto exclusions, if on one side you exclude, and on the other you try to homogenize, its a big contradiction. So I say, if they don't accept my support inside the Mayan *pueblo* because I don't look like a woman from *Conavigua*[7] ... I give my support where I can which can be in the [women's movement] where they accept me for my identity as a woman. [...] I don't leave my Mayan identity aside from the other parts of me. [...] My

> work implies a permanent revision, a permanent study of myself and what I am doing. (Manuela)

While the organizations offered a safe haven, they also set up criterion for who gained entry and who deserved expulsion. Manuela's reflections over her own alienation and exclusion from a subject position in which she invested eloquently reveals the conundrum of conducting identity politics in all sites, even marginalized ones.

NOTES

1 By making this distinction between organizing for 'practical' reasons and then struggling for wider political goals through the venue of an organization, I am not distinguishing between 'practical' and 'strategic' gender issues (Peterson and Runyan, 1993: 121–3).
2 Onelia explains how the decision to join the organization pained her mother and her brothers. Her mother feared that she too would be 'disappeared'.
3 Rosa explained that when she began working for human rights she received threats because 'woman didn't have the right to organize men'.
4 See chapter 8.
5 A main slogan for one of the largest *campesino* organizations reads: 'The salvaging of the culture and the struggle for land is the struggle for life and peace!'
6 Slogans to be repeated at the first national meeting for the creation of the '*Defensoria de la Mujer Maya*' (1995) included: 'As women, Mayans, and Poor, we search for equal rights!'
7 *Conavigua* is a widow's organization made up almost exclusively of Mayan women (who wear their *traje*).

7

The political economy of Mayan women

> The *pueblos* live in poverty ... they hardly have food for the day ... This is poverty for me, because there is not adequate food for a human being. (Onelia)

> I see that my enemies are not only the army or the Patrollers anymore ... The enemies have increased. The army, the CACIF, the *Finqueros*, the *Jaguar Justiciero* ... the groups that are not in accordance with the Mayan revindications in this country.[1] (Mercedes)

> We need to struggle to respect the culture and inside of the culture, the principal for us ... is the land, because without land we can do nothing. (Onelia)

THE CONTEXT OF 'POLITICAL ECONOMY' connotes a vast array of intersecting relations and actors which, together, form the conjuncture within which the narrators identify themselves as poor and without resources (i.e. land). These relations and actors can be quite difficult to pin down as they take form in diverse and disparate discourses (Enloe, 1990). Nevertheless, Guatemala's recent politico-economic history, as the narrators recalled it, revolved largely around the politics involved in land distribution, the legacy of colonialism, the 'threat' of communism and the politico-economic tactics used to 'fight' it. Locating themselves as subjects within such relations played an integral part in the depictions of themselves and their struggles as Mayan women, borne out of a triple oppression.

In general, the narrators explained that Mayan women, in particular, suffered from the unequal distribution of resources, land, knowledge, and power in Guatemala during the three-decade-long 'dirty' war. Indeed, the imbeddedness of the Mayan *pueblos* within the political economy of Guatemala was greatly apparent in the narratives. Some narrators talked directly about the discourse of globalized political economy and how related articulations of this discourse affected their lives and sense of security. Some identified, for example, the linkages between the price of corn as governed by NAFTA, Mayan spirituality and connection to the land as a fundament of collective identity, land distribution as a part of national politics, and the gendered laws regulating land inheritance as part of an interwoven dynamic.

Specifically, they emphasized the centrality of Mayan claims for the right to land and sustainable livelihoods: living off the land as peasants remained in the early 1990s intrinsic to the identity of the Mayan *pueblo*.[2] The cultivation of corn and the dependence of the land not only embodied the continuous struggle for survival, but also had strong religious and existential connotations (Edmonson, 1993; Wilson, 1995). Thus, the importance of the land transcends its role for subsistence (Green, 1999: 17). The threat of having to abandon one's community because of repression, or to make an income, was often expressed as a threat extending to the essence of the Mayan culture. Many Mayans linked their identity so absolutely to the land, that without land, they held, the Mayan people were existentially at risk.

Poverty

The narrators talked of their experiences of poverty and the hindrances of being poor as involving all aspects of their lives. Without economic resources, basic needs – food, potable water, and health care – become momentous hurdles, which were often impossible to surmount. In this sense, poverty and the relations between the 'rich' and the 'poor' provided a discursive framework for their struggles in the various contexts of their lives.

According to the narrators, poverty presented a life with little opportunity. The narrators identified themselves as those who had been able to extract themselves from the quagmire of poverty, at least in their choices to devote themselves to their struggles instead of solely to the basic survival of themselves and their families. Many talked of poverty as if it were a beast that had almost caught them within its jaws. Yet, because of a variety of circumstances, they had managed to escape. This beast already robbed many of their childhood, and threatened them with critical illnesses. It was capable of completely divesting them of their humanity. In fact, it threatened the survival of the *pueblo* and therefore represented a primary threat to the people as well as the culture. Onelia explained, for instance, how poverty could be exemplified in parents' inability to provide for their children. Poverty, in effect, killed.

> If the parents hardly can get food, how are they going to get enough for an education, for clothes for their children ... because they can not give their children medicine, they die. (Onelia)

Being poor meant that one's future was threatened, both in terms of the possibilities one had in life and because of the peril to the future of one's children. Both literally and metaphorically, children were dying. Not being able to provide for the survival of one's children – the future generation – meant the most primary task of existence could not be fulfilled.

The narrators also talked of their experiences as children, and deplored the loss of their childhood to poverty. They constructed a 'discourse of danger' around the condition of poverty (and those who were responsible for causing it.) The primary – and one could say, metaphorical – victim in many of these stories was the lost child. (As I will explore in later sections, the metaphor of 'childhood', albeit together with one of 'wise antiquity', could also be stretched to include the identity of the Mayan *pueblo* as a collective.) Diana explained that she had no childhood in the 'true' sense of the word. My guess is that she meant a time when she could play, be 'herself', *develop*, have her basic needs provided for, and her future before her, unlimited. She began her testimony by defining 'her story about her life of sadness, a life in which she could not enjoy her childhood because of the situation of poverty in which she lived', a life which forced her to 'join her father in the fields, working long days, cleaning rice'(Diana). Diana then explained how her missing childhood pained her and acted as a motivating force in her life and struggles.

Diana continued her description of her 'life of sadness' with a story about sickness as a casualty of being poor. She thus further constructed the discourse of danger mentioned above. She explained how, because of poverty, her mother was malnourished, sick, and 'lost many babies'. Diana repeatedly returned to her mother's frailty and how poverty killed her little siblings as a cardinal exemplification of the situation of want and lack in her *pueblo*. This experience came to be one of the nodular moments in her narrative and constituted her struggles, as well as informed her sense of herself as a political subject. She situated herself and her political work in the organization (*campesino*/Mayan) through representations of her impoverished childhood.

Many of the other narrators also mobilized the venue of poverty and the 'rich–poor' dichotomy in order to situate their political identification as well as their assignment of threat and definition of the enemy. Leticia, for example, engaged in a long description about the differences between rich and poor. She explained to me how the rich *were* (like dogs) and described the manner in which *they* wielded their power over the poor. She exclaimed:

> We do not have the ability to do all that we want to, but we are struggling while they are profiting from us. If one tries to claim ones rights, one is sequestered or shot. (Leticia)

Being poor was thus juxtaposed with being rich and was necessarily also its opposing counterpart. While the rich were like dogs, the poor were their morally superior prey.

Many of the narrators discursively named poverty as an existential threat to the Mayan culture. The condition of poverty, they explained, compelled them to cleave to a culture that felt as if it were under the threat of disappearance. For instance, several narrators addressed the problems that they (and the *pueblo* in general) faced because *traje* had become so expensive in relation to '*ropa Americana*'.[3] As explored in chapter 5, *traje* bore a large symbolic weight in the reconstruction of a resistant ethnic-gender identity in the constitutive racist power relations between Mayan and *Ladinos*, as well as those between Mayans and the army/government. Wearing *traje* became an act of resistance against the decaying of the culture from both political denouncement, as well as the insidious forces of exigency. Hence, traje, as a critical symbol of the antiquity of the Mayan culture, gained in importance in the face of both economic and political attacks. Onelia, for example, attempted to clarify for me what made someone Mayan as opposed to Ladina. When I asked Onelia if a woman could still be Mayan if she stopped wearing *traje*, she explained:

> Yes, she can continue being Mayan. That is, more than anything else for the Maya is their thinking, no? Their vision, their way of seeing the world ... Poverty in itself makes it so that [*traje*] is lost ... one feels that when on wears [*traje*] one identifies with something. Me, when I wear a tee shirt, I do not feel the same. (Onelia)

She then explained that although being Mayan resided in one's mentality and not in one's exterior, it was nevertheless still important to wear *traje* in order to combat *Ladino*ization. Poverty sufficed as an acceptable reason to abandon ones traditional clothes as compared with 'opportunistic' reasons (such as assimilation in *Ladino* society). She explained that it was difficult for her to buy *traje* for her sisters because it was very expensive (300 *quetzals* – around 20 US$ altogether). However, she proclaimed, she would never consider buying '*ropa Americana*' for them. Many others, however, were both less fortunate and less determined to make the necessary sacrifices and efforts needed to continue wearing the expensive *traje* and therewith maintain a symbolic pillar of Mayan culture. The conditions of poverty thus complemented the forces of racism and repression in the society.

Social reproduction and the 'triple workday'

> In the rural areas ... the women do most of the work. This is why we say that women have a triple workday: One workday when she gets up at 4:00 in the morning to make the breakfast and do the housework. She starts her second workday when she has to go to work in the plantations beside her husband. The third workday is on her little plot of land ... Finally it is the woman who goes to bed last. After every one else has fallen asleep, she goes to sleep herself. (Diana)

Many of the narrators mirrored the common official declaration that women (mostly Mayan) worked a triple workday. Throughout their texts, they established women's role as the guarantors of basic needs of the family and social producers.

These roles, however, rendered them particularly vulnerable to destitution. The women often bore the heaviest burden of poverty, and the children suffered the highest price.[4] Onelia explained:

> When my father and my brothers went to the *finca* to work, we [her mother and she] were in charge of doing the work in the house. At our house, there was a small plot of land where we could grow vegetables. [...] What six brothers can earn at the *finca* is not enough for anything because when they returned we would see if there were debts because one buys corn, returns to pay it off and ... so we had to work on both ends. (Onelia)

Diana demonstrated that although poverty was an overlying force in the life of the whole family, it struck in particular, uneven, and gendered ways in the household. Diana reflected an understanding that prevailed generally. Through conversations with several women, I understood that, especially in the rural areas, women and girls ate 'last' in households where food was scarce. This assertion was reiterated by several of the narrators. Of course these situations differed from family to family, depending upon a host of different factors. For instance, Diana, Mercedes, and Onelia emphasized that families in which both the men and the women were 'organized', the burden of the household work was more evenly shared by the men than in families where the men and women were not organized. On the whole, they explained, there was more gender (as well as 'race') equality among those who were organized in the popular movement.

Furthermore, the narrators clarified that even a triple workday was not enough to provide for the needs of a family.[5] Many women therefore developed alternative livelihood strategies. Many supplemented their incomes by weaving fabrics or making handicrafts for sale to others or for the tourist industry. Some also brought small amounts of their surplus produce to the markets for sale. Every town had their market days and many times women would travel far with heavy burdens in order to make a small profit from selling their produce. Furthermore, women and children were also charged with procuring firewood for cooking and potable water for the household. These were often difficult to find close by. Many women's triple workday thus became even a quadruple workday, because they would be forced out of necessity to engage in this 'informal economy' in addition to their other labor.

Hence, one could say that survival depended upon the conditions of a market agroexport-based economy. Women depended largely on having access to a market in which to sell their goods in order to supplement the income they earned through a day time job, or subsistence agriculture. This situation was, of course, exacerbated in the case of female-headed households. The Violence killed many men and left many women widowed and responsible for children and the elderly.[6] Or, men left the women to care for the families for a variety of other reasons (e.g. work in other areas of the country such as on the plantations, or for another woman or family, or because they deemed the responsibility too demanding.)[7] Often, lack of land augmented the immediacy of their needs.

Because women were often responsible for the subsistence of their families, they were rendered extremely susceptible to ramifications of the fluctuations of the globalized economy. Many of the narrators explicitly represented their vulnerability to the consequences of economic policies adopted by the Guatemalan government, as well as NAFTA. Leticia, for instance, implicitly named preground corn (*maseca*) produced in Mexico as a threat to Mayan women's livelihood and traditional subsistence strategies, to their very survival as Mayans.[8]

> We spend a lot for fertilizer ... It is very expensive. And the government asked for already ground corn this year. We did not know that it came from Mexico, '*maseca*' they say, so this is what the government did to us, they asked for a lot, they have made propaganda. In the stores there where we live, they sell [*maseca*]. The corn that we sell is sold at eighty *centavos* a pound. Now they say that [its only worth] thirty-five or forty, so now one can't buy anything with this money. Before one had a little bit of corn to go and sell. Now, no. (Leticia)

Leticia thus situated herself not only in terms of the economic policies of the Guatemalan state, but also in relation to NAFTA and the global political economy.

The narrators mourned the loss of their (collective) future as well as their past. The distress involved in not being able to secure basic human needs (i.e. food, clean water, shelter, clothing, medicine) as well as a host of other needs (as defined by the narrators) such as education, decent living conditions, and basic respect in society reoccurred as an ongoing theme throughout the narratives. They identified this lack as a source of danger, and its alleviation as a component of a secure future. They thus placed themselves visibly within the global political economy. Positioning themselves in a discourse that traditionally ignored them also gave them a site from which to participate as active subjects, not just as victims.

Working in the plantations

> In the Costa Sur there were no massacres but there was a situation of marginalization, exploitation on the part of the *patrones* because the majority of the *fincas* are in the Costa Sur ... The worst problem is with the *finqueros*, because they have the majority of the land. So, the *campesinos* who are there are forced to submit ourselves under the order of the patron. (Diana)

As noted above, the living conditions of many of the narrators made basic survival difficult. In their texts, they explained that many people left their homes to find work on large coffee or banana plantations (*fincas*). Seasonal work on the plantations offered a means to combat extreme poverty and to provide an income with which to purchase basic goods in a market economy. Diana, for example, explained that her family (father) decided that they could not rent land for their livelihood anymore because it was too expensive. Instead, they went to work on a *finca* to harvest coffee when Diana was eight years old. Similarly, Mercedes explained: 'We did not have land ... We were forced to work in the *fincas*' (Mercedes).

Although perhaps necessary, work in the *fincas* did not successfully alleviate many of the problems of poverty and hardship. Life on a *finca* was unpleasant, at best, and deadly, at worst. When describing their experiences, the narrators employed potent language to portray the extremity of the living conditions in the barracks. The *finca* was described as a holding pen for animals, a place where human dignity was desecrated and destroyed – a site of danger on myriad levels. Lourdes explained that when working on the *finca* one had to rise at one or two in the morning. Lack of food forced the women to spend time looking for edible food (i.e. greens). She stated: 'The boss treats you badly; he does not pay you for the work you have done. There is no place to go, and everyone lives on top of each other'(Lourdes). Diana stated, for instance, that they 'were robbed at the finca' of both human decency and of money:

> [There] arrived a moment when we became discouraged ... [because of the] bad conditions: (rain, cold food, rising early in the morning) and the salary did not cover our expenses. (Diana)

Lourdes' and Diana's descriptions were mirrored in many of the other testimonies. Rosa explained, for example, that she began working at the *finca* when she was seven years old. She connected this moment, her recollections of herself as a child, and the beginning of the Oppression. When addressing these linkages, she organized her text around herself as a little girl, representing innocence and purity. She stated, 'I was a child, a pure child' (Rosa). She explained that the Violence, the economic hardship her family faced, as well her treatment at the *finca* were all manifestations of 'living under a capitalist system'(Rosa). She then further elaborated that the Mayan people had been living under this 'system' 'since the invasion' (the '500 years'). She claimed that she, in particular, 'lived under this system (in flesh and blood) in the many years I worked in the Costa Sur at the *finca*' (Rosa). Rosa centered her descriptions of the *finca* on the 'conditions of being a child'. She thus established that the combined effects of the Violence and life on the finca destroyed her childhood (as well as her innocence and purity), and her health as an adult (chapter 4). Within the *finca*, she was deprived of her very humanity.

> Even today I remember all this ... [it was as if] we, the children, weren't human beings. We had no rights, no education, poor health ... Children didn't earn a cent ... In the *finca*, we lived like animals, children died, [received] no medical attention, returned home sick. There was no [medical] treatment in the communities ... This is how my

> health and my development as a girl began to deteriorate ... the root of why I do not have good health now. (Rosa)

Rosa conveyed that the forces of capitalism and its intermingling with racism, colonialism and sexism took her childhood, and made her sick. The *finca* seems to have played an important symbolic role in Rosa's narrative: the miserable living conditions for everyone, but especially children, represented the disastrously insecure conditions of life in general for the Mayan *pueblo*. The ramifications of these relationships still plagued her and provided the vector for her struggle.

The narrators established that life in the *finca*, like life in the family, community, organization, and society in general followed the dictates of the ruling gender discourses. For example, women, in their role as social reproducers, were responsible for the well-being of their families at the *finca*. They were paid less for the same work and otherwise marginalized. The narrators explained that those who worked on the plantations were in positions of extreme vulnerability in terms of job security and working conditions (e.g. pesticide poisoning, disease, and fatigue). They were also subject to death threats for joining unions or making demands of any sort on the plantation administrators or owners. Such vulnerability placed in high relief the particularly gendered power relations at play in the site of the *finca*.

When talking of their experiences in the *finca*, many of the narrators also articulated their sense of threat and danger as directly related to their being women in sexualized, subordinate positions to those in power as well as to the men with whom they worked. Diana, Leticia, and Delia, for instance, all punctuated their stories with accounts of sexual harassment and rape. They explained that women were not safe from the sexual abuse of the administrators and the 'patron'. Through this naming of danger, they also established themselves as women who struggle for security from such harms. Diana most succinctly relayed these gendered power relationships. She recounted her personal experience as an example of how women, as a collective group, were abused at the *finca*:

> A group of us organized because we only were earning four *quetzals* and the administrator arrived and changed our tasks. Men were earning seven *quetzals*, so I said to the *compañeras*, let's organize and demand at least six ... The administrator changed our task from six *holladas* [a measurement] a day to twenty ... So, I ended up earning less. I said to the *compañeras*, 'I can't continue like this. I may be very poor and in need of much but not because of that should I be killed ... [It is] better to kill me all at once with a bullet than in this form' ... So we went to talk to the administrator and he said ok, I'll change your tasks, but now you have another task: have sex with me ... So, this is the way in which women are abused sexually ... I have been almost raped at least two times. (Diana)

Diana continued her account by telling me how her observations and experience of these relationships led her to reject the subjugation that her position at the finca implied:

> A moment arrived when I said no, I want to do more, to study. It's better if I go and see what I can do ... I had seen the situation of the youths – sexual abuse in the *fincas*, pregnant at fourteen, fifteen years old. Prostitution was one of the only options to escape the *finca* ... [The situation was the] same in the houses [working as a domestic worker.] (Diana)

Diana's naming of the specifically sexualized and gendered danger that women faced in the *finca* as a motivating force for her to study and to 'see what she could do' allowed entry into how she related her life choices to the threats she perceived. Her identity as a woman, who would rather die from 'a bullet' than be killed by the abuse and the oppression in the *finca*, emerged through this text.

Rosa also located a threat to the Mayan culture in the ramifications of the living conditions on the *finca*. She talked of how the ways in which people were forced to live alienated them from the customs and traditions that were crucial to the Mayan culture. She drew upon the example of having been forced to eat rancid, machine-made *tortillas* – *tortillas* made by men instead of, according to tradition, by women:

> The *tortillas* were made by men with an apparatus ... There were machines to make the *tortillas*. *Tortillas* made by a machinc lose all the flavor of the corn. (Rosa)

In attempting to interpret the weight she gives to the distasteful, heinous and humiliating act of being forced to consume these *tortillas* (her facial expression when describing the *tortillas* indicated utmost disdain) I recognized a subtext that evoked the symbolic importance of corn and the *tortilla*.[9] Through desecrating the *tortilla*, work on the *finca* also (symbolically and practically) destroyed a cornerstone of Mayan identity.

Violence and repression

In Guatemala, it is often difficult to understand, or even discern, the relationships between those few who maintain positions of power in the society. For instance, the large landowners (*latifundistas*) have historically collaborated with different sections of the army (even officers have been landowners or have 'moonlighted' for them (Jonas, 1991: 93; Kramer, 1994; Schirmer, 1998). Workers on the *finca* therefore posed a threat to the government by their organizing and so engaging in (perceived) subversive behavior, especially since many of the earlier leaders of organizations/unions among factory workers espoused what were seen as communist and subversive ideas. They also threatened the individual economic interests of those who profited from the *fincas*/companies. Claims for land rights, for example, threatened the government because they posed an ideological and economic challenge to the state, as well as a personal economic threat to many in power – rendering the people doubly vulnerable. The repression and counter-insurgency tactics continued and were played out among players on the scene of the *fincas*.

Gloria spoke of the difficulty she faced in organizing workers on the *fincas*. As in the context of the family/community, the army/government considered the joining of an organization on the plantation as a subversive act. Organizing either in terms of 'worker rights' or 'the rights to land' upset the division of power/resources and therewith the political order upon which the economics of national identity were based. She explained:

> It is difficult to organize in [my] region ... because there are many *finqueros* that do not let people in. [They ask] 'Why are you going to visit these people? To change their ideas? To turn them against us?' (Gloria)

According to many of the texts, danger did not just reside in the injurious environment of the *finca*, but also in the imminent violence of the landowners and their collaborators. When the workers claimed their rights through the union or the *campesino* organizations, the landowners would retaliate through threats of violence. Sometimes, it was not even necessary actively to challenge the landowners; one's presence in an area which was subject to land disputes sufficed to incite the landowners. Hence, the narrators explained that working on the *finca* also involved possibly placing oneself in the line of direct violence.

Delia, for instance, relayed how the owners of the *finca* in their community harassed the villagers by flying airplanes overhead and threatening them. She explained that their menacing presence had to do with 'conflicts over land'. I then asked who was threatening her and her family when she referred to (death) threats that she had received. She responded:

> All of the [19]80s until the 90s, it was the army who was eliminating the people, sequestering and killing the people. This happened. But now it is calming a bit. Now it is not the army ... who are threatening us. It is the owner of the land because he has appropriated land which is not his ... And now it effects us because a [juridical] ruling came out in our favor. So, because of this, they are eliminating the people ... Yesterday, twelve people came on behalf of the boss and said that they are going to fight us with machetes, with clubs. That is why they came here, for the land, they said. (Delia)

'People of corn': the politics of land distribution

The picture on the jacket cover of the two-volume series *500 Years of Struggle for Land* (*500 Anos de Lucha por la Tierra*) depicts a ground-view of a cornfield (Cambranes, 1992). Yellow ears of corn are scattered on the brown earth and several kernels have loosened and fallen on the ground. Splotches of bright red blood thickly cover portions of the corncobs. Above the earth, the green cornstalks reach upward into a clear blue sky. The absence of the people whose blood was spilled only augments the eeriness and symbolic power of the painting/photograph. The volumes address a span of 500 years, and the publication dates 1992. The '500 years' frame the legacy of colonialism in Guatemala in terms of violent and repressive struggles for land.

I chose to describe this image because it represents a commonly held reading of the history of politics in Guatemala where struggles over land distribution played (and continue to play) a critical role. As noted in the introduction, access to fertile land has been a central issue around which the violent international political economics framing life in Guatemala have revolved. Following the political mood in the beginning of the 1990s, many of the people who had previously forged their struggles in terms of their identities as peasants (class), began explicitly to link political claims around access to land with gendered/cultural rights, environmental concerns, and Mayan spirituality. The narrators' texts reflected this move. They reconfigured a discourse of danger to reflect the multifaceted effects of their lack of land and thus reconstituted themselves as political subjects who could not be reduced simply to a peasant class without cultural uniqueness. In the following paragraphs, I will explore some of the ways in which the narrators spoke of their relationship to the land and the threats that befell them in terms of their identification of themselves as 'people of corn'.

Lack of land

Access to fertile land could ensure many of the basic needs for a family; lack of land often meant poverty and destitution. When reflecting upon their situations of poverty, the need to work on the *finca*, or more generally, upon their position in the global political economy, many of the narrators intimated their relationship to the land as pivotal. When I asked Delia, for example, if her family owned land when she was a child, she responded:

> No, before, there was none. There was nothing, only a ravine. My father wanted to farm but there was no place, or that is, there was no land. (Delia)

She continued explaining that when one had no land, even to rent, then there was no food. Several other narrators (e.g. Diana, Rosa, and Lourdes) also spoke of the difficulties involved when their families were barely able to rent land upon which to grow their crops. They were often forced into seasonal labor on the *fincas* in order to pay the rent on their plots.

Maria, Johanna, and Amara, all members of returnee organizations (based either in returnee communities on the borders between Guatemala and Mexico, or in the refugee camps in Mexico), also oriented much of their testimonies around their connections to the land. For them, their concerns involved attaining fertile land in order to rebuild their lives upon their return to Guatemala. They focused on the problems that awaited them because access to land was exceedingly difficult and expensive (chapter 8). Lourdes explained, for instance, that 'internally displaced' families also encountered much difficulty around land ownership. She described how her family was forced from their land in the highlands because the Repression was too formidable. They emigrated to the Costa Sur and consequently abandoned their land which was subsequently used by the military and the PACs during the period the family was 'displaced'. When the Repression had calmed, Lourdes' father decided to attempt to relocate back to his family's plot of land. According to Lourdes, this involved great uncertainty and danger. She explained:

> We lived a life in the Costa that was very difficult ... My father had to think, 'My land is mine because I bought it and how am I going to leave it to my children? What will I do? How can I work here? The life is very difficult.' So, according to the culture, he had to do a ceremony to get rid of all the fear that he had and all the badness that the people had in their heads ... so that the people who were patrolling would calm down and no longer do these things. So he did this so that afterwards all the people in his family would not be afraid to move back to the house. (Lourdes)

Lourdes then explained that when her family returned, the army and patrollers were angry and threatened them with 'their arms in their hands' because they 'wanted the land for themselves'(Lourdes). She emphasized how she and her family continually lived under the threat of the patrollers accusing them of some subversive activity because they wanted revenge for their having taken their land back. She thus illustrated how blurry the boundaries between economic and political interests were regarding particular struggles (Paul and Demerest, 1992: 126–7).

GENDER AND LAND RIGHTS[10]

Many of the narrators (especially Maria, Johanna, and Amara because of their involvement in refugee organizations, and Carmen, because of her involvement working with widows) explicitly identified women's lack of access to land as a primary source of insecurity in their lives and in women's lives more generally. Carmen explained what happened to her after her husband had been 'disappeared':

> I suffered a lot because of my situation ... I have a father-in-law who has a lot of land but he does not want to share it with my children ... A woman does not count, only a son. But when his son died, we women with our children, we are not taken into account. (Carmen)

She was left destitute and without recourse. She explained to me that luckily, she encountered other widows in the same situation and together they began petitioning the government for financial assistance and loans in order to build a house.

Amara worked with economic co-operatives of people intending to return from refugee camps in Mexico. These co-operatives negotiated loans together to purchase collective land where they could resettle upon returning to Guatemala. She explained, however, that women also had been marginalized in the laborious and complicated process of 'returning':

> Women have not had a voice and have not been able to vote on questions having to do with land. Only the man [has voted]. So, the thoughts of [the organization] are that the woman also has to sign the loan together with the man. [...] Also there are problems within the family when the man is left with the land and the women ends up in the street. ... This is a problem for the woman. The woman does more work than the man, and she is not taken into account. But, who does the most work and who maintains the man? The woman. So, why is the woman not recognized? (Amara)

Amara attempted to redress these injustices by joining other women in Mexico and making claims on both the men and those organizing the returns (i.e. UNHCR), so that the women also could actively participate in choreographing their return. Hence both Carmen and Amara formed an organization of women in vulnerable living conditions and named their insecurity in issues of land tenure as a primary threat to their future as Mayan women *campesinas*.

In general, the narrators established that the centrality of land, both symbolically and concretely, fueled many of their struggles. When I asked Delia if she could explain to me what had been important for her in her struggle, she replied:

> I think that all of the women ... want to earn their own land, because there is nowhere to live, nowhere to farm. Yes, they need one, two, three rows of corn, three rows of coffee, two or three rows of tomato. They need to cultivate tomato, beans, corn, everything, chili, to have something to eat, yes; they want to gain this land. (Delia)

Homesteading identity

In chapter 5, I addressed how many of the interviews evoked representations of the land as the source and homestead of Mayan identity, culture, and spirituality. In the following paragraphs, I intend to elaborate on this theme, in the context of the globalized political economy.

The majority of the narrators drew attention to the inseparability of the Mayan culture, spirituality and the land. The precolonial culture, at least according to its mythic representation, placed living in harmony with the land and with other members of the community (i.e. men and women) at the center of its cosmovision.[11] This view of Mayan antiquity anchored much of the ideals for Mayan identity. Hence, land and the rituals surrounding its use and veneration became cornerstones of much of the Mayan movement in the early 1990s. The move away from a class-based analysis in terms of explaining the exploitation of peasants cleared room for a more explicit marriage of the Mayan movement with the *campesino* movement.[12] When many of the narrators talked of the threat of no land, they articulated their sense of threat as extending to the essence of the Mayan culture. Many linked their identity so absolutely to the land, that without land, they explained, the Mayan people were existentially at risk. Onelia elaborated:

> We need to struggle to respect the culture and inside of the culture the principal for us ... is the land, because without land we can do nothing, without land we cannot redeem the culture because for us the land is the mother. Without the land we cannot rise up because we nourish ourselves from her, and from there we practice our religion. The Mayan religion for us is the relation with nature, with the trees, with the birds, with all of this. ... Through this we communicate with God. So, for us to rescue our culture, we have to rescue the land. (Onelia)

Onelia seemed to articulate that, without land, 'they' simply can not *be Mayan*; therefore, they cannot exist as known and familiar subjects.

Several of the narrators underscored that even though many organizations ostensibly focused on rights to land or *campesino* rights, they also embraced and incorporated cultural claims as well as, for some, gender-specific claims. For example, the three main national *campesino* organizations included the gendered cultural connections to the land as one of their main claims. Diana, a leader of a *campesino* organization, explained to me the connections that she drew between the distinct, yet wholly integrated tenets of her struggle. She linked justice and equality between *Ladinos* and Mayans, land tenure, gender relations, spirituality, and environmental degradation as inter-related and crucial parts of her struggle. Hence, when she fought for the rights to land, she also struggled for the revindication of the Mayan culture, as well as respect for women and nature. Discursively, she connected the 'roots' of these different systems of oppression to the Spanish invasion and the consequent loss of land for the Mayan people. However, it is unclear in her analysis just how she drew the line of causality. Nevertheless, even if the invasion brought with it these other relations of ruling (racism and sexism), the land question appeared so fundamental in her analysis that its resolution held the key to the solution of the other problems. In any case, sexism and racism could not be extracted from the Mayan *pueblo*'s relations with the land and therewith their rights to land tenure.

Diana's tripartite construction of her struggle invoked the triple identity, which was discursively linked with her triple struggle. Furthermore, she identified a three-part threat – stemming from the 'Spanish invasion' – that were the counterparts to her struggles, and constitutive of her political identity constellations.

Linking struggles

In the course of conducting the interviews, I became increasingly aware of the intricate and multidimensional linkages between the narrators' identities as Mayan, women and *campesinas*, of their triple identity. How did being Mayan relate to being *campesina*, to being poor, to being a woman? Was there any way to unravel some different threads of identification processes in order to understand how the narrators composed their triple identity?[13] I will continue to address these questions in the following chapter. However, I approach them now because it is in reading the context of the international political economy that my comprehen-sion fell frustratingly short in understanding how the narrators viewed the connections between being Mayan and being *campesina*. Where did the dividing lines between these identifications fall? Could poor *Ladinos* also be considered *campesinas* in the same way that Mayans were? How did middle-class Mayans fall into systems of classification? What were the different mechanisms of inclusion/exclusion at play? And, how were these identities represented in the narrators' discourses of danger/safety?

A uniform answer to these questions is clearly impossible. Instead, dwelling in the seeming messiness of these identifications might hint at the inherent leakiness of identity categories, no matter how circumscribed or secure they appear. Importantly, however, no matter how confusing the relationships between these mutually constitutive subject positions seemed to me, they appeared to be relatively unproblematic to the narrators. Although each narrator applied different methods of distinguishing between identity categories, the divergent systems made sense to the narrators themselves.[14] Onelia, for example, explained that, for the sake of clarity, one added the term 'indigenous' to *campesina* to distinguish between the poor peasant *Ladinas* and the peasant Mayans. For her, however, this distinction was barely necessary since the majority of all peasants were Mayan or of Mayan descent. She explained that the identity of a *campesino* had to do with 'the relationship with the land, the agriculture, all this, his relation to the fields'. She continued:

> A *campesino* is someone who dedicates himself daily to working. [He is] indigenous, because a long time ago, we were all Mayan. Apart from having a culture, we are also peasants. That is, we work the land. So, to say that we are indigenous and *campesinos*, that we use these two names, is because it is certain that the majority of us are Mayans and we are the majority of the *campesinos*. But there are poor *Ladinos* also among the *campesinos* or that is there are poor *Ladinos* who do not have any money who work in the field. [...] A *campesino* identifies himself with his machete, his hoe, with the land and with his daily work ... This is the same meaning [that the ancestors gave]. although before, they did not talk much about being *campesino* as separate from being Mayan, No, for us they are the same because, at least in my *pueblo*, there were no *Ladinos*. So, all we had were Mayans. (Onelia)

Although Onelia's explanation holds many nuances, one aspect seems to dominate her reading. She emphasized the relationship between the land and poverty as the pinnacle of the identity category, '*campesino*'. She further explained: 'Unfortunately, there are no rich *campesinos* here, almost the majority of *campesinos* are poor ... So here in Guatemala ... the one who identifies [himself] as *campesino* ... is poor and works the land' (Onelia). Hence, for Onelia, the line of demarcation for identifying oneself as *campesino* convened with that of identifying oneself as Mayan, but left space for poor *Ladinos* as well. As for middle-class Mayans, Onelia seems to articulate, they were so few, and their heritage was so imbedded in the land, that they could not disengage themselves from their history as peasants, or as 'people of corn'. A Mayan was also always a *campesino* in terms of his/her relation to the land and its place in the Mayan culture, spirituality and history.

Diana, on the other hand, employed another set of criteria to distinguish what the identity category '*campesino*' included:

> A *campesina* is someone who has migrated from her community to the city, does not use her *traje*, or speak her own language, and denies being indigenous. She is *campesina* because she's lost her identity as an indigenous ... its the same Maya, but she has lost part of her culture. (Diana)

Diana incorporated the essence of *campesinidad* in the identity category 'Mayan'. A Mayan's connection to the land was given and rooted in history. Diana seems to connote that there was no need for a Mayan to identify herself as *campesina*, in the sense described above by Onelia, because the identity category 'Mayan' included these meanings. Hence, when someone (who according to Diana was originally Mayan) identified herself as *campesina*, she denied her indigenous heritage. For a Mayan to claim political identity based on her position as *campesina* fomented *Ladino*ization and thus crossed important boundaries discerning Us from Them. Nonetheless, allegiances between Mayans and poor *Ladino campesinos* were possible based on struggles around land and a common identity of being poor. Such allegiances need not threaten specific political Mayan claims or Mayan's unique identification with the land upon which they rested.

Onelia also condoned coalition building across 'cultural' lines. She clearly explained why, according to her, allegiances with poor *Ladinos* were acceptable (although distinctions between Mayans and *Ladinos* remained).

> We are Mayan in my community ... what is different in my community is that we do not reject the *Ladinos* because I believe that my people have the idea that there are poor *Ladinos*. So we do not speak about this [racism?]. Instead, we say 'rich and poor'. There are groups in the community who work for the rescue of the culture because they say that it is the rich who want to terminate our culture and that we should maintain and rescue that which we have lost. (Onelia)

Learning from the differences in the above meanings the narrators give to the identity '*campesina*', I concede that the web of the different, yet related, subject positioning that made up the triple identity Mayan-woman-poor/*campesina* remained quite tangled. Moreover, I am further convinced that the particular identity constellation 'Mayan-woman-poor', acted as a unifying framework for political identity, yet it was in constant motion and under continual reconstruction (Ferguson, 1993). Its meaning shifted both in relation to context, as well as to the specific site of the narrator. The question of 'how' the narrators imbued these identifications with positive meanings comes to mind. It is necessary, therefore, to discuss ways in which some of the narrators reconfigured this tripartite identity as a vehicle of political (subaltern) identity in relation to the global political economy.

Many of the narrators drew upon their vision of Mayan women's role in history in order to conjure an archetype for revindicating contemporary Mayan women's role in agriculture. They also used these 'myths' to redefine Mayan women as productive actors within the political economy. For instance, Susanna commented on the 'role of women according to the Mayan *pueblo*'

> Women developed many roles in agriculture. Agriculture was very important in the epoch of the matriarchy, because it was the woman who played the most important role in the family. However, ['modern'] work is what changed everything. New work arose for the men ... So ... these changes have made it so that now the woman is discriminated against ... She does not have the same ability to do other work that the man has. According to my criterion, the woman should play the same roles as the man equally, like many have already demonstrated. (Susanna)

In chapter 5, I discussed how many of the narrators located sexism on a trajectory of the colonial/*Ladino* project. Here, Susanna shifted this type of argument and designated sexism as a derivative of 'modernity'. Instead of comingling explanations of gender relations with discussions of culture, she talked of gender relations as also part of a system of power relations – of the 'global political economy'. She emphasized the constellation class-gender more explicitly in this discourse than that of race/culture-gender. However, by extrapolating the relations between the specific identities created in terms of class and gender, I do not intend to ignore other constellations of mutually constitutive identifications that also came into play in her text. Nevertheless, her emphasis on how gender relations within the Mayan *pueblo* had altered in the wake of a modernizing project may allow entry into how she conceived of how her different identifications (and therewith the different conceptions of both danger and well-being) formed her struggles.

According to Susanna, the 'changing of work' placed men's activity in the modern, formal work sector (on plantations, etc.) She implied that women remained mired in the informal/private spheres where their work was not valued in economic terms; consequently, women's status (and mobility) *vis-à-vis* men declined. Susanna implied that this rupture in the 'traditional' division of labor within the Mayan *pueblo* led to inequality between men and women – an inequality that then informed gender relations in other contexts. Susanna mobilized, or brought to the fore, the particular identity constellation 'gender-class' in her effort to redress these harmful power relations. Her struggle as a *campesina*-woman therefore included an attempt to alter the site of the Mayan *pueblo*, and Mayan women in particular, in relation to the governing power relations of the global political economy. A symbolic 'return' to the homeland of the ancient Mayan *pueblo* guided the venue of the struggle in which land redistribution and peasants' rights were nodular.

Rosa also looked 'backwards' for beacons to more desirable gender relations for Mayan women. When talking about discrimination of women because of the 'capitalist society' she stated that the goal of Mayan women today should be to 'recuperate the role played by the ancestors'. Similarly, Diana also looked to the past for answers to Mayan women's marginalization. This homeward glance guided the path of her struggle, and cast a spotlight on the perpetrators of her in/securities. Diana stated:

> Our struggles now are revindicating struggles against a structure which does not recognize the work of women. It is we women who work more than men and it is work that is not paid. That is why we want to initiate youths [into the struggle] whose eyes are more open to the situation ... to teach the importance of the role women play [...] Our struggle is not against the men, but instead it is against a system. [We want] to do the work together ... for a better society. This is our perspective as *campesina* Maya women. [We struggle also] to revindicate or recuperate our customs, which have been lost a lot, above everywhere else in the Costa Sur [Because of the dominance of the large landowners there]. (Diana)

Diana stated clearly that she did not see herself as struggling against men; nor did she imply in this context that she was struggling exclusively against the *Ladinos* or even the government/army. Instead, she talked of a 'structure' that did not value the work of women. Diana, however, did not seem to place workings of the *Ladino* society or even sexism in her organization, family, and community as 'outside' this structure. She emphasized the specific power relations which devalued Mayan women's work within these other sites as well, yet concentrated on how the interacting power discourses of sexism, racism, *and* classism particularly marginalized women in terms of the political economy. She constructed her tripartate identity constellation *and* exemplified its hyphen points by, for instance un-packing the connections between different concrete threats.

Diana explained, for example, that there was no place for women to grow cotton to weave *huipiles* and that the costs of obtaining thread became prohibitive in juxtaposition to costs of '*ropa Americana*' and therefore decreased Maya women's status within the Mayan community. The lack of land thus also influenced the 'loss of culture' and fostered sexism. She also explained that because of the influence of a globalized (Americanized) pop culture, Mayan youths listened to 'rap' or 'English' music, instead of to the traditional marimba of Guatemala. (She clarified, that 'really, we, in our condition in Guatemala do not understand [this music]'.) Diana continued saying that 'there was more respect before' (i.e. for the land, for the cosmovision which speaks of the balance with nature and between men and women). She claimed that 'certain rituals and values have been lost'. Like Rosa and Susanna above, she linked the decline of Mayan girls' 'decency' – and the increase in sexism – to the impact of these globalized cultural forces. The economic interests that determined the agrarian policy of the country, as well as those that produced and marketed a globalized youth culture, were part of the same 'structure' that 'devalued Mayan women's work' and that coconstructed their triple identity as Mayan-women-poor.

Notes

1 'By February 1989, there were announcements of at least four death squads operating in Guatemala: *Jaguar Justiciero*, *Los Commandos Urbanos Revolucionarios*, *El Frente Contra la Delinquencia*, and *El Moviemento Armado Centroamericano* (El Grafico, 1989)' (Schirmer, 1998: 223). Also see REMHI/ODHAG (1999: 110–11). The *Jaguar Justicero* is a 'privitized' death squad, which threatened human rights workers and other members of organizations (REMHI/ODHAG, 1999: 111).

2 The identity as peasants is so strong that many families who have too little land to live on and rely on income from other sources still try to cultivate a few corn-plants and refer to themselves as peasants.

3 '*Ropa Americana*' refers to inexpensive used clothing that comes from the US through various charities.

4 For further discussions of the genderings of economic insecurity see e.g. Benería and Feldman (1992); Boserup (1970); Jackson and Pearson (1998); Kandiyoti (1985); Kabeer (1994); Marchand and Parpart (1995); Sen and Grown (1987).

5 See Blandón (1993); Cabrera Pérez-Arminán (1992: 69); Coincedencia de Mujeres (1991); Garcia et al. (1991).

6 Green cites an estimate of 80,000 widows and 250,000 orphans as a result of the Violence (Green, 1996: 4).

7 The narrators often cited a 'commonly held' understanding that many men were not reliable as providers for the family. They explained this in terms of alcoholism, unemployment, and a 'culture of machismo' (stemming from the *Ladino* society).

8 A leader of ALMG stated: 'A woman is not a woman until she makes tortillas' (cited in Nelson, 1999: 165). See also Green (1999: 18). Corn was also the staple of diet and traditional land cultivation. Often families subsisted on a diet of little more than tortillas.

9 Ibid.

10 For a further discussion of problems around gender and land tenure in Guatemala, see Calder Chaves (1998); COINDE, (1993); Mama Maquin (1994); Worby, (1998).

11 According to a pamphlet written by Majawil Q'ij, on 'The Rights of the Mayan Woman', the Mayan cosmovision rested on a balance between men and women, with corn in the center of a circle of balance and harmony.

12 There were many points of contention between those who organized specifically around land rights and those who organized around the revindication of Mayan culture more generally. See Bastos and Camus (1993, 1995).

13 See discussion on identity formation (p. 32) and chapter 2, fn. 30.

14 Some of the narrators' explanations were so confusing to me that I could make no sense of them. Diana talked of *campesinidad* as having to do with the relationship with the earth. Onelia also talked of *campesinidad* meaning those Mayans who had moved into the city and who refused to admit that they were indigenous.

8

Mayan women as citizens – Guatemala: a nation-state?

> Not everyone sees the same Guatemala. I feel a part of Guatemala, but I feel part of an exploited *pueblo*, part of a *pueblo* that is discriminated against and repressed ... CACIF feels Guatemalan, but as an exploiter, an oppressor. So, there is so much difference that we cannot see it in the same way. (Onelia)

> Being Guatemalan is what motivates my struggles. (Manuela)

Guatemala 1985–1990s: negotiating peace

ESPECIALLY SINCE 1992, the Guatemalan government has been forced to recognize the emerging salience of the Mayan *pueblo* as an internationally backed, widespread political player on the national arena. However, as Nelson aptly points out, the Mayan *pueblo*'s relationship to the state was ambiguous and contradictory, as was the state's relationship to its indigenous majority (Nelson, 1999: 77).[1]

During the time of fieldwork, there was an ongoing debate among intellectuals, movement leaders, and the policy elite about the character of national identity, *Ladino* identity, and Mayan-ness.[2] Basically, there was a widespread sense that the close of the civil war and the peace process created a space for redefining political identity in the geopolitical space of Guatemala. A *Ladino* (counter-insurgency) state made up of, and representing 'the rich', and defining itself against the poor, indigenous majority no longer was politically or economically viable. The meaning of national identity was, of course, highly contested. What did being Guatemalan mean and to whom in the political conjuncture of the early 1990s? Many of the debates centered on issues of multiculturalism and the construction/absence of a *Ladino* identity in relation to (an also contested) Mayan-ness (Nelson, 1999: 182).

At the time of the interviews, the indigenous heritage was marked as a commodity of the Guatemalan state; it bestowed its proud, grand, and ancient heritage on the necessary myth of origins of Guatemalan new nationalism. For instance, in 1995, a large economic corporation, Occidente sponsored a series of extra editions on 'Identity' (which highlighted a different indigenous ethnic identity every week) in *Prensa Libre*, one of the biggest national newspapers. On the last page, they placed a large one-page advertisement, which referred to 'our grand culture and heritage'. One featured a picture of a Mayan hieroglyphic and stated 'Our nationality is carved in solid rock. We feel a great pride for our past, confidence in the present and security in the future (*Prensa Libre*, 3 June 1995, '*Identidad*' Vol. 4 'Tzutujil'.) 'We are all Guatemalans!', the army, the business community, and the government claimed through the public media. Even on the walls surrounding the army barracks outside of Santa Cruz de Quiche, one could see the words 'We are all Guatemalans!' painted in black.[3] Several complementary discursive strategies were at work in these types of slogans: a redefinition of the Guatemalan nation which linked it to a glorious past (and thus exonerated it partly from its recent tainted history); a homogenizing move whereby the government/army attempted to 'swallow–up' and neutralize any opposing identities; and a silencing of dissident voices through appropriation of the Mayan discourse (Nelson, 1999: 76–7).

As noted above, shortly after I conducted the interviews, the civil war officially ended. After seven years of negotiations, on 4 December 1996, the umbrella guerilla organization URNG and the government signed a peace agreement. The process of redefining 'Guatemala' as a political community that had begun during the peace process and the 'democratic opening' intensified.

In this chapter, I will address how the narrators made sense of their relationship to Guatemala as both a geographic territory and an 'imagined community' (Anderson, 1991). The narrators all spoke of the Guatemalan nation-state project as a site of danger and a source of harm. However – to my surprise – they also expressed a strong identification with the idea of Guatemala as a possible site of inclusiveness and security. An overwhelming 'nationalism' ordered their yearnings for an embracing and just political community. In order to grasp this seeming conundrum, I benefited from Nelson's referral to a 'double helix of attraction and repulsion', which characterized the peoples' relationship with the failed nation-state project of Guatemala. She explains:

> Pulling the state apart – marking it with a small *s*, or dismissing it as a fiction – does not account for the 'peculiar sacred and erotic attractions, even thralldom, combined with disgust, which the state holds for its subjects'. (Taussig 1992: 111, cited in Nelson, 1999: 77)

At the time of the interviews, the Mayan *pueblo* was making political claims on the nation-state as a collective cultural group for the first time in the recent history of Guatemala. The Mayan organizations, in spite of differences in scope and extent of their claims, coincided in wanting participation within the nation-state, not secession. However, they demanded that the constitutional rights of citizens also be theirs, implying both a change from political corruption and clientilism, and an end to repression, discrimination, and exclusion. This has been described as the 'right to have rights', the right to be recognized as a legitimate member of the political community (Jelin, 1990). It has also implied a 'regionalization' and a revamping of a centralized system of political representation (ARIIP).

Thus, Mayan demands could be said to reaffirm the nation-state as a legitimate political and social unit, expressing identification and loyalty with this 'imagined community'. In this way, the Guatemalan popular movements were bounded in claims and political imagination by the borders of the Guatemalan state, and indeed by the discourse of state sovereignty. However, the Mayan movements also challenged the structures of the nation-state to allow instead for multicultural plurality and autonomy. They claimed, in different forms, collective rights for indigenous peoples for local self-determination and ethnically based representation in political bodies on regional and national levels. They demanded recognized, respected, and equal political identity within the only plausible unit of international politics: the state.

Exclusion

> I believe that ... the government defines us as the most backwards, the most stupid, that we do not know anything. They treat us this way. They discriminate against us, [because they say] ... that we are underdeveloped, that we are the ones who are responsible for the poverty here in Guatemala. There is no land because we are many. We do not have anywhere to live, so we are responsible for all the poverty in Guatemala. (Mercedes)

Throughout the texts, the narrators all explicitly situated themselves in an oppositional relation to the Guatemalan state. They explained that they were excluded as equal members of society – and even blamed for Guatemala's 'underdevelopment'.

Mayan pueblo

> Up until now, the concept that they have, the army, about us the Mayans, is that we are the most backwards, that we do not know anything, and also that we are the communists in Guatemala, that we are the subversives. They say it at any moment, in the newspapers, on the radio, in our faces directly. (Mercedes)

In this citation, Mercedes explained how she imagined the army/state viewed the Mayan *pueblo*. She named herself as a threat, as 'communist', as 'subversive' in relationship to the security of the state. This assessment informed how she situated herself as a member of the Mayan *pueblo* in relationship to the

Guatemalan nation-state project. In explaining to me how the Mayan pueblo represented a threat and danger to the army/state, she constituted herself – albeit through the Other's eyes – as outside the nation. The presumed 'backwardness' of Mayans also provided an explanation for the way in which they were poorly treated by the state. She explained that this naming of the Mayan *pueblo* occurred through the important (and censored) channels for information in Guatemala: the newspapers and the radio. Hence these negative definitions of the Mayan *pueblo* became public commodities and gained the status of public truths. This informed not only how people identified/ing as Mayans understood themselves, but also how they viewed the army/state, and how the Other saw them. However, such naming 'in our faces' also drafted a partial blueprint for resistance.

Onelia explained how there was a 'grand injustice' in Guatemala that must be redressed. She identified herself as a Mayan woman and explained that Mayan women were the victims of 'injustices'; they therefore must engage in certain 'clear' struggles:

> We ... have said that we have to be clear as Mayan women, we have to be clear that our struggle is against the grand injustice in Guatemala. Our struggle is to rescue the Mother Earth, rescue the culture as Mayan women, have an education, better health and food. All these things and much more, including the same rights that the laws mention, but are never complied with. All this ... respect towards the Mayan woman, that discrimination is terminated, exploitation, all these things which are so big ... are injustices to us as Mayan women. (Onelia)

Onelia explained that the struggle of Mayan women included ensuring the 'rights that the ... laws mentioned' (Onelia). The government should guarantee these rights; yet, the government/army did not comply with the laws that would offer protection and opportunity for Mayan women. In fact, as exhibited by many of the discussions in the earlier chapters, the army/state deemed Mayan women as threats to national security especially during the most violent years of the war. The laws of the state were not there for the safekeeping of Mayan women. National security discourses more than excluded Mayan women; the identity 'Mayan women' can be thus seen as a 'constitutive outside' to that of 'Guatemala'.

Mercedes also explained how Mayan women and the Mayan *pueblo* more generally were excluded from participating actively in public politics:

> [The state and the army] have not taken women into account, the women in all of Guatemala, the Mayas ... It does not suit them to gain our participation, because we are going to fight for our rights and we are going to take away the power of this thinking that they have ... Every time any woman or any organization says anything good about their rights ... they are called a communist. To them, to be a communist is to be against the laws to be against all the rights of a country. How are they going to accept the rights that we state? They do not want them; they do not want to accept them. (Mercedes)

Mercedes highlighted a common appeal to the 'rights' of the Mayan peoples or the 'rights' of women. In many cases, the narrators specified human rights and adopted the discourse of 'human rights' as it was articulated by NGOs and within the popular movement. Other times, 'rights' seemed to be more generalized and to belong within a discourse of citizenship. In the above citation, Mercedes appeared to be explaining that she would struggle for her rights as a citizen of Guatemala – those rights that were protected by the Guatemalan constitution and safeguarded by Guatemalan laws. Yet, anyone who challenged the state by appealing to their rights *vis-à-vis* the state hazarded a claim to citizenship. Mercedes connoted that Mayan women were doubly excluded. The Mayan people, because of their very 'Mayan-ness' (as defined by the Other and the self), resided outside the realm of citizenship. If a Mayan women were to make political claims based on an idea of her rights as a citizen, she would be immediately considered subversive, a communist. The Mayan peoples therefore could not possibly be citizens of the nation-state project as it was comprised at the close of the war; at best, they remained anomalies that both reinforced the 'normal' and haunted the cohesiveness of the subject 'Guatemala'. The concept/practice of citizenship and the rights/duties inherent to it had no room for people whose political identity resided outside of the narrow and rigid confines of the hierarchies of national identity. Nor did citzenship allow for the inclusion of those 'internal others' (the backwards, poor, stupid, uncivilized, homeless, etc.) who enabled the establishment of 'The Citizen' through the example of their deviance.

Gender

> After a little while when the Repression was over, men arrived in our houses ... They asked us questions ... and said that the government was going to send help to those who are widows ... So we felt that it was certain that the government was going to send food and there was nothing ... The government was going to send money to pay for our husbands' debts ... nothing ... And every time, every time, the army would arrive. (Carmen)

As has been discussed at length in earlier chapters, women suffered specific threats and insecurities *because* they were women (CEH, 1999; REMHI/ODHAG (1999: 73–104). In the above citation, Carmen explained that the particular ramifications of the violence for widowed women were blatantly ignored by the state. When the state neglected to address their needs for survival, many felt the need to organize to make better their claims on the state. The state then considered them guerillas and subversive. Carmen, for example, explained that during the Violence, the daily activities of women were seen as subversive acts. For instance, she was accused of spying when she was 'out with her cows in the path'. When she became known as an 'organizer', she became even more suspect (REMHI/ODHAG, 1999: 73–104).

Onelia further expounded upon the state/army's exclusion of Mayan women by highlighting the government's attempts to separate women from men, and effectively separate women from their communities – from their culture, from themselves as valid subjects of security.

> Our struggle will not be against the man, but against injustice, because many times ... these objectives get deviated ... But, we do not lose sight of our struggle ... against the state ... At the level of the state they have tried to get us off track ... They have a *procuraduria* of the Woman, Offices of Women. They are giving education to the woman to mislead them. ... They tell them that they have the right to, and should reject the man, fight with him or do the same as he does. 'You have to have freedom.' Many times this freedom is converted into '*libertinaje*'.[4] It's certain that we are not slaves of anyone, but ... many times the education that they are giving is to have us remain struggling against the man. [It's important not to be misled] because the state has a principal objective to create divisions between men and women. (Onelia)

Later, Onelia alluded to the exclusion of Mayan women from the government's definition of women's identity as it was articulated in the Office of Women. Mayan women's own identification *as women* did not resonate with that of the government (and the *Ladina* feminists). Mayan women's concerns therefore could not be addressed *as women's concerns* because they did not fit into the narrow definition of women sanctioned by the state/army (read: *Ladina*); they were not properly 'hailed into place'. In this sense, even the small room allowed 'women' by the state/army, refused Mayan women's entry. Onelia concluded that the state (at that time) could not view her, or Mayan women more generally, as participating, political subjects, but only as sources of danger to the nation and therefore targets of national security policy. The narrators explained that a political identity as 'woman', without its defining counterpart, 'Mayan/*campesina*', was not a viable venue for the assurance of Mayan women's well-being. Hence, like Onelia, many of the narrators definitively distinguished between themselves as 'women' and as 'Mayan women' in terms of their place in the nation-state.

For instance, Susanna described how she believed that the state/army viewed women. Although Susanna, like Mercedes (above), did not explicitly differentiate between 'women' (read: *Ladina*) and 'Mayan women', it was understood that when she talked of the communities, she referred to Mayan women. However, both women definitively conveyed that the army and the government did not value women/Mayan women. Susanna clarified:

> The government gives work to men not woman, believes that men have more capacity than women and that woman are limited ... I have realized that [the army] treats [women] as objects in many communities ... the army acts with so much freedom, rapes girls or the *Señoras*. They believe that the army is everything and can do everything and treat women like this. (Susanna)

There were indeed distinctions between femininities sanctioned by the state (certain articulations of *Ladina* femininity), and those that posed threats to the state. These distinctions informed mechanisms of inclusion/exclusion within the Mayan movement, the women's movement, and within the state itself. Although the narrators emphasized that it was impossible to separate one's identification as a woman, from one's Mayan-ness, or *campesina*-ness, many claimed that their ulterior expressions of femininity were explicitly political and challenged the state in multiple ways.

Campesinidad

The narrators also emphasized how their status/identity as *campesinas* implied an inherent exclusion from the state as equal citizens. Mercedes explained how she had never felt part of the political project of Guatemala.

> From all my experience up until today ... I have not felt part of the political project of the country because we have never been taken into account. Every time we arrive as a *campesino* organization to the government to tell them that we want land, that we want salaries, that we do not want deaths, they do not pay attention to us. They do not listen. They never receive us. So how could one be part of a project, of the policy of a government in this way? One can not. ... We do not have this participation. Yes there are some indigenous, but they are there as adornments, not as people. (Mercedes)

'We' in Mercedes' text referred to the *campesinos* and more explicitly, *campesino* organizations. Mercedes explained that the state offered no venue for participation for the formation or even the critique of policy. According to Mercedes, when the organization presented their claims upon the state, they were perceived as threatening national security. Hence, when Mercedes articulated *campesinas*' (security) needs, such as 'not wanting deaths', these very expressions threatened the security of the national project. According to Mercedes, the state/army read the act of building a collective that expressed a common voice of dissent as evidence of subversion. Therefore, any critique arising out of one's identification as *campesino* could only threaten the state because the state depended upon the definition of 'backward' or 'poor' (and so on) *campesino* as one of its 'constitutional Others'. Reading from the texts, one assumes that any other expression of what it meant to be *campesino* threatened the order of identity established by the particular configurations of the national project. Therefore, *campesinos*/Mayas could not participate in politics 'as people', only as 'adornments', or as 'resources to exploit'.

Leticia referred to the women/*campesinas* as 'staircases' for those in government and 'the army'. Women's suffering resulted from the government's neglect of the *campesinas*.

> We ... women suffer a lot here in Guatemala. This is certain because they say that we are marginalized because the government ... in Guatemala is not interested in the *campesinos*. What most interests them is only to make their propaganda ... We serve as

> the staircase for them and when they arrive in power they do not remember us anymore. This is the big discrimination that they inflict upon us here in Guatemala – the government and the army as well. (Leticia)

As discussed above, Leticia was new to the popular/cultural movement and explained to me that she was learning her place and to name her experiences through the meetings and seminars that she attended. She was in the process of learning to navigate her voice within the discourses of the Mayan/*campesina*/ women's movement. In this statement, for instance, she talked of discrimination against women/*campesinas*, yet it was clear that she remained on somewhat shaky footing in articulating the 'discourse of danger' that constituted the 'we' (*campesina*/Mayan/women). She expressed herself by partially repeating what 'they said'. Nevertheless, it was also clear that her new discourse resonated with her experiences as a poor indigenous woman. Although not quite comfortably, she articulated this discourse to give form and logic to the pain she experienced. She thus molded who she was in relation to the exclusion and vulnerability she named. The obvious scaffolding that upholds her narrative, however, hints at the discursive work involved in making sense of (and thus giving meaning to) one's life, pains and indeed self, in hers as well as other in/security discourses.

Carmen expressed what transgressing the confines of her place in Guatemala meant concretely. She explained that she had been accused of being a traitor to Guatemala.

> I received a threat ... They said ... this *Señora*, 'Carmen', is selling the *pueblo* of Guatemala ... It is a threat because someone is saying that we are receiving money because the people are organizing, but it is not so ... They say: 'they are going to cook your *tamalitos*.' What is the *tamalito*?' It is an assassination ... My '*tamal*' is when I am dead ... Every time I am in a meeting, a course on health, etc., there are threats. (Carmen)

By recalling how the state/army accused her of 'selling' the *pueblo* of Guatemala, Carmen identified tactics of terror and discipline. The signifier '*pueblo*', when modifying 'Guatemala' reclaimed the legitimate right to collective identity and sense of community from those who were organizing and the larger communities they represented (Mayans/women/*campesinas*). It forced a shift in alliance from an ulterior collective identification to an identification with the *pueblo* of Guatemala. It thus effectively disrupted the feeling of belonging and unity that the term *pueblo* connoted. Through a coercive shift in identification, this accusation evacuated Carmen from the inside of the community she was organizing, and placed her on the outside, as an excommunicated traitor. Carmen's recollection of this statement further deprived her of her dissenting political identity by undermining and subverting the identity of 'poor', of '*campesina*' of 'marginalized'. If Carmen were 'selling' her *pueblo*, she was not poor and one of the 'people'; she crossed the border into enemy territory – the enemy named by the people, the rich exploiters of *campesinas*. This discursive tactic of counter-insurgency successfully smudged the lines between Us and Them and turned friend into foe and foe into ally. However, Carmen's discursive strategy in recalling and subverting this statement should not go unrecognized.

Like Carmen, many of the narrators drew attention to their implicit place on the marginal 'inside' of the nation, as 'the most backward and poor', as a 'resource to exploit'. Onelia explained when talking of the state's view of the *campesinos*: 'I can not give an exact definition of what the state thinks, the question is that the state looks at us all in the same way: that which is to exploit, and exploit and nothing more' (Onelia). Onelia implied that the state was dependent upon the subordinate position of the *campesinos*. In this sense, she conceded that *campesinas* as a collective group did indeed occupy an important position in the national project of Guatemala. However, the significance of the site '*campesina*', according to Onelia's reading of the state, lay in its very subordination. Onelia rejected this position and sought instead to redefine the meaning of *campesina*/Mayan/women. Reconfiguring their allotted place within Guatemala entailed substantially reforming the national political project(s) as such. She explained:

> Not everyone sees the same Guatemala. I feel a part of Guatemala but I feel part of an exploited *pueblo*, part of a *pueblo* that is discriminated against and repressed. [...] CACIF feels Guatemalan, but as an exploiter, an oppressor. So there is so much difference that we can not see it in the same way. (Onelia)

FLIGHT/EXILE

During the most violent years, the army often descended upon the villages with the orders to burn and destroy everything and everyone in its path (REMHI/ODHAG, 1999; Schirmer, 1998). Those who survived these massacres fled or hid, and then often began a life in exile. Several of the narrators experienced such trauma first hand. Recalling these experiences and the powerful threat of the army acted as nodule moments in their narratives. Many of the narrators, such as Andrea, Amara, Maria, and Johanna, were forced into an extreme situation of flight and then exile. However, not all of them were forced to flee the military. Many also left their homes and their villages because they felt that opportunities were limited for them there, as was the case for Manuela. She explained that she was faced with two choices: to stay in her community and, even indirectly, collaborate with the military and comply with the stereotypes that she was trying so hard to break, or to leave, to resist, to place herself in exile from her home and her community.

In all of the texts, exile involved painful separation from family and community. Because of their work of resistance in 'exile' many could not visit their families and be in their communities. Rosa, for example, explained that she went and visited her family under constant surveillance by the PACs. Andrea could not return to her village, because it was raized; she did not want to go back now; she had nothing left but painful memories. Hence, most of the narrators 'fled' their circumstances – be it to the capital or the mountains and the Communitites of People in Resistance (CPRs). They came to inhabit a place of exile and exclusion from the nation-state, either metaphorically or concretely (i.e. in the refugee camps in Mexico.) Being violently displaced, symbolically and physically, concretized the exclusion from legitimate identity and the (political) life of Guatemala.

Andrea, for instance, relayed how the army attacked her village and she fled. She saw her little sister murdered and was lost without clothes or food. She explained how women who were also lost in the jungle could not give birth and were forced to bring their babies into the world 'like animals'. She talked about the role of Mayan women as 'mothers' and how she struggled to revive these roles. Threat, flight and displacement from her village, her family, her childhood, the roles of Mayan women, and then even the geographic/political territory of Guatemala ran as a defining theme in her narrative, placing her and her *pueblo* in an all-pervasive state of exile. It was this state which she sought to redress.

Amara also graphically explained her flight from Guatemala as one of desperation and last resources:

> We realized that we could not live on our land although it pained us to leave ... We thought, 'what are we going to do?' because we could not continue suffering under bullets and the rain, day and night with helicopters shooting at us ... Many people died of sadness and hunger. We ... decided to look for a place where we could be 'a little calm'. We could endure no more ... We left for the border of Mexico ... But the army arrived. [...] They did not respect the border, but instead they went up to where the people were ... Some people were killed ... We survived these torments. We will never forget them. They follow us, we remember ... Through all of this, the army has been very close to the camps where the refugees live ... always threatening. (Amara)

The threat of the army pursued Amara to the borders of Guatemala and even pervaded these borders, inflicting its harm both psychologically and directly. She portrayed a sense of being forever prey to the guardians of the state: she was chased out, tracked down, an outlaw. She sought security then beyond the protection of the violent state, through her temporary identity as 'exiled' future citizen of the imagined state which would welcome and protect her.

The theme of being uprooted appeared in almost all of the narratives, either in terms of cultural purging or displacement.[5] In chapter 4, I discussed the narrators' recollections of the army's policy of dividing communities and families as a counter-insurgency tactic of terror. The resulting division of families and communities when many people were forced to flee recurred as an integral theme of harm and the anguish of exile. Mercedes was 'internally' displaced and spent several years in exile outside of Guatemala. She often turned to the intricate details explaining the whereabouts of family members, and the trauma of separation and reunification. For Mercedes, the necessity of flight and hiding unraveled the fabric of her family and homestead. Her displacement then occurred not only in terms of being severed from her home village and the 'home' of Guatemala, but also from the safety of familiar relations and known contexts.

Johanna also talked of the mutilation of the familiar and the perpetuation of loss, symbolically and directly illustrated by the cleavage of intimate, meaning-sustaining relations.

> When we left, some of my relatives stayed ... We have suffered greatly. We could not go to Mexico, the whole family together. Lost relatives have stayed ... I am not the first; there are many mothers, many fathers, who have been left without their children, without their brothers. Many *compañeras* are left widowed ... too many widows. Too many *compañeras* who, when they were pregnant, they took out the baby before it was born and left them shot. All this suffering in Guatemala! (Johanna)

Redefining identity

As has been discussed throughout this book, the narrators coincided in expressing that they sought to reconstruct a collective identity, which rejected the harmful circumscription of their identity that the Guatemalan state/army re-enforced. This entailed carving out a space for ulterior communities within the geopolitical territory called Guatemala and reconfiguring the power relations that excluded Mayan women from acting as valid political subjects within Guatemala.

Elena explains how she repositioned herself within her community/world and assessed who she was from that venue instead of through the eyes of the dominant society. She explained that, in terms of being Guatemalan, she was 'nothing', yet inside her 'group' she was 'something rather important ...' (Elena). She was a subject warranting security.

> [I am] nothing as a Guatemalan. But now, inside of my world, my community, my group, I consider that I am good enough and that I do well enough ... I have my aspirations, I would like to ... work in a ministerial post, give my contribution, make reconstructions, change many things. I have not been able to because they do not value me ... But I do it from my community ... so inside of my group I feel as if I am something rather important, that I am giving a lot, but inside the Guatemalan society, nothing. (Elena)

Establishing a clear inside/outside dichotomy, Elena worked to 'contribute' to her community on the 'inside' because the 'Guatemalan Society' (on the outside) excluded her and named her as 'nothing'. In order for her to be able eventually to contribute to the Guatemalan society, she explained, she must first establish herself within the 'internal' community and then fortify this community. She evoked a discourse of danger where those in power existentially annulled her as a subject. She did not exist. This discursive move informed the lines of demarcation between her 'world' and the hostile excluders. In her world she existed, was seen and was even important.

Elena then explained that she hoped that her world would one day become strong enough that the outside would be forced to recognize Mayan women not as deviant, but as legitimate and equal citizens of a shared polity.

> One day, I feel that our attempts, our struggles will be listened to, but to get there, there is a lot missing. I feel that we are in a process as well. But one day we will have the laws in our hands ... We will have made them for ourselves ... The *Ladinos* will realize that we also are very capable even to the point that they make official our languages, that the society will be egalitarian for everyone ... Things can change. We can contribute more. Yet, all those who ... have tried to give their contributions as Mayan are not heard. We have to do it as a group ... in order to really succeed ... Although the Mayan population is the majority, the spaces that they have given us are very few ... They are tiny spaces that we, the indigenous, have in the life of Guatemala. (Elena)

Elena called for a transgression of the 'spaces' that Mayans accessed in Guatemalan society. She sought to engage the power of a large collective to demand that the *Ladinos* recognize Mayans' capability and treat them as equal. Elena's declaration called forth the Mayan *pueblo*'s independence and strength. However, she also ceded agency to the *Ladinos*, by, for instance, challenging them to 'make official our languages'. Her narrative here seems to disclose tension within its logics: on the one hand, she called for equality within the existing discourses of Guatemalan society; on the other hand, she called for autonomy to create their 'own' laws within (and therewith constituting) a multicultural society. Such tension might hint at the ambiguous processes of rearticulating sovereignty discussed in chapter 2. Yet despite this tension, Elena presented a clear vision of the need to anchor a collective identity outside of the legitimate hierarchies of identity established by Guatemalan national security, yet inside Guatemala's national borders.

Mercedes' narrative was less seemingly conflicted, and took the agency of the Mayan *pueblo* as its point of departure.

> The popular movement is a unity between organizations and the Mayan *pueblo*. The civil patrols were created to divide the civil population between Mayas and *Ladinos*, so that they kill each other. Our struggle, rooted in all of this, is to clarify ... the laws, the rights, that which brings us to this division. We have explained to the population and it has begun to pay attention, comprehend, and respond. ... It doesn't matter what religion, or ethnia [one is] in the face of a struggle. I believe [this struggle] is ... generalized in all of the country and even more now that there are many Mayan organizations that work for the values and the rights of indigenous *pueblos* ... There is much space now and much work to be done. I believe that the Mayan *pueblo* has learned things. There is much missing, but we are prepared to learn and to do that which is left for us to do. (Mercedes)

The Mayan *pueblo*'s values and rights demanded a central position in Mercedes' text above. Through the power of knowledge (and the help of democratic opening), the popular movement created space within Guatemala to demand the values and the rights of the Mayan *pueblo*. In framing her demands as such, she sought a rightful place besides the *Ladinos* in a legally reformed national society.

As I have discussed previously (chapter 6), much of the narrators' discourse subverted the dominating truths that the *Ladino* society was superior, more civilized, cultured. During the time of the interviews, the peace negotiations spurred a widespread dialogue about requestioning national identity. Siglio XXI, one of the biggest national newspapers, printed a debate series addressing the issue of identity, both national and Mayan. Concurrently, the state/army/ruling coalitions engaged in a process of explicitly appealing to all 'Guatemalans' in an attempt to over-ride any (dangerous) divisions in national society.[6] (The slogan I referred to earlier, '*Somos todos Guatemaltecos!*' ('We are all Guatemalan!') was just one explicit manifestation of this maxim.) This 'national' appeal appeared to be a milder (at least less directly violent) form of homogenizing the population than those tactics employed during the Violence. Onelia addressed this debate as follows:

> It suits them [the state] to say that ... 'We are all Guatemalan' because they cannot identify with a culture ... I have heard much in the university, for example: 'We, the *Ladinos*, we are not from here or from there, nor do we know from where we come. [...] We indigenous know where we come from. We are from these lands. Our grandparents lived here when the Spanish came to invade. We are in accordance with ... seeing us all as equal in Guatemala. That is good, [and] respects ... development. Yet we can not say that [our] identity is the same; it is not the same. (Onelia)

Onelia accepted the confines of the political imaginary that the representatives of the state articulated, yet she rejected the superimposition of over-riding political/cultural identification with the nation-state. Her text implied that her identity as a Mayan woman must define her participation in the national identity. She might be Guatemalan, yet her Mayan-ness informed her definition of *Guatemalidad* (Guatemalan-ness). She thus established a new meaning to being Guatemalan (to national identity) and therewith, to an alternative discourse of in/security.

Onelia continued explaining that the identification 'Guatemalan' did not reflect who she was in terms of her past or her future. A national identity was inadequate to encompass all of who she was.

> For me, it is important; I feel good to say where I am from, to say from which culture, from which roots. Because at least I have this identification, and I know that my culture should be as my grandparents were ... If I only say 'Guatemalan', it is not part of my identity, because I am Guatemalan but, as for culture ... one [knows] if one is Mayan or not. (Onelia)

Onelia thus not only separated her national citizenship from her culture, she also situated her culture in a time before the modern state, before the 'Spanish came to invade'. One could then surmise that the *Ladinos* were the cultural outsiders, not the Mayans. Belonging to the national political community seemed to be important in that it opened the possibility of enforcing certain rights, but, in terms of meaningful community, it offered little. Minimum safety resided in the substantiality of these rights and values, but the establishment of herself as a valid subject of security could be achieved through belonging to the cultural community.

Mercedes explained what belonging to this cultural community meant. Mayans were special within the territory of Guatemala as well as within the world at large. Mayans could not be subsumed under the general identity category 'Guatemalan': 'in Guatemala we understand that [as] Mayan, we have our own rights and our own customs also. So this differentiates us from any other language or group in any other part of the world' (Mercedes). Elena further rewrote the dramatic script between *Ladinos* and Mayans in the context of Guatemalan society. She called for an 'awakening' so that the Mayan pueblo would resist the divisionary tactics of the state and develop a unified whole political subject which could then be secured:

> In a world where the means of communication ... education ... the media are manipulated, where we practically have sold our eyes [being told] that everything is very beautiful ... that as indigenous, we are not capable, that the women can not do anything. If we continue to see the things like this ... our consciousness will remain sleeping ... Who will be the ones steering all of society? Only this way are we going to wake up, and to realize. We are going to organize, it is necessary that we indigenous are united to reach our own development because if we do not organize, we will not be united, and we will not succeed in much, because they will always have us so divided, separated. (Elena)

Claiming space in the nation

In 1995, the Mayan movement focused its claims on the state around the ARIIP. Although many leaders of the Mayan movement helped draft the agreement, they also skeptically awaited how the government would adopt the constitutional reforms and implement the necessary changes in policy that complying with the agreement would entail (Jonas, 2000: 189). Despite much skepticism and wariness, many placed much hope in the ARIIP. Both symbolically and in terms of direct political reform, it was the only viable blueprint for providing a political space for the Mayan *pueblo* in a peaceful and just Guatemala.

For instance, when talking of the myriad atrocities that the army/state inflicted upon the Mayan people, Onelia brought up the ARIIP as the venue for redressing these harms, as the venue for assuring security.

> The army gathers up the people and tortures them as if they were a tree ... All this [the respect of her grandparents] was lost because of the imposition of other cultures, which has made us lose ours. But now with the new accords, [we need to] make all that is written on paper be put into practice. (Onelia)

Despite her apparent confidence in the import of the ARIIP, Onelia also alluded to wariness as to how the accord would be implemented.

Susanna, on the other hand, discussed the ARIIP as possible fuel for the continued divisions of Guatemalan society into Mayans and *Ladinos*, whereby the *Ladinos* would maintain their superiority. She talked about a 'backlash' of sorts, where *Ladinos* might react to the 'politics of separateness'. She feared that *Ladinos* would interpret the ARIIP as implying special rights and allowances for Mayans in the Guatemalan society. At the same time, she rejected the discursive move to homogenize the population and to negate the history of discrimination imbued in the statement 'We are all Guatemalan':

> The *Ladinos* are so accustomed to discriminating against the Mayans that they think that now that we are going to be equal, things will be reversed, that now the one who will be discriminated against will be the *Ladino*. Because they have said that ... if a man rapes a Mayan woman he will be punished twice ... Why do they say 'We are all Guatemalan?' It would mean that there has not been discrimination. Yet, the discrimination has always been given. (Susanna)

Susanna's fears regarding the impact of the ARIIP in *Ladino*–Mayan relations, as well as relations within the women's movement more specifically, underscored her sense of its status as a watershed in the history of Guatemala. As Susanna implied, the ARIIP named the Mayan *pueblo* as distinct within the Guatemalan society, thereby also naming the power relations that this distinction implied. Yet she also rejected the image of the Mayan *pueblo* as a marginalized part of the Guatemalan nation-state that needed protection. This image bore with it an inherently unequal relationship of power where the Mayan *pueblo* remained subject to the dominance of the state. 'We, the Mayans do not need protection, but we need respect.'

Claiming citizenship

The ARIIP could be seen as an expression of many years of struggling against the exclusionary politics of the counter-insurgency state. The acceptance of it placed the indigenous *pueblos* on the map of legitimate citizenship in Guatemala, both in terms of national politics, but also in international institutions (Jonas, 2000). However, at the time of the interviews (and even at the time of writing this book), the reality of participation and equal citizenship remained in imprecise principles in the accord. Incorporation and implementation into policy, juridical reform, and discursive transformation remained elusive.

Susan Jonas refers to the 'Realm of the Imaginario' and the construction of citizenship in her book on the peace process (Jonas, 2000: 232). She explains that the peace process provided an opening in which the population was able to imagine an inclusive nation based on an alternative form of democracy. This imaginario was not purely symbolic, it also constituted a potent counter-hegemonic act of resistance against the violence of nation-hood articulated by the state (Jonas, 2000: 233). The narrators continually articulated their goals to claim their legitimate agency and rights as citizens of a Guatemala in the making, as citizens of this imaginary realm.

Leticia, for example, forcefully asserted herself as a participating member of the polity by explaining to me her intentions to vote in the up-coming national election:

> I am against this Rios Mont.[7] I do not like him because I know that he is a big liar ... I do not agree (with him.) Now, I am registered [to vote.] I am going to vote this year, but null! I am not going to vote for anybody. They are all the same. This is what I am thinking because I see how they act poorly with the people. (Leticia)

Leticia's tone when making these claims rang quite defiant and triumphant. She explained to me that she was very happy to be registered finally to vote (after decades of not voting), and that she was going to make her voice heard. Her words above implied that she placed her newly formed political self as a legitimate national actor. She belonged to the national ('imagined') community enough to register her vote, express her opinion, her dissatisfaction, and her criticisms through perhaps the most powerful vote of all: a presently absent one.

Leticia then went on to explain that 'now with human rights, one can defend oneself', provide security. She used her status as a citizen – and thereby her entitlement to protection under the international convention of Human Rights, and the monitoring of the United Nations – openly to challenge the state. However, she chose to do so from within the constitutional and juridical structures of that very state, thus refuting the identity of outlaw, subversive, property (of men) etc, that the government labeled her (in her eyes). She thus claimed her space and registered her political opinion in content and in action. Gloria's words below alluded to how the people's awareness of their rights and the laws of Guatemala posed a threat to the state by offering a counter-narrative to the state's constitutive discourses of danger:

> I think that while the people were uniting there already was another perspective ... In the demands of the communities, the people do not remain quiet. They say, 'Look, they violated my human rights; look, they have not given me this and it's the obligation of the state to provide these things. That is [what one can] read in the political constitution. Now I can claim this.' (Gloria)

Gloria's appropriation of the constitution of Guatemala as a means for her protection from the army/state offered a powerful blow to the dominant narratives of state security. These narratives read the state's violent actions against the Mayan population as a necessary measure for the protection of national security. Drawing on the constitution changed the defining roles of ally and enemy. Her claim for rights can also be read as a claim for the right to be a valid subject of security.

Returning

> We, who are making these demands ... we are rightful citizens of Guatemala. (Johanna)

> When I was in Mexico, I did not feel anything ... I felt unhappy because neither could I say that I was in Guatemala, nor could I say that I was Mexican, or anything. Nor could I say that I had rights as a Guatemalan, I couldn't, I only knew that I was Guatemalan that I was in a foreign country. That's all. But I kept the memory of Guatemala, of my country, it was never erased from my mind, I always thought I'd return. (Maria)

Returning to Guatemala after years in exile promised a homecoming, an end to a fierce sense of estrangement. Many of the narrators expressed a great longing for a homeland that was, of course, fraught with trepidation and fear. Guatemala may have been the site of a sanctuary remembered, but it was also the place of trauma and violence. Furthermore, the future in Guatemala was uncertain and threatening. Nevertheless, the narrators (especially Amara, Andrea, Elena, Johanna, Maria, and Mercedes) talked of their connection with Guatemala as a profound aspect of who they were and who they sought to be. Moreover, they spoke of their lives in exile as a continually suspended time, a time in between the past and the future, a time of waiting. A return to Guatemala meant the possibility of continuing the natural progression of their lives and the lives of their children. Once again we can surmise that the narrators longed for the symbolic promise of immortality and implied ultimate security offered by national belonging.

Johanna spoke of the process of deciding whether to return to Guatemala from Mexico. Her words exemplified much of what was at stake in returning to Guatemala.

> Yes I am afraid of the army; that I die. I am not afraid but the fear that I have is that they will kill my children ... Because if they kill one of my children, it's like at once killing all of us because they kill our own blood ... We say: 'Lets go, let's not go ...' Yes, I want to go to Guatemala. I would like to go scream that they should fulfill our rights ... But my children say no, my old man also says no, that he is afraid ... Its a fear but also a challenge ... It is a challenge to return to our *patria* [native land/mother country], to continue surviving, to see afterwards [if we'll get] the right to a plot of land. If we leave our children, who are still young, and if we die in Guatemala, we, the old ones, will never recognize our rights in Guatemala ... We will not leave them

> anything. They are going to spend their whole lives working in Mexico, in little plots of land. They will never produce. If ... there is peace here in Guatemala, then we will be able to live freely. (Johanna)

Johanna's deliberations shed light on the extreme complexity involved in the decision to return. In addition to the fear that she and many others expressed, Johanna's vision of Guatemala as the site of 'rights' stood in high relief in the above text. She talked of Guatemala as the only possible place where she and her family could 'live freely', and 'produce'. Only in Guatemala did she possess the potential to have rights, to be respected, to be able to provide for her family, and perhaps most importantly, be protected. Although Johanna and many others had never experienced a period of tranquility and belonging in the nation-state as such, the potential of inclusion loomed large in their narratives. This potential ordered the nostalgia of a lost homeland and a future homestead. Guatemala, the wayward state, the delinquent *patria*, might be reformed and adhere to its duties to govern and secure its citizens.

Mexico offered a temporary refuge; yet, Mexico could never provide a home. Johanna linked the meaning of home with notions of citizenship and the rights that citizenship granted. She explained:

> We are Guatemalans ... We want to be here in Guatemala because it's our *patria* and we want to be beneath the jungle, which protects us. ... If we were to stay there [Mexico], it would mean that we conform to being isolated ... from Guatemala. And, besides we do not have rights ... In Mexico, they are not throwing us out by force, but more than anything we want to be in Guatemala, although we suffer from many things. (Johanna)

Johanna clearly linked 'being in your *patria*' and, legally, having the right to demand one's rights. The Guatemalan state/army had been the one to violate her rights and force her into exile – a site of statelessness – in order to survive. Johanna nevertheless emphasized her right to have rights in Guatemala because of her legal status as a citizen. Hence, even if these rights were not respected, their very potential was more desirable than remaining relatively physically secure, yet without rights, and therewith, legitimate political identity.

The discourses of human rights and state sovereignty thus informed many of the narrators' imaginations for political identity formation and the attachment of belonging. Their connection to Guatemala as a geopolitical territory was inseparable from their connection to and sense of belonging with their *pueblo* and the physical land expressed in a nostalgic sense of home and self. These discourses also informed historical memory and the perennialness of the categories of modernity. Johanna, for instance, argued that the indigenous have rights in Guatemala because they built Guatemala during the ancient Mayan civilization. According to this reasoning, the Mayan *pueblo* had first rights to the modern construct of the political territory known as Guatemala. She explained as follows:

> We have our rights in Guatemala, we have to go demand our rights, we are not going to fight with arms or anything, we are going to fight that we have our rights as the humans that we are and as builders of the *patria*. (Johanna)

Amara also expressed her identity as a political subject with rights. She could make demands around the ordering of her life in Guatemala. Her text connoted a strong will to participate in deciding over her future and not be at the hand of patronage and goodwill of a 'foreign' state. She longed to belong again to a 'we' as an active, respected citizen:

> The people thought that they needed to return, because they know that this is their land and this is their country ... they were born here and they can demand their rights for the land. The government has to resepect them as Guatemalan citizens ... one cannot become Mexican. (Amara)

The idea of citizenship in many (exiled) narratives also involved participating in defining the terms of return. Becoming a subject and an agent in one's own 'rebirthing' into the nation of Guatemala therefore included informing the content of what it meant to be a citizen. It also entailed molding one's own identity constellation within the category 'citizen of Guatemala'. Amara, Johanna, and Maria spoke, for instance, of the process of constructing themselves as gendered, culturally specific citizen-agents in this pilgrimage of return. Maria stated, for example:

> The idea to have an organization of women was so that ... they have participation in the making of decisions equal to the men ... about returning, and choosing the area where they return to. No more, were the men going to bring the women like little dogs, no. It was our objective that we have our own point of view, that we visit the land, make decisions, and participate in all of the dialogues with the government. (Maria)

Returning, however, was clearly a difficult endeavor in the texts. It was a trial, a feat, a challenge that demanded great courage. Maria remarked how the courage to return came from their own suffering, as well as the knowledge about suffering that they acquired when leaders from the popular movement came to educate the refugees. Suffering and experiences of danger and fear became channeled into the creation of a returning citizen who would reclaim her rights to be a valid subject of security from *her* delinquent state.

> [I have developed] because of the same suffering ... It is certain that I am not going to revive my children ... or all who have already died. But with the struggle ... to demand from the government that they give us our rights, we are also reviving the blood of our ancestors who are already dead, our children. It is certain that the blood of our children remains in the jungle, thrown who knows where, but with our struggle we are ... remembering the martyrs who existed and still exist in our hearts. This is what gives us the most force, yes, for me, this is what gives me force. (Maria)

Revisioning Guatemala

Claiming space in the Guatemalan nation involved establishing oneself as citizen and demanding that the rights of citizenship also belong to Mayan/*campesina*/ returnee/women. However, upon claiming that they belong as equal, participating, political subjects in the nation-state, the narrators also profoundly altered the vision of the nation itself. By changing the dividing lines between Us and Them, deviant and normal, outlaw and citizen, they prescribed a dramatic rewriting of the script of Guatemalan nationalism and therewith national security policy. Hence, although their political imagination was reigned in by the discursive confines of the idea of the nation-state in an international system of states, they refused the Guatemalan state as it had been constructed. Instead, they called for political imaginings based on a nationalism for a Guatemala-in-the-making, as well as a Guatemala-of-the-grand-(Mayan) past.

The narrators, for similar reasons, saw Guatemala's counter-insurgency state as a failed project built upon different interlocking systems of exclusion and violence. In the name of development and security, the state/army committed atrocities against them and their communities. In their texts they began to evoke notions of a drastically reformed Guatemala where such violence could/would not occur. Susanna, for instance, painted a vivid image of the contamination of the Guatemalan nation-state project. Implicit in her criticism was a view of a different Guatemala, partially a relic of the past, yet also a 'clean' ideal as opposed to the 'contaminated' disastrous reality. She explained:

> To be Guatemalan is to have the luck to live in a country where everything is a disaster but one manages to survive ... There is so much violence ... Yet, one ... wants to do much, but there are many things to be done and one does not know where to begin ... Now everything is contaminated. (Susanna)

Guatemala, as a political body, was overwhelmed with disaster and contamination; it suffered from a pervasive cancer. According to Susanna, the people who lived there did not know how to approach the magnitude of the problems or where to begin to alleviate their misery.

Yet, as discussed above, the peace negotiations, the ARIIP, and the repatriation processes all offered venues to redefine what Guatemalan citizenship meant. This entailed reformulating what the nation was, who one was in relation to this 'imagined community', who/what was safe and what one, as a citizen, must fear. The ARIIP addressed many aspects of these questions in its general blueprint for the creation of a pluri-ethnic society. However, as I have attempted to show in this work, the narrators spoke from multiple and shifting identities. The ARIIP therefore offered a discourse, which gave them a language for articulating their own fears and desires. By reproducing this discourse in their own stories they gained political validity and confidence, because their stories also reflected the experiences of Mayan women more generally.

Diana, for instance, explained to me what being Guatemalan meant to her. She linked being Guatemalan with being Mayan (speaking Mayan languages and wearing *traje*).

> Guatemala is one of the countries which has the largest indigenous population ... For this, I feel proud to be Guatemalan because Guatemala has more than twenty-three languages, which existed when our forefathers did. So for me, Guatemala has a very large meaning [in the] identification of the indigenous *pueblos* ... [I identify] myself as Guatemalan. The population that is indigenous ... should represent themselves with their *traje*, their language, as the majority of the population. (Diana)

Diana seemed to take for granted that the political unit of significance was the geopolitical territory known as Guatemala. She called on the indigenous people to represent themselves within this unit 'with their *traje* and language as the majority of the population'. However, in naming the indigenous people as the majority of the population (which should *represent* itself) she dramatically altered the politico-cultural makeup of Guatemala as it had been articulated in the dominant national discourses. The 'Guatemala' she elicited was a place where the 'population' included those who had a distinct cultural identity, yet were not deviant, tokens, or subversives. They were, instead, the majority, and therefore, the norm – safe.

Diana therefore insisted on rewriting the power dynamics that were imbued in the statement, 'We are all Guatemalan', cited above. Instead of whitewashing difference, her plea 'normalized' it. Manuela also addressed difference, rejecting the homogenizing moves of the nation-state, which, from its sovereign position, defined the terms of politics, of being human:

> We are human beings, we are persons who have our own values ... ways of life, organization, and relation with the cosmos ... So our demand as a people, as a *pueblo*, is not to have access to the civilization in the terms that they conceive of civilization ... but that they recognize that we are civilized according to our own criterion and our own values. (Manuela)

In addition to demanding a place in the nation on their own terms, Manuela also sought to stretch and reconfigure the confines of 'Guatemala' to make room for difference. She centered difference inside the nation:

> We are born in this country ... We feel like Guatemalan women ... although I don't know where the name Guatemala came from ... But we identify ourselves 'we are Mayan-kaqchikel women'. Because we are inside the territory of Guatemala, that's why we say 'Guatemalan'. Because, in fact, we are part of Guatemala ... Our demands are that we participate, that our rights are respected *as* Mayan women and that we contribute to the society, that we are taken into account, acknowledged. (Manuela)

Manuela continued, explaining that her social commitment and every relationship that she had occurred within the conceptual context of Guatemala.

Guatemala was comprised of many different people with distinct identifications ('rich and poor', '*Ladinos*, and indigenous, and blacks', and 'also men and women'). Manuela explained that relationships of power transgressed different constellations of identities. She stated: 'There are different forms of oppression exercised by different subjects to different subjects.' Here, she did not employ the discursive move common in the narratives of reading different discourses/relations of power only through the grammar of the dominant Mayan discourse, which was built around the relationships *Ladino*/Maya or colonizors/victims (see chapter 6). Instead, she explained that she felt like 'ethnicity and gender had arrived late to the party'. Class analysis, she explained elsewhere, had previously dominated the discourses of the popular movement; the naming of oppression as related to racism or sexism was subordinate to that of classism.

Although Manuela explained above that she identified herself as a Guatemalan woman and a Mayan-kaqchikel woman, she did not explicitly create a hierarchy between these subject positions. She spoke of her identities as complementary aspects that became activated in different situations. Nevertheless, they were always a part of her; they always 'fit'. In the following citation, she spoke of her 'triple identity' in relation to the political climate in Guatemala.

> Guatemala is a society so politicized, so that even when people say 'I'm not political' they are expressing a position ... My identity has these three components ... these three parts which contain others ... [Q: The others fit inside?] They fit, they fit perfectly, and at least if tomorrow it occurs to me that they don't fit, I may add another ... They fit because they are wide. (Manuela)

Manuela implied that identification had become so politically charged in Guatemala because of the historical conjuncture, that to explicitly identify oneself at all in Guatemala was a political act. If that identity did not fit into the idea of citizenship and nationality defined by the state/army, then one was, per definition, challenging the state. Furthermore, placing one's different subject positions in a lateral relationship instead of a vertical one challenged the hierarchy of identities upon which state sovereignty and security depended, and thus redefined in/security.

Manuela consciously raised these challenges against 'homogenization', and called for a nationalism that tolerated fluidity and multiplicity, both on the part of those in power and in terms of those who resisted. She explained:

> Historically we've been the most affected by the general situation of social exclusion that exists. So, this has led to us uniting, in the sense of becoming cohesive as a group or as movements. However, there are respectable differences ... The role that the social movement should play now is not the same as before ... It is not a struggle of sectors. Now it has to be a struggle for all the people, and in which all the people feel represented. It is very difficult, but what are we going to construct? ... We have been

> saying for many years that Guatemala is not a homogenous reality, that there is diversity ... Yet in practice, very few assume this. (Manuela)

Manuela continued the theme of 'struggling against stereotypes' that was discussed in chapter 6. In her discussions about discourses within the social movements (specifically, the Mayan and women's movements), she navigated among different exclusionary practices, and spurned being forced to comply with rigid criteria of belonging. Manuela therefore warned against repeating much of the logic of sovereignty and discourses of danger that fix subject positions in rigid categories of inside (read: same, limited, safe) and outside (read: foreign, different, dangerous.) Instead, she revisioned an idea of Guatemala that took as its point of departure the contingency of political and social life. She explained:

> There are three official visions of Guatemala: 1) folkloric; 2) vision of the garbage dumps, which exploits the needs of the people to attract pity from the international community; 3) vision of Zone Ten [where the rich people live] ... But I do not like any of these visions of Guatemala, because none reflect what Guatemala really is. They reduce it to a small vision which responds to certain interests ... Yet, a whole *pueblo* is struggling not because we want pity, but respect, because we do not want to be underdeveloped ... We simply want to be left in peace so that we can develop into what we want ... We want to construct a Guatemala which opposes stereotypes ... I believe that what should be salvaged [is] the people who are changing, and who want to change things. (Manuela)

Manuela refuted stereotypes and embraced change as the basis of desired politics, even the basis for security. Her need for fluidity, however, was unique among the narrators. The majority acted within a discourse that demanded more distinct boundaries, closed categories, and discouraged transgressions, at least as a political stance.

Writing a future

> In my future, I want Guatemala to be happy. I want the army to be reduced more than anything else, because the army gives much sadness. It is made up of people of our own race, our people. Many times these same people are obligated to hurt their own race. I do not want this to continue like this. I want to live in a different country so that we young people have more opportunity to work, and express ourselves freely. (Susanna)

The articulation of a desired future can represent the framework for our political imagination, and therewith, inform possible answers to the critical questions that govern our lives. Such questions include basic inquiries about who we are in relation to others, and where danger and safety may reside. I therefore concluded the interviews with a question about the narrators' desired future.

The majority of the narrators situated their desired futures in terms of the Guatemalan nation-state project. The picture they painted of the future was often rather vague in details, yet nevertheless, it reflected a strong conviction about the areas of society that must be reformed. These reforms 'naturally' would take place within the juridical (and discursive) framework of 'Guatemala'. For example, they articulated a vision of a society without discrimination, violence, exploitation, and militarization. Maria stated:

> Future? That its a better country ... no militarization because that is the most cruel thing there is ... That the military would disappear, the rich disappear, that there would be equality, we would all be brothers, no discrimination, exploitation, an agrarian reform, good distribution of resources. (Maria)

Equality also loomed large as a desired goal; the narrators called for agrarian reform, the equal distribution of resources, abolishment of the rich (class), and conscious participation in 'economic, social and cultural development' (Gloria). Onelia called for health clinics and for the people to 'live more humanely'. Onelia, also summoned an image of unity among the different factions of the social movement, as well as all of the country. She also demanded state-recognized political participation of Mayan women.

Above all, the narrators colluded in their belief that the Mayan *pueblo* belonged in the political landscape of Guatemala, yet they knew that this landscape must undergo major transformation. For example, when talking about creating peace and a desirable future in Guatemala, Diana spoke of the problem of redistributing the resources of the country. She explained that there was a concentration of wealth and power at the top of a cupola, which defined a structure of power relations 'that include(d) sexism, racism etc. to keep it going' (Diana). Achieving peace in a desirable future meant rectifying these different interrelated relations of power. How, for example, Diana would identify herself in such new power configurations remained to be seen.

By proposing that a future Guatemala would contain all of the above attributes (marking a safe site), the narrators also indicated who they strove to be in this political configuration. By nature of striving after what they did not have, they rejected the position that they already occupied. Onelia explained her desires for the future:

> [My desire is] that my great grandchildren do not live the same [situation] that we are living because it is sad and painful. At least, in the future one does not think about a sequestration happening, that there were massacres here but that they will be thinking about a development, and this would not only benefit the Mayan *pueblo*, it would benefit the whole country. (Onelia)

Onelia named sadness and pain as the basic characteristic of 'the situation that [she] is living'. Security and contentment resided, then, in a developed Guatemala where the Mayan *pueblo* would participate equally along with the *Ladinos* and the violence (manifested in sequestration and massacres) would cease. Hence, the vision of the future and what dangers one wanted to alleviate was informed by one's subject position in the moment of imagining the future.

When imagining, the narrators placed themselves in a Guatemalan nation-state project that could ensure both their participation and their security, and provide the framework for their identity constellations. Maria talked of Guatemala as if it were the 'Promised Land' of her nostalgia and her future. Since she had not yet returned, it was a Promised-Land-in-the-making: 'I feel proud of being Guatemalan, of being in my country, I feel happy. Here is my land ... here is everything; I need to be in my country' (Maria). In this imagined Guatemala, she would be happy; Guatemala would belong to her and she would belong in it. Mercedes also owned Guatemala, pledging her allegiance 'until she dies':

> To be a citizen of Guatemala, with all the rights, which the law says. To be Guatemalan is [also] to feel part and to be part of the whole life of a country. In this sense ... to be Guatemalan because its my country, I was born here, I continue living here, and continue my support until I die, this is to feel part of a country, to defend the life of a country. (Mercedes)

The Guatemala to which she was loyal would include her as a citizen, name her an 'insider' and allow her to be a provider of security, 'to defend the life of the country', instead of being its enemy.

Notes

1 See e.g. Fischer and Brown (1996); Jonas (2000); Smith (1990); Solares (1993).

2 See Avancso, 'Foro de La Etnia a La Nacion' Guatemala City, August, 1995; various articles in the national Newspapers *Prensa Libre* and *Siglio XXI* during period June–August 1995.

3 Quiche suffered some of the most brutal violence during the late 1980s. The very barracks where this slogan was painted was also the site of imprisonment of 'disappeared' peoples, as well as torture. One narrator explained that she could hear screams coming from within these walls at night. A climate of violence and oppression continued in Quiche throughout the early 1990s. In 1995, when I conducted interviews in Quiche, I was harassed by civil patrollers blocking my way and asking me my business. Armed soldiers could be seen at various points in the area.

4 '*Libertinaje*' is a term that connotes a sexual and moral free-for-all.

5 The complementary pair of 'losing one's roots' and 'rescuing one's roots' also appears in all of the narratives.

6 These moves resonated with the creation of the 'model peasants' in the Model Villages.

7 General Efraín Rios Mont was responsible for brutal counter-insurgency tactics in the early 1980s after winning power through a military coup. He was elected to a seat in the provisional parliament in 1994 and attempted to run for presidency in 1995. At the time of the interviews, many feared his return to a position of power in the country.

9

Closing comments

> Perhaps they don't have a name for that which makes me who I am, or makes me think what I think, or feel what I feel. (Manuela)

> If the Mayan *pueblo* fortifies itself ... and wins space and revindication in the Guatemalan society – as if it were a homogenous entity, as if it were a thing – what will happen when it already has all these revindications? [...] All these contradictions will continue then, and worse, worse because there will be women who will have known beyond that which is trying to homogenize them. (Manuela)

IT HAS BECOME INCREASINGLY OBVIOUS that people come into conflict with each other over issues related to identity. In many different parts of the world, the hegemonic political identification with the nation-state may be losing a competition for loyalty and allegiance among other competing identities – identities that both follow and subvert the logic of state sovereignty. Attempts to broaden the concept of in/security to reflect this conceptual dearth have set the stage for an unpacking and rethinking of this central concept/practice, thus opening possibilities for taking into account the centrality of identity, and the plurality of struggle and conflict.

'Security', as it has been conceived in mainstream IR and among the architects of most national security policies, has been inadequate in explaining or prescribing solutions for many of the most pressing and violent conflicts within states, between states, and beyond states. The devastation of violence and war which permeates the societies of what many classify as 'new wars', as well as the threat of widespread violence stemming from globalized terrorism, and the 'war on terror' resist simple remedies, old panaceas, and unbefitting logics (Gökay and Walker, 2002; Kaldor, 1999). Indeed the stronghold that the 'logic of sovereignty' holds over ways of thinking about and practicing in/security might disenable novel and constructive ways of addressing recent and ongoing conflicts in many parts of the world, as well as Mayan women's hybrid experiences of violence.

Indeed, the acuity of the Mayan *pueblo*'s demands for 'rights and identity' affirm that massive social and political transformation is certainly necessary for the resolving of direct conflict, insidious violence, and exclusion.

I suggest that the articulations of in/securities discussed in this book merit serious attention in the consideration of a palatable response to the 'culture of violence and fear' that has defined life not only in Guatemala, but also in many other sites globally. The narrators' articulations of in/security provide clues as to what people in diverse violent situations and at the collusion of different systems of oppression find important and even essential for their safety and well-being. These articulations can provide insight into the mechanisms of how danger and safety are reproduced, and therefore how we can better address the in/security of people in diverse situations.

This book was motivated by two inter-related concerns: first, it reflects a preoccupation with the very real violence that many Mayan women have endured and that somehow gets left out of most discussions on security in theories about modern politics, and surely in policy formation. It matters that people like Mayan women suffer multiple and persistent harms. Second, the violent ramifications of the paradox of in/security are often repeated in the very sites of marginality where people attempt to procure safety and resist the violence and exclusion inflicted by hegemonic practices of securing national (or other dominant identities), such as evidenced in many of the narrator's testimonies. This conundrum resounds in many of the bloody struggles, dubiously called 'ethnic conflicts', of today.

In order to consider the puzzles that these concerns raise, I have sought to unpack the dominant logic of in/security as we have been taught to imagine it through reading in/security as inscribed in Mayan women's narratives in resistance. Through different, yet related trajectories, the different chapters of the book have traced how these narratives both reinstate and disrupt dominant stories about security in global politics. This 'concluding' chapter will offer further reflection over what reading these narratives might tell us about these crucial queries.

Representing Mayan women

The spatio-temporal contexts discussed in chapters 4–8 have illustrated how the narrators' evocations of in/security were multiple, hybrid, contradictory, contingent, crafted out of discourse, and defined in direct relation to their identity constellations. Throughout these different chapters, I have sought to reveal how they called forth experiences of violence and harm and thereby imbued the political subject 'Mayan woman' with meaning. Recollections of these experiences served to define who the narrator was in relation to others, and to clarify what she considered security and insecurity. The chapters highlighted how in different ways, the narrators navigated their texts around the violent experiences they endured at the confluence of various discourses such as colonialism, nationalism, racism, classism, and sexism. They identified these discourses and their particular articulations as threats and connected their experiences with that of the collective, as 'women', 'Mayans', and 'poor/*campesinas*'. Through remembering and recounting their struggles they constructed themselves in their narratives as political subjects who experienced vast insecurities directly related to the identities that they articulated.

These marginalized ethnic and gendered identities were formed in relation to the dominant and 'legitimate' political subjects in the hegemonic discourses that defined political life (Nelson, 1999: 76–7). Their narratives, however were not merely reflections of the dominant discourse. They created a marginalized account, which both challenged and surpassed the dominant ones. They also established themselves as subjects in resistance who contested the disciplinary tactics of the dominant discourses. Their struggles for security (safety, and well-being) were therefore not only reactions to harmful threats, but were also borne out of who they were and strove to be. They thereby gave new meanings to being a 'Mayan woman' in the different contexts that informed their lives and struggles.

Hence, the Mayan women I interviewed were not fully 'hailed into place' by the hegemonic discourse of nation-state security. Neither, however, were they cemented into static roles by the dominant Mayanist discourse, which elevated them as symbols and repositories of their culture. Instead, they crafted their own hybrid political identity that rearticulated the subject positions that were already determined through divergent discourses. The narrators embraced the identity constellation 'Mayan-women-poor', yet redefined its meaning from one of subordination to one of resistance and agency.

In sum, specific understandings of sovereignty crafted out of its 'grid of intelligibility' defined what it meant to aspire to some other identity and to resist the identities fashioned by hegemonic powers (Dillon, 2004; Radcliffe and Westwood, 1993: 13; Walker, 1993: 179). In their attempts to resist the violence they experienced and to struggle for security of their triple identity, they also re-enacted harmful exclusions and inclusions, thus rearticulating some of the injurious workings of discourses of danger/safety that, I argue, are attendant to the dominant logic of in/security. While not resolving the conundrum of in/security, these rearticulations offer some apertures through which to reconsider it.

Revisiting security studies

In concluding this book, I find myself resisting the question: 'What has my research on Mayan women's in/security narratives brought to the study of security?' This question seems to concede that focusing on Mayan women's in/security must be somehow justified as a valid subject for research relevant to understanding security and global politics (Zalewski, 2005). However, as Zalewski implies, resisting the move to justify or legitimate the boundaries of the 'field' need not necessarily entail refusing to engage with it at all: instead, it may mean both disturbing and destabilizing its dominant stories. One way is to devise a methodology for studying security in sites whose very inclusion onto the playing field of IR forces us to rethink our tattered 'rulebooks'.[1] By paying careful attention to the specific contexts and subject positions inscribed within marginalized discourses, one can perhaps begin to understand better the contingency and multiplicity of in/security and identity, as well as what might be at stake in attempts to represent a subject in order to secure it.

Another way of disturbing the violent logic of in/security is to take seriously Mayan women's narratives *as* valid texts about in/security – texts which transform the knowledge of modern politics, and reveal its scaffolding as constructions that need not take the form they do. This book does this in at least four ways.

First, I have sought to make clear that the Mayan women I interviewed are indeed valid political subjects whose in/security is not located outside of global politics: Mayan women were already 'there', even in accepted so-called security politics (Enloe, 1990). For instance, areas as diverse as the Guatemalan state security policy, Nicaraguan elections, US foreign policy, German and Israeli arms sales, NAFTA, multinational corporations, structural adjustment programs, United Nations' Convention 169, and Human Rights commissions, all made an appearance in the narratives and informed the in/security-identity of the narrators. The narrators clearly showed how those processes traditionally (and 'alternatively') considered relevant to security studies also constitute many Mayan women's lives and struggles. The enactments of Guatemalan state security policy was only the most obvious of these. Leticia's naming of the mass production of preground corn (*maseca*) as dictated by agreements through NAFTA as a source of threat to Mayan women provides another example. Indeed, accounts such as these reveal how in/security in global politics is already gendered and, in many instances, includes subaltern women by their very exclusion and silencing (Pin-Fat and Stern, 2005).

Second, reading Mayan women's narratives also exposes the limitations of the accepted understandings and practices of security: Mayan women's in/securities cannot be reduced to a location, level, or category ultimately determined by the logic of state sovereignty. Their narratives disrupt the familiar relationships that provide many of the building blocs for our understandings and practice of politics, political community, identification, and conceptions of in/security. Indeed, the very attempt to reduce Mayan women's in/security to the familiar category of, for example, 'individual in state' or 'human' can be read as crafted out of the same logic of security and violence that has so greatly punctuated their lives. Their narratives suggest that the assumed dividing lines engraved in security as we have been taught to imagine it (e.g. those between domestic and foreign, inside and outside, Us and Them, protector and protected, citizen and enemy, victim and perpetrator, civil and military, etc.) not only poorly reflect Mayan women's accounts but may also make it more difficult for adequate response to their pleas for safety.

For example, in the context of organizations and political movements, we saw how the narrators established that they contended with an existence of overriding insecurity in terms of direct threats to their lives. Yet, it is important to remember that they chose to risk their lives in order to struggle for the security of the larger collective, both in terms of its survival as a (sovereign) collective into the future, and in terms of the lives of its individual members. The narrators expressed that they rejected a possibly solitary site in which they were threatened by the army/PACs/state/*patrones* and joined together with other persons who had experienced similar insecurities, even if this meant placing their individual lives in greater danger. They thus discursively shifted their 'subjectivity' from their personal bodies onto the collective body of their organization and *pueblo*. Within this context, they re-presented how they had constructed a political identity almost inseparable from the others in their collective – both in the past and the present – and in direct relation to those (or that) which threatened them. Security, for them, involved belonging to this collective.

Additionally, many of the narrators spoke of their sense that the decaying forces of poverty eroded their humanity. Security, they seemed to imply, resided in being able to regain human dignity. This would be achieved not only through the provisions for basic needs and for the procurement of a future (i.e. education), but through the vector of culture. Without their identity and its markings in society, they lacked humanity and remained victims, 'dogs', positioned at a disadvantage in the globalized political economy at the conflux of related violent discourses. The narratives thus complicate familiar notions of 'individual' or 'human' security.

Moreover, in the context of the family and community, many narrators focused on the threats to the hearth of their identity when Mayan boys returned 'home' after having spent time in the army and PACs. The returning boys represented how the army/state had succeeded in planting the 'enemy within' and divesting the Mayan boys, the future generation, of their culture and their sense of community and family, rendering them both 'foreign' and in danger of losing themselves. Some spoke of boys returning home and disrespecting their mothers who represented the core of Mayan cultural identity and embodied the linchpin of resistance. They thus named disrespect against the mother's, and community's, cultural expression as a threat to *her* gender identity (which was marked by her *traje*, as well as her role as a mother). The boys were thus at once both enemy and self, perpetrator and victim. The narrators' representations of the complex and crisscrossing power relations which informed the difficulties involved in Mayan boys' return provide an excellent example of how the prevailing categories through which we understand or practice in/security poorly correspond to in/security as Mayan women 'spoke' it.

Third, the intricate and inseparable relationship between in/security and identity explored in post-structural security studies is cast in a different light when one pays attention to marginalized security discourses. The identities articulated in Mayan women's in/security narratives – as well as the in/securities that were co-constructed along with these identity positions – were multiple, complementary, informed each other, and at times even implied contradictions. The different chapters underscored the complexity, hybridity, and contingency of security (as an ontological condition of identity) and drew attention to the oft-violent conflict and marginalization that occurs at the intersection of identities and in attempts at securing identity positions.

For instance, in addition to the obvious insecurities (such as fear of torture, death, rape, the razing of villages, or other forms of violence), the narrators also evoked other threats and dangers in the context of family/community that were tied to their sense of themselves as political subjects. They located the 'birth' of their political selves in moments of extreme violence at the hands of the army/state and thus established themselves and their struggles in their communities (*pueblo*) and in opposition to the violent domination of the army. Yet their security-identity constellations included other relationships. As we saw in the context of *Ladino*-Maya relations, many defined themselves as a proud and defiant Mayans in relation to their oppressors, the *Ladinos* through the naming of danger and harm. Similarly, as we will recall, Leticia's identity as a Mayan women in resistance was produced in relation to 'men' as the enemy. Rosa, for instance, expressed similar dynamics in the construction of her identity as Mayan-*campesina* in the face of the 'rich'.

The narrators also showed how their multiple identities both informed each other, and implied contradictions, which they sought to resolve. As we saw in the context of Maya-*Ladino* relations, the narrators established that security resided in maintaining firm boundaries between Us and Them, the Mayas and the *Ladinos*. Yet, in the context of the family/community many expressed how they felt insecure in the presence of (Mayan) men who could harm them physically. Moreover, they articulated that insecurity also resided in the confines of a gender identity that did not allow them a sense of well-being within themselves. Security, on the other hand, involved an opportunity for well-being, a chance to reconstruct a gender identity that did not build upon 'stereotypes' dictated by the state, the community, the relations in their family, or by men. Yet, they attributed harmful sexism manifested in Mayan communities to the Spanish invasion. They talked of the triple oppression women bore. Security entailed maintaining a sense that the Mayan community was coherent, it also entailed ridding the Mayan community of the ills of colonial sexism. Similarly, the gender ideologies that the narrators defined as harmful were informed by *Ladino*-Maya relations, or further back in history, by the relations of ruling in colonialism. The narrators established that the *Ladino* view of Mayan women had influenced the Mayan men. Hence, the gendered political identity of *Ladinos* in relation to Mayans also were implicated in the threats that the narrators identified 'inside' their families.

In the context of the organizations and political movement, we saw how the narrators made claims for security as 'Mayan women', re-presenting dominant Mayan discourses in their texts, and imbuing the meaning of 'Mayan woman' differently, even in inharmonious and opposing ways. Through recalling their engagement with their specific organizations (and the umbrella movements), they presented themselves as architects of the political space they demanded, both within these movements, and in the Guatemalan society at large. In so doing, they linked their different struggles and negotiated (more or less successfully) the disparate trajectories of their struggles and identities. Within this context, they re-presented how they had constructed a political identity almost inseparable from the others in their collective, both in the past and the present, and in direct relation to those who (or that which) threatened them. Security, for them, involved belonging to this collective. It also involved finding a space in which to share their experiences with others and to grow into political subjects of their own making.

Fourth, the narratives reveal how discourses of danger and the mechanisms of inclusion and exclusion that foster violence in conflicts over national securities and identities also resound in security discourses in marginal sites (e.g. as was expressed in the need for cohesion in the Mayan *pueblo* in the face of its enemies).

In all of the texts, the narrators articulated an acute threat to the Mayan *pueblo*. For many, security resided in not rupturing the unity of the group, which provided the base of their identity. We thus can see how the narrators' notion of safety resonated with the promise of a sovereign and cohesive 'subject' which *could* be rendered secure. Focusing on sexism within the Mayan community might have meant turning allies into The Enemy in their discussions with me through discourses of danger. For instance, many explained how sexism was not 'theirs': 'The discrimination comes from the Spanish. We can not blame the elders, they are not guilty.' Naming sexism in the community – 'the inside' – threatened the necessity of a maintaining a unified front against the *Ladino* society and in relation to all other outsiders, both well-meaning and outwardly dangerous.

The narrators underscored their experiences of discrimination and exclusion, expressing the pain they felt as subjugated persons in hierarchical relations of power and resources. They established that security resided in maintaining firm boundaries between Us and Them, the Mayas and the *Ladinos*. However, simply maintaining boundaries would not redress racism. The narrators revealed that they struggled for security through redefining and subverting the harmful meanings attached to being Mayan in *Ladino* society and in the Guatemalan state. They sought security in reconstructing an 'old' political identity partly in resistance to the inherited identities dictated by racism. This political identity was imbedded in a collective movement for reconstruction and 'revindication' of a group identity that was linked to a grand and majestic past, and affirmed as sovereign and constant throughout history – and which 'belonged' within the borders of the Guatemalan state. As we saw, perhaps most strongly in the testimonies of those longing to 'return' to Guatemala, the modern sovereign state of Guatemala defined the perimeters for their future hopes and desires. Yet, they also explained that they were engaged in specific political projects for safety and security – namely respect for their difference and 'identity' and the 'rights' that this respect grants. The narrators thus, as Shaw discusses, 'politicized sovereignty', and sought 'to rearticulate it as a terrain of political possibility' (Shaw, 2004).

As we saw in the context of the organization, for many, securing their identities involved circumscribing them and constructing strict lines of demarcation between inside and outside, belonging and betraying. In Elena's testimony, for instance, safety resided also in limiting those who shared the same identity categories, lest they 'decay the culture'. Many narrators, (especially Elena and Onelia) warned against the traitorous act of crossing over the boundaries that protected the Mayan *pueblo* and Mayan women from the perilous influences of *Ladino*ization.

One narrator (Manuela), however, recounted her experiences of exclusion from the Mayan movement as personally painful and politically harmful. She identified the threat of homogenization and exclusion *from this site of resistance* (the Mayan movement) as her primary insecurity in this context. For her, security also implied the freedom to struggle for transformation without limiting herself and others within strictly defined identity categories. Manuela's subjectivity clearly 'leaked' over the boundaries containing the dominant representations of Mayan women; she, therefore, simultaneously posed a threat to others, and was rendered unsafe herself. Exploring how these potentially violent mechanisms work in these sites also discloses openings for possible resistance, which I will return to below.

Throughout the different chapters, I have sought to show how Mayan women's in/security discourses can be seen as unsettling rearticulations of dominant stories about security. When considered together, the insights gained from reading these narratives prompt additional questions about the puzzles which motivated my writing this book. The remainder of this chapter will therefore offer further reflection prompted by these insights. In particular, I aim to reconsider the relationship between identity, subjectivity, and in/security in order to explore the conundrum of security and the violence that seems to go hand in hand with struggles for security. Primarily: what might the elision of subjectivity into identity mean for the enactment of violence in the name of security? The discourses of danger/safety against which the narratives were written, as well as those which figure as central within the narratives, suggest that discourses of danger (and safety) collapse all that 'we' are (subjectivity) into representations of who 'we' are (identity) and thereby reproduce violence (Dillon, 1996: 35). Given the insights gained from reading Mayan women's narratives, I suggest that the notion that a political community could possibly act as cohesive subject, as it is often depicted, partly rests on the conflation of identity and subjectivity. How might such mechanisms work? And why so they seem to reproduce violence?

Discourses of danger: a logic of violence

In the different chapters of this book, we have seen how danger resides in the foreign – as it appears in the dominant logic of security, and importantly, as it reappears in Mayan women's narratives. Instances of disharmony within the 'subject of security' can be seen as attributed predominantly to 'outside' influences. Threat, danger and in/security engrave the dividing lines between an identifiable 'us' from an identifiable 'them', as well as the criterion for selfhood which establish normalcy from deviance. Such criteria for 'normalcy' often leads to a hierarchy of other identity categories (in terms of the state, this implies the hegemony of national identity as crucial for security; in terms of Mayan women, this often necessitated an over-riding identification with the Mayan *pueblo*). Many of the narrators saw themselves as part of a marginalized and threatened collective identity and found it difficult to challenge the rigid borders of their over-riding identity with the group. Threats to their identity *as* members of the Mayan *pueblo*, for instance, often also inscribed boundaries of inside-outside which regulated what this identity meant. Recalling Dillon's discussion of Hobbes may shed some light on these processes: if the inside does not remain a unified political subject in the face of the outside, the 'edifice' may crumble (quoted in Dillon, 1990–91: 106).

The narratives underscored how discourses of danger require the naming of the subject of security as well as the source of threat and danger. Yet, they also suggest that the naming of the subject of security can never be complete. This was perhaps most telling in Manuela's testimony, although similar insight can be gained from the other narrators as well. Indeed, I suggest that the spillage or excess of subjectivity that can not be fully represented makes the securing of identity impossible.[2] Following this logic, representations of a subject will be haunted with supplementary or excluded voices – 'What about "me'?' – that will inevitably clamor for attention even in the most careful attempts at representation. (These voices may perform within the 'self' that is supposedly represented, or resound in the constitutive outside – in the body of the Other.) Mayan women's narratives pose this question in myriad ways in response to the many discourses of power which harm and exclude them, including Guatemalan state-sanctioned security-identity policies. However, as we have also seen, their discourses of danger have produced additional excluded Others. I posit therefore that discourses of danger/safety work to conceal the excess of subjectivity, thus paving the way for the violence that pervades the struggle for security of identity, masquerading as subjectivity. What might this mean?

The narratives suggest that the very immediate violence that pervades global politics – and that many Mayan women experienced – make the seduction of the promise of security, emancipation, deliverance from danger and oppression imminently compelling, if not necessary. The assurance of security demands, however, a representation of the subject of security. Discourses of danger must then work to conceal the inherent impossibility of their own foundational suppositions. Hence: the conundrum of the (necessary) fantasy of the politics of representation and the promise of security.

Post-colonial and feminist scholars have in various ways grappled with the confines and possibilities of enacting identity (or subject positions) as a politics of resistance.[3] Debates within much post-colonial literature revolve around 'identity' as a perhaps necessary yet also dangerous place from which to speak (Williams and Chrisman, 1994). Furthermore, there has been a detailed and rich discussion within feminist theory about the politics surrounding the pinning down of subjects and the 'dangers of representational politics' – also in relation to the writing of security.[4] I am not attempting to debate the issue of 'strategic essentialism' as a viable venue of resistance (or even to explore if whether or not framing the questions in this way is at all helpful). Instead, I have drawn upon the insights gleaned from this body of work to inquire into how discourses of in/security are particularly disposed to produce danger and violence and how the dominant logic of in/security discourses can be reconstituted – and unsettled – in marginal sites, such as the narratives of Mayan women.

As noted in chapter two, critical theorists have argued convincingly that the 'paradox of sovereignty' inscribes 'the political' and forecloses possible alternatives to the basic questions of modern politics (Connolly, 2004; Edkins and Pin-Fat, 1999). Whether or not the myth of state-sovereignty maintains a stronghold on the political imagination of people and communities in disparate sites remains a vital question in the exploration of possible alternative imaginaries. Instead of attempting to address this question here, however, I will instead simply reassert that many attempts at making a 'we' – a metaphoric community of belonging – seem to follow the logic or grammar of sovereignty.

As we have seen, in the formation of a collective 'we' the collective is painted as a political, cultural, religious, or gendered 'subject': the Guatemalan state, the Mayan community, Women. Representations of the 'we' as subject often portray sovereign cohesion, despite the perhaps changing form of the contours framing it. In the words of Homi Bhaba, in asking how to understand the "homogeneity' of modernity – the people ...:

> we may begin by questioning that progressive metaphor of modern social cohesion – the many as one – shared by the organic theories of holism and community and by theorists who treat gender, class or race as social totalities that are expressive of unitary collective experiences. (Bhaba, 1994: 142)

Any notion of a 'we' as 'the many as one' arguably rests on the assumption that identity formations are similar in an individual and a state (or other form of collective 'we'.) This move is made possible through the logic of modern sovereignty which grounds the analogy of political community, (such as a state, ethnic' group or nation) as individual – an analogy, which has been well discussed and criticized elsewhere (RIS, vol. 30, no. 2, April 2004; Tickner, 1993).

In identifying oneself/being identified with the collective, 'I' shall become 'we': representations of the subject are painted with the colors of collective identities. This 'we', being a metaphorical construction, appears to be not only fundamentally singular, but also representable. Most importantly, the metaphorical 'we' promises correspondence with more than just the inscription of the imagined community as subject; people are often willing to die and kill for it (Anderson, 1991). In the inscription of in/security discourses, those collective identities that are to be secured – the 'we' of the subject of security – necessarily become more cemented or 'entrenched' since so much is at stake in their definition[5] – and in their the symbolic correspondence to the 'real'.[6] A defined national (or gendered ethnic) identity comes to stand for not only what the community *is*, but also who the members of this particular community *are*. Yet what of the excess that does not fit into the label 'we'? Mayan women, and the Mayan movement more generally, certainly figure as 'excess' over the label 'Guatemalan' in the architecture of Guatemalan security policy. Moreover, the narrators navigated 'excesses', anomalies, contradictions, through their naming of in/securities in the different contexts of their lives, hinting at the gaps and lacunae in their cohesive representations. Manuela so eloquently drew attention to such excesses when she said: 'Perhaps they do not have a name for that which makes me who I am.'

Hence, as many of the narrators remind us, the process of identification can never be complete, for similarity or wholeness is only constructed through difference and is, in effect, 'a fantasy'. One might say that wholeness, or, in other words, complete representation, is impossible. Hall states:

> Identification … is lodged in contingency. Once secured, it does not obliterate difference. The total merging it suggests is, in fact, a fantasy of incorporation … Identification is, then, a process of articulation, a suturing, an over-determination not a subsumption. There is always too much or too little – an over-determination or a lack, but never a proper fit, a totality. Like all signifying practices, it is subject to the play of difference. It obeys the logic of more-than-one. And since, as a process, it operates across difference, it entails discursive work, the binding and marking of symbolic boundaries, the production of 'frontier effects'. It requires what is left outside, its constitutive outside, to consolidate the process. (Hall, 1996: 3)

I suggest that through the writing of in/security, identities are taken to be accurate representations of the subject and discursively elide into *being* the subject. Yet, the in/security narratives explored in the previous chapters suggest that representing subjectivity, as well as attempts to secure these representations, can only be seen as (im)possible. Drawing on the later work of Wittgenstein, Pin-Fat explains that, according to an '(im)possible dynamic', 'what counts as possible depends upon what is already tacitly accepted as impossible' (Pin-Fat, 2000: 664).[7] Representing and securing the 'subject of security' can be seen as (im)possible for two reasons: first, insecurity is the inevitable supplement to security; and second, subjectivity can never be fully represented (and therewith secured). Identity, no matter how mobile or multiple it may be, can never represent the 'excess' of subjectivity. Arguably, as is evident in the harmful realities of conflict, the promise of security bears with it a logic, or grammar of violence; violence occurs (in part) through the concealment of these two inherent (im)possibilities. This concealment, I suggest, is enacted through the politics of naming a 'we' as a viable subject of security, albeit ultimately unsuccessfully. By exploring these (im)possibilities and the moves that conceal them, one might better understand how violent mechanisms of inclusion/exclusion often seem to be part and parcel of the enactment of (identity) politics in the name of securing political subjects or communities in both hegemonic and resistant sites, such as Mayan women's narratives.

Concealing (im)possibilities, assuring deliverance, re-enacting violence

We saw in different ways throughout the previous chapters how when discourses of in/security are enacted and alterity is explicitly marked with danger, the boundaries of identity become more heavily guarded and policed. Thus, through processes of politization,[8] identity categories become more fixed or stable. Importantly, the fixing of identity relies on the *being* of the subject of security as already established as foundational through the narrative of it 'always already having been' (Campbell, 1999: 24). The narrators' insistence on their identity as constant throughout a long and proud history provides support for this supposition. According to such logic, only – perhaps – the subject's 'correct' identity remains disputable. As Edkins reminds us, at the moment of securitization, 'the political' is effectively foreclosed and all that remains is the following of a script (Edkins, 1999: 1–17). A familiar plot is enacted: clear boundaries between a safe (and knowable) inside and dangerous outside are drawn. Security narratives produce a mythical (and 'mystical'[9]) subject that is represented through identity – a 'we' to be secured that must be both fundamentally singular and hegemonic (within the confines of the subject of security). This implies that representations of the subject are framed through discourses of danger in terms of the temporally marked boundaries that establish self from Other – as seemingly representable and securable identity categories.

Yet, I propose, these descriptions of the content of identity resound with their limiting fixity; answers to questions of identity ('Who am I?' or 'Who are we?'), must be inevitably incomplete and limiting, as Manuela's words testify. Violence occurs then in the attempt to close down/off subjectivity into a representable identity that can be secured through the naming of danger and the complementary construction of identity/difference (Connolly, 1991).

Both the theoretical inquiry which set the stage for the subsequent reading of the narrators texts, and the texts themselves, suggest that the writing of in/security discourses conceal both the (im)possibility of security and the excess – the spillage of a subjectivity that will always be more and beyond any attempt to represent it through the politics of naming. The logic of concealment appears as follows: in order for the 'subject of security' to be 'securable', it must then be circumscribed, contained, namable, with contours dividing the included from the excluded. Through eliding subjectivity into these supposedly securable identities, excess can be either unacknowledged or placed 'outside' of the subject (in the form of the Other). Securing the subject then requires the 'policing' of boundaries and the 'taming' or homogenization of an imagined 'self'. Arguably, this occurs more or less violently; in extreme cases the border guards 'secure' these boundaries through tactics that result in killing in the name of 'cleansing' (as did the Guatemalan army). However, as Dillon (1996) has argued, insecurity, as a supplement to security, haunts these dividing lines, making their ultimate security impossible. Discourses of in/security, then, conceal the unavoidable deferral of security through evocations of danger and threat that shall be overcome and disarmed.

The (im)possibility of security and the fantasy of representation

I have argued above that identity can be understood as the naming of a subject position, as a representation of the 'subject'. The identities we call forth, or that are inherited or imposed upon us stand for a (necessary) attempt to name and represent subjectivity. That 'subjectivity' is constituted through the process of naming, however, does not imply that they are one and the same; subjectivity will always spill over (Edkins, 1999: 99). Any seemingly coherent representation is always an unstable configuration in so far as 'it' is constituted by, and indeed haunted by, that which is excluded.[10] The voices that can be seen as saying 'what about me' disturb and unsettle the ordering and seemingly stable foundations of the subject of security – and indeed of the possibility of security – by revealing them as essentially unstable. The 'picture of the subject', which shall be secured, can never be big or broad enough: security will be forever unattainable.

Thus, calls for attention to identity as the 'new' or critical subject of security risk setting the stage for upholding the notion that security is ever possible, and for a never-ending search for pinning down that which is to be secured – the subject of security. Yet, as I argued above, insecurity can only be the inevitable supplement to any attempt to secure the subject of security, no matter how detailed, varied or multiple the identity categories may be that are enacted to 'capture' or represent it, such as the in/security narratives of the Mayan women I interviewed. The problem seems to lie in its framing: no matter how many dues are paid to multiplicity or difference (i.e. in moving from a focus on the military security of states, to a breakdown of spheres of security into levels and areas ((Buzan, 1983; 1991)) to a focus on societal or national identity ((Buzan et al., 1998)) to an attempt to reflect the hybrid and multiple sites of security in much feminist work, including this book[11]), security remains illusory. Security always carries with it its own undoing, thus ensuring that the act of securing must endure. Sylvester explains 'there simply can be no coherent statement inscription or morality that makes the definitive home, covers all the contingencies of contingent existence, and thereby ends insecurity. Security is always partial and therefore strategy is always, as a result, somewhat undecidable' (Sylvester, 1994: 183).

Following this logic, threat and danger will always loom and are indeed integral, as a 'constitutive outside' to security and safety. The security of identity therefore precludes its closure (Butler, 1990: 126). Hence although the fixing of identity through politicization of marginal identities (i.e. ethnic identity) may serve as a viable counter-force to the politics that arise out of securing hegemonic identity categories (i.e. national identity), identity politics (by enacting rigid and closed identity categories) may also render insecure the very people it aims to protect.

In sum, throughout this book I have argued that in/security is hybrid, composed within discourse, and that the naming of in/security is mutually constitutive with processes of identification. The different chapters explored the complexity of and violence embedded in what can be seen as the (im)possibility of the promise of security and the fantasy of representation. In the above section I have suggested that violence occurs when discourses of danger conceal these (im)possibilities through the co-constitutive process of, first, veiling the insecurity that is implicated in security, and second, the conflation of subjectivity and identity. These discursive moves make it possible to cast a metaphoric 'we' as a subject of security.

In giving the representation of a 'whole' political community the status of corresponding with the soul or core of the substance (which *is* that community), the possibility of its ultimate existential 'security' makes sense. If we know what *Guatemalidad* or Mayan-ness is then we can surely secure it. The trick, so the story goes, is to find the most real representation (multiple, hybrid, or deep) that captures the *being* of the community. Articulations of identity thus serve to denote the (im)possible subject into securable representations (the content of identity categories), such as 'we Guatemalans' or even 'we who have suffered for 500 years' that can be confined and safeguarded against those who are not and have not. Yet, I propose, these discursive sleights of hand never quite work: Mayan women's in/security narratives suggest that violence is both subverted, as well as enacted and reproduced in efforts to procure safety – even in resistance.

Both despite and because of the inevitable failure of such discursive maneuverings, Mayan women's in/security narratives offer a site to view the conflux of dominance and contestation – and the ripples of resistance produced at these junctures. Their anomalous, problematic, and indeed 'untidy' accounts of in/security thus dislodge security as it has been written by the logic of modern state sovereignty and reveal some of the patterns of sedimentation, as well as the dust particles that inevitably fall from even the most solid foundations.[12]

Resistance: subverting subordination – negotiating identity

The in/security narratives that figure in this book serve as anomalies and contestations to the dominant stories of security; similarly, the 'securing' moves within these narratives also produce their own anomalies and contestations. Such ripples of resistance also dislodge security as it has been written by the logic of modern state sovereignty. As we will recall, Dillon reassures us that grids of intelligibility, such as those that circumscribe the (im)possibility of security, transmute. Although, 'sovereignty remains central ... to the political imaginary of the modern', the 'modern' is constantly renegotiated, rearticulated, and therewith transformed even by those voices that claim their political status as borne out of traditionality (Dillon, 2004: 46).

In Guatemala, the perceived threats to the state inscribed boundaries of difference (i.e. *Ladino* vs Mayan), which reproduced hierarchical divisions that distinguished the self (*Guatemalidad*) from the enemy (the majority of the people). A similar dynamic, although certainly much less violent, occurred within the popular/Mayan movements; dynamics of inclusion/exclusion thus informed the politics of dominance and of resistance in Guatemala. The preceding chapters showed how, in different ways, the narrators navigated among the rocky shoals of their hybrid identities, multiple struggles, and their contingent, and sometimes contradictory naming of danger and desires for safety, thus disclosing the layers of shifting sediment under seemingly solid representations of the subjects of security: 'Mayan women'.

The narrators linked their struggles and subject positions into a comprehensive whole. This, however, was not without conflict and tension. The lines between 'us' and 'them' blurred, for example, when many Mayan teenagers were forced to join the army. Similarly, loyalties may have been confounded when the narrators were subject to physical abuse from their husbands, and Ladina women offered solidarity and support in the name of 'women's rights'. When made rigid and when regulated by the dominant in/security discourse, the categories of nationalism/ethnic and gender identity severely constricted the realm of possible resolutions to the very urgent problems of danger and threat (Parker et al., 1992: 14). Yet, these blurrings (or leakiness) also provided a space in which the narrators could reimagine both their struggles and themselves as political subjects.

In the simple and tremendously courageous act of becoming politically active – in constructing themselves as political subjects – these women challenged many of the disciplining forces of in/security both 'inside' the community, and 'outside', as well as those which insist on an 'inside' and an 'outside'. Their struggle for security and agency could not be removed from the dominant in/security discourses that informed their lives. Yet, despite the endurance of such constructions, their political identity also attested to a profound challenge to these very forces. By refusing to accept the content of the inherited identity categories ascribed to them by confluent discourses, the narrators gave their own meanings to the subject position 'Mayan woman'. The narrators all rejected the hierarchies of identity positions that were dictated by the dominant discourses, and resolutely maintained the multiplicity of their struggles and the hybridity of their in/securities. Manuela, in particular, refused a pinning down of who she was and for what she struggled. Hence, although their attempts at cohesive resistant narratives reinstated the paradox of sovereignty and indeed in/security, these resistant moves also left space for an engagement in 'the political', as Edkins defines it (Edkins, 1999: 2). I propose that instead of reading seemingly contradictory claims as incommensurable, one can read these seeming contrasts as open, and importantly, not yet decided 'or technologized' political spaces.

By tenaciously making claims from a triple identity, and refusing a disjoining of their struggles into distinct parts, they validated the hyphen marks between their subject positions and rendered these marks 'political', that is, those linking the identity constellation Mayan-woman-poor. From the site of their hyphenated identity, they rewrote their own representations of in/security. They thus altered relations between the margins and the hegemonic discourses that harmed them (Schirmer, 1993: 62). Hence, attention to the boundaries and borderlands between and within inherited identities – as well as between and within the different discourses which reproduce them – may disclose regulatory self-Other dichotomies, and even partially disarm dominant in/security discourses. Through their evocations of the very multiplicity and contextuality of their in/security, the narrators renegotiated the tensions in different loci of danger, threat, and political strategy. These very tensions reveal some of the otherwise obscured scaffolding of the workings of discourses of danger. I suggest then that by carefully paying attention to the conjuring moves that create the seeming possibility of secure subjects, we can begin to resist the seductions of a logic that also inflicts harm.

Concluding thoughts

Although the narrators' 'subjugated' knowledges may not provide new or conclusive answers to critical questions of politics, or to the puzzles I posed in the beginning of this book, they might be able to help those working in these fields to rethink the connections between security and identity. Treating Mayan women's narratives as a valid point of departure for reading in/security-identity as a discursive practice highlights the contingencies of all 'stories' about in/security-identity and opens up the possibility that these stories could be written differently. Ultimately, my intent has been to challenge the limitations of political imaginaries that expunge from consideration the in/securities Mayan women name because they represent (im)possible subjects of security.

While writing this book, I have sought to resist reproducing secure representations of Mayan women's in/security and to remain open to the surprises and indeed the contestations or excess in the texts and in my representations of the narrators' words. The narratives both unsettle and re-enact many discourses at once, inviting many entry points for reflection and meaning. Without being 'representative', or generalizable, contingent readings help us make sense of both ourselves and the world as we have lived it, live it, and hope to live it.

Crucially, the in/security narratives cited in this book are also life stories about the people I interviewed. They are stories with great power, wisdom, and 'truths' about in/security. They are stories about the narrators themselves, their lives, Guatemala, the Mayan peoples, the global political economy, the power relations inherent in 'conducting research' – as well as much, much more. They are also stories of resistance and of hope: Diana's words (upon reflecting over reading the transcript of her interview) therefore offer a fitting conclusion to this book:

> In reality, I was surprised by what I said in these moments. I have never talked of my life, I've only suffered ... But to tell about it in this way in a detailed manner, no [...] I've never described the story which I have lived ... sometimes I think: during my thirty-three years, I ask myself, What I have done? How have I advanced? Sometimes, I do not

find the answer, because for me the years have been short ... And according to me I have not done anything. But seeing the questions that I have written here made me think. Really, I have lived through a difficult time in my life. [Now] ... I continue living the problems maybe in a different way, [reading this text] has made me refresh my memory. I say: 'I am a woman and I have done something and in this moment my visions are already wider about how to help other *compañeras* to not, perhaps, follow in the same condition ... I felt, on the one hand, sad, and wanted to cry in remembering my history, but at the same time, I felt glad because I have done something ... I am able to aid my *pueblo*. (Diana)

Notes

1 See e.g. Jabri and O'Gorman (1999); Krause and Williams (1997); Milliken (1999); and Weldes et al. (1999).

2 See also e.g Campbell (1992); Connolly (1991); Der Derian (1995); Dillon (1990–91; 1996); Jabri and O' Gorman (1999); Krause and Williams (1997); Sylvester (1994); Weldes et al. (1999).

3 E.g. Bhaba (1994); Chow (1993); Fanon (1952); Hall (1996); Narayan and Harding (2000); Edkins, Persram and Pin-Fat (1999); Spivak (1988).

4 For a range of different approaches see e.g. Barrett and Phillips (1992); Butler (1990, 1993); Jabri (1998); Lugones and Spelman (1983); Masters (2002); Shutte (2002); Trihn T. Minh-ha, (1989).

5 See Connolly (1991); Hekman (1999: 18–19).

6 See Edkins (1999: 113); Zizek (1989: 173).

7 Pin-Fat further describes this dynamic: 'Implicated in these enabling possibilities is also that which is necessarily excluded in specific articulations ... That is to say, the impossible. Whether implicitly, or explicitly, what is taken to be possible not only implies what shall be taken as impossible, but more importantly, what shall be kept at bay, excluded, as the 'outside'. Indeed, we contend that articulations of the possible are privileged as legitimate but that this can only be adequately understood by paying attention to the role that the impossible plays' (Pin-Fat and Stern, 2005)

8 What Edkins calls 'depolitization' – or arguably, 'securitization', according to Waever. Edkins (1999); Waever (1995).

9 See Pin-Fat (2005) for a discussion of the state as 'mystical'.

10 I am borrowing some of the basic logic (as well as several phrasings) of this argument from Pin-Fat and Stern (2005).

11 Feminist accounts of security include: Blanchard (2003); Cohn (1993); Elshtain (1987); Enloe (1988, 1990, 1993); Peterson and Runyan (1993); Pettman (1996); Reardon (1985, 1993); Tickner (1993, 2001); Wibben (2002).

12 The following poem is cited in Zalewski (2005): 'Local women said: no matter How you sprinkled it, everytime,/You'd sweep a concrete floor,/You'd get more off it./ As if, deep down,/ There was only dust.' (Second stanza from the poem 'Wings' by John O'Donohue.)

References

Abiri, E., 2000, *The Securitisation of Migration*, PhD dissertation, Gothenburg, Department of Peace and Development Research, Göteborg University.

Ackerly, B., M. Stern and J. True (eds), 2005, *Feminist Methodologies for International Relations*, Cambridge University Press (forthcoming).

Acuerdo Sobre identidad y Derechos de los Pueblos Indígenas, 31 March 1995, Gobeirno de la República de Guatemala y la Unidad Revolucionaria Nacional Guatemalteca.

Albert, M., D. Jackson and Y. Lapid, 2001, *Identities, Borders, Orders: Rethinking International Relations Theory*, Minneapolis, University of Minnesota Press.

Alvarez, S. and A. Escobar, 1991, *The Making of Social Movements in Latin America: Identity, Strategy, and Democracy*, Boulder, Westview Press.

Amnesty International, 1987, *Guatemala: The Human Rights Record*, London, Amnesty International Publications.

Anderson, B., 1991, *Imagined Communities: Reflections on the Origin and Spread of Nationalism*, New York, Verso.

Anthias, F. and Nira Yuval-Davis (eds), 1989, *Woman-Nation-State*, London, Macmillan.

——, 1992, *Racialized Boundaries*, London, Routledge.

Anzaldúa, G., 1987, *Borderlands/La Frontera: The New Meztiza*, San Francisco, Aunt Lute Books.

Appiah, K., 1992, *In My Father's House: Africa in the Philosohpy of Culture*, Oxford, Oxford University Press.

Arias, A (ed.), 2001, *The Rigoberta Menchú Controversy*, Minneapolis, University of Minnesota Press.

Asemblea de la Sociedad Civil, 1994, Coordinación de Organizaciones del Pueblo Maya de Guatemala, 'Identidad y derechos de los pueblos indígenas', Propuesta para las negociacones de paz Gobierno-UNRG.

——, 1994b, Sector de Mujeres, Mujeres Mayas de Guatemala, 'Identidad y derechos de los pueblos mayas', Propuesta para las negociacones de paz Gobierno-UNRG.

Ashley, R. and R. B. J. Walker, 1990, 'Reading dissidence/writing the discipline: crisis and the question of sovereignty in international studies', *International Studies Quarterly*, 34, 3.

AVANCSO, 1995, 'De la etnia a la nación: la discusión sobre la identidad nacional base necesaria en la construcción de la paz y la democracia en Guatemala', Guatemala, 18–20 Julio 1995, Asociacíon para el Avance de las Ciencias Sociales en Guatemala. AVANCSO, vol. pup. seriada: No. 11, Marzo 1996.

Barrett, M. and A. Phillips, 1992, *Destabilizing Theory*, Stanford, Stanford University Press.

Barry, T., 1987, *Roots of Rebellion: Land and Hunger in Central America*, Boston, South End Press.

Bartelson, J., 1995, *A Geneaology of Sovereignty*, Cambridge, Cambridge University Press.

Barth, F., 1969, *The Social Organization of Cultural Difference*, Oslo, Universitetsförlaget.

Bastos, S. and M. Camus, 1993, *Quebrando el Silencio: Organizaciones del Pueblo Maya y Sus Demandas (1986–1992)*, Guatemala, Flacso.

——, 1995, *Abriendo Caminos: Las Organizaciones Mayas desde el Nobel hasta el Acuerdo de Derechos Indígenas*, Guatemala, Flacso.

Behar, R., 1993, *Translated Woman: Crossing the Border with Esperanza's Story*, Boston, Beacon Press.

Beneria, L. and S. Feldman (eds), 1992, *Unequal Burden, Economic Crises, Persistent Poverty and Women's Work*, Boulder, Westview Press.

Bhaba, H., 1994, *The Location of Culture*, New York, Routledge.

Blanchard, E., 2003, 'Gender, international relations, and the development of feminist security theory', *Signs*, 28, 4.

Blandón. M. T., 1993, *Encuentro Centroamericano de Mujeres: Historia de Género-Una Nueva Mujer, un Nuevo Poder*, Nicaragua, CEM.

Booth, K. (ed.), 1998, *Statecraft and Security: The Cold War and Beyond*, Cambridge, Cambridge University Press.

Booth, K. and T. Dunne (eds), 2002, *Worlds in Collision: Terror and the Future of Global Order*, London, Palgrave Macmillan.

Boserup, E., 1970, *Women's Role in Economic Development*, London, George Allen and Unwin.

Bouta, T. and G. Frerks, 2002, *Women's Roles in Conflict Resolution and Post Conflict Reconstruction*, Netherlands Institute of International Relations.

Brah, A., 1993, 'Re-framing Europe: en-gendered racisms, ethnicities and nationalisms in contemporary Western Europe', *Feminist Review*, 45.

Brignoli, H. P., 1985, *Breve Historia de Centro-América*, Madrid, Alianza Editorial.

Brown, W., 1988, *Manhood and Politics: A Feminist Reading in Political Theory*, New Jersey, Rowman and Littlefield.

Brundtland, G., 1987, *Our Common Future, World Commission on Environment and Development*, Oxford, Oxford University Press.

Bruner, J., 1990, *Acts of Meaning*, Cambridge, Harvard University Press.

Bull, H., 1977, *The Anarchical Society: A Study of Order in World Politics*, London, Macmillan.

Butler, J., 1990, *Gender Trouble: Feminism and the Subversion of Identity*, New York, Routledge.

——, 1993, *Bodies That Matter: On the Discursive Limits of 'Sex'*, New York and London, Routledge.

——, 2004, *Undoing Gender*, London, Routledge.

Buzan, B., 1983, 1991, *Peoples, States and Fear*, Brighton, Weatsheaf Books.

Buzan, B. and O. Waever, 2003, *Regions and Powers: The Structure of International Security*, Cambridge, Cambridge University Press.

Buzan, B., O. Waever and J. de Wilde, 1998, *Security: A New Framework for Analysis*, Boulder: Lynne Rienner.

Cabrera Pérez-Armiñán, M. L., 1992, *Tradición y Cambio de La Mujer K'Iche'*, Guatemala, Idesac.

Calder Chaves, E., 1998, 'NGOs and cooperatives, working with populations affected by the Civil War in Guatemala', paper prepared for the Inter-Regional Consultation, 3.

Cambranes, J. C. (ed.), 1992, *500 Años de Lucha por la Tierra: Estudios Sobre Propiedad y Reforma Agraria en Guatemala*, Volumen 1 y 2, Guatemala, Flasco.

Campbell, D., 1992, *Writing Security: United States Foreign Policy and the Politics of Identity*, Minneapolis, University of Minnesota Press.

——, 1998, *National Reconstruction: Violence, Identity and Justice in Bosnia*, Minneapolis, University of Minnesota Press.

——, 1999, 'Violence, justice and identity', in J. Edkins, N. Pershram and V. Pin-Fat (eds), *Sovereignty and Subjectivity*, London, Lynne Rienner.

Campbell, D. and M. Dillon (eds), 1993, *The Political Subject of Violence*, Manchester, Manchester University Press.

Carr, E. H., 1939, *The Twenty Years Crisis: An Introduction to the Study of International Relations*, London, Macmillan

Carmack, R., 1992, *Harvest of Violence: The Mayan Indians and the Guatemalan Crisis*, Norman and London, University of Oklahoma Press.

CEH, 1999, *Guatemala: Memory of Silence*, Guatemala, CEH.

Chatterjee, P., 1993, *The Nation and its Fragments: Colonial and Postcolonial Histories*, Princeton, Princeton University Press.

Chow, R., 1993, *Writing Diaspora: Tactics of Intervention in Contemporary Cultural Studies*, Bloomington, Indiana University Press.

Clifford, J. and G. E. Marcus, 1986, *Writing Culture*, Berkeley, University of California Press.

Cohn, C., 1987, 'Sex and death in the rational world of defense intellectuals', *Signs*, 12, 4.

——, 1993, 'War, wimps, and women: talking gender and thinking war', in M. Cooke and A. Woolacott (eds), *Gendering War Talk*, Princeton, Princeton University Press.

Coincidencia de Mujeres, 1992, *Memorias de Comision Guatemalteca Preencuentro*, 'Trabaha de grupos IV: refleciones sobre la realidad de la mujer maya', I Encuento Centroamericano de mujeres, Guatemala.

COINDE (Consejo de Instituciones de Desarrollo), 1993, *Diagnóstico sobre refugiados, retornados y despiazados de Guatemala*, Guatemala.

Cojti Cuxil, D., 1991, *Configuración del Pensiamento Político del Pueblo Maya, Quetzaltenango*, Asociación de Escritores Mayances de Guatemala.

Connell, R. W., 1995, *Masculinities*, London, Polity Press.

Connolly, W., 1991, *Identity/Difference*, Ithaca, Cornell University Press.

——, 2004, 'The complexity of sovereingty', in J. Edkins, V. Pin-Fat and M. Shapiro (eds), *Sovereign Lives: Power in Global Politics*, London, Routledge.

Der Derian, J., 1995, 'The value of security: Hobbes, Marx, Nietsche, and Baudrillard', in R. D. Lipchutz (ed.), *On Security*, New York, Columbia University Press.

Der Derian, J. and M. J. Shapiro, 1989, *International/Intertextual Relations: Postmodern Readings of World Politics*, Lexington, Lexington Books.

Derrida, J., 1981, *Dissemination*, trans. Barbara Johnson, Chicago, University of Chicago Press.

Díaz-Polanco, H., 1997, *Indigenous Peoples in Latin America: The Quest for Self-Determination*, Latin American Perspectives Series, 18, Boulder, Westview Press.

Dillon, G. M., 1990–91, 'The alliance of security and subjectivity', *Current Research on Peace and Violence*, Tampere Peace Research Institute, XIII, 3.

——, 1996, *Politics of Security*, London and New York, Routledge.

——, 2004, 'Correlating sovereign and biopower', in J. Edkins, V. Pin-Fat, V. and M. Shapiro (eds), *Sovereign Lives: Power in Global Politics*, London, Routledge.

Doty, R. L., 1996, *Imperial Encounters: The Politics of Representation in North-South Relations*, Minneapolis, University of Minnesota Press.

Edkins, J., 1999, *Post-Structuralism and International Relations: Bringing the Political Back In*, London, Lynne Rienner.

——, 2004, *Trauma and the Memory of Politics*, Cambridge, Cambridge University Press.

Edkins, J., N. Persram and V. Pin-Fat (eds), 1999, *Sovereignty and Subjectivity*, London, Lynne Rienner.

Edkins J. and V. Pin-Fat, 1999, 'The subject of the political', in J. Edkins, N. Persram and V. Pin-Fat (eds), *Sovereignty and Subjectivity*, London, Lynne Rienner.

——, 2004, 'Introduction: life power, resistance', in J. Edkins, V. Pin-Fat, and M. Shapiro (eds), *Sovereign Lives: Power in Global Politics*, London, Routledge.

Edkins, J., V. Pin-Fat, and M. Shapiro (eds), 2004, *Sovereign Lives: Power in Global Politics*, London, Routledge.

Edmonson, M. 1982, *Ancient Future of the Itza: Book of Chilam Balam of Tizimin*, Austin, University of Texas Press.

El Bushra, 2003, *Women Building Peace – Sharing Know How*, London, International Alert.

El Jack, 2003, *Gender and Armed Conflict*, BRIDGE, Institute of Development Studies, University of Sussex, Brighton.

Elshtain, J. B., 1987, *Women and War*, London, The Harvester Press.

Enloe, C., 1988, *Does Khaki Become You? The Militarization of Women's Lives*, London, Pandora Press/HarperCollins.

——, 1990, *Bananas, Beaches and Bases: Making Feminist Sense of International Politics*, Berkeley, University of California Press.

——, 1993, *The Morning After: Sexual Politics at the End of the Cold War*, Berkeley, University of California Press.

——, 2000, *Maneuvers: The International Politics of Militarizing Women's Lives*, Berkeley, University of California Press.

Eriksen, T. H., 1993, *Ethnicity and Nationalism*, London, Pluto Press.

Eriksson Baaz, M., 2004, *The Paternalism of Partnership: A Postcolonial Reading of Development Aid*, London, Zed Books

Erwér, M., 2003, *Challenging the Gender Paradox: Women's Collective Agency in the Transformation of Kerala Politics*, Göteborg, Padrigu Papers.

Falk, R., 1995, *On Human Governance: Toward a New Global Politics*, Cambridge, Polity Press.

Fanon, F., 1952, *Black Skins, White Mask*, London, Pluto Classics.

Feminist Review, 1993, Vols 44–5.

Ferguson, K. E., 1993, *The Man Question: Visions of Subjectivity in Feminist Theory*, Berkeley, University of California Press.

Fischer, E. F. and M. R. Brown (eds), 1996, *Maya Cultural Activism in Guatemala*, Austin, University of Texas Press.

Flax, J., 1987, 'Postmodernism and gender relations in feminist theory', *Signs*, 12, 4.

Fonow, M. and J. Cook, 1991, *Beyond Methodology: Feminist Scholarship as Lived Research*, Bloomington, Indiana University Press.

Foucault, M., 1980, *Power/Knowledge*, ed. Colin Gordon, New York, Pantheon Books.

Fraser, A., 1999, 'Becoming human: the origins and development of women's human rights', *Human Rights Quarterly*, 21.

Garcia, A. I. and Gomarez, E., 1989, *Mujeres Centroamericanas: Tomo II, Efectos del Conflicto*, San José, Costa Rica, CSUCA, FLACSO, Universidad para la Paz.

Garcia, R. (ed.), 1988, *Central America: Crisis and Possibilities*, Stockholm: Institute of Latin American Studies.

Gluck, S. and D. Patai (eds), 1991, *Women's Words: The Feminist Practice of Oral History*, New York, Routledge.

Gramajo Morales, H. A., 1995, *De La Guerra ... A La Guerra*, Guatemala, Fondo de Cultura Editorial.

Green, L., 1999, *Fear as a Way of Life: Mayan Widows in Rural Guatemala*, New York, Columbia University Press.

Gökay and Walker, 2002, *11 September 2001, War, Terror, Judgement*, Keele, European Research Center.

Goldstein, J., 2001, *War and Gender*, Cambridge, Cambridge University Press.

Gugelberger, Georg M. (ed.), 1996, *The Real Thing: Testimonial Discourse and Latin America*, Durham, Duke University Press.

Guzzini, S. and D. Jung, 2003, *Contemporary Security Analysis and Copenhagen Peace Research*, New International Relations Studies, London: Routledge.

Hall, S., 1996, 'Introduction: who needs identity', in S. Hall and P. du Gay (eds), *Questions of Cultural Identity*, London, Sage.

Handy, J., 1984, *Gift of the Devil: History of Guatemala*, USA, South End Press.

Hansen, T. and F. Stepputat (eds), 2001, *States of Imagination: Ethnographic Explorations of the Post-Colonial State*, Durham, Duke University Press.

Hansen, L., 2000, 'The little mermaid's silent security dilemma and the absence of gender in the Copenhagen School', *Millenium*, 29, 2.

Harbury, J., 1994, *Bridge of Courage*, Monroe, Common Courage Press.

Hekman, S. (ed.), 1999, *Feminism, Identity, and Difference*, London, Frank Cass.

Hettne, B., 2001, *Kultur, Säkerhet, Hållbar Samhällsutveckling, Riksbankens Jubileumsfond*, Stockholm, Gidlunds Förlag.

——, 2003, *Culture, Security and Sustainable Social Development*, Södertälje, Gidlunds Förlag.

Hoogensen, G. and S. V. Rottem, 2004, 'Gender and the subject of security', *Security Dialogue*, 35, 2.

Hooks, M., 1993, *Guatemalan Women Speak*, Introduction by Rigoberta Menchú, Washington DC, EPICA.

Hooper, C., 2001, *Manly States: Masculinities, International Relations, and Gender Politics*, New York, Columbia University Press.

Huntington, S., 1998, *The Clash of Civilizations*, New York, Simon & Schuster.

Ibarra, C. F., 1991, *El Recurso del miedo, Ensayo sobre el estado y terror en Guatemala*, EDUCA, Costa Rica.

Imber, M., 1994, *Environment, Security, and UN Reform*, Basingstoke, Macmillan.

Ivison, D., P. Patton and W. Sanders (eds), 2000, *Political Theory and the Rights of Indigenous Peoples*, Cambridge, Cambridge University Press.

Jabri, V., 1998, 'Uni(form) instrumentalities and war's abject', *Millennium: Journal of International Studies*, 27, 4.

Jabri, V. and E. O'Gorman, 1999, *Women, Culture, and International Relations*, Boulder, Lynne Rienner.

Jackson, C. and R. Pearson, 1998, *Feminist Visions of Development: Gender, Analysis and Policy*, New York, Routledge.

Jahn, E., P. Lemaitre and O. Waever, 1987, *European Security—Problems of Research on Non-Military Aspects*, Copenhagen Papers, University of Copenhagen, The Center of Peace and Conflict Research.

Jayawardena, K., 1986, *Feminism and Nationalism in the Third World*, London, Zed Books.

Jelin, E., 1990, *Women and Social Change in Latin America*, London, Zed Books.

Johansen, R. C., 1982, 'Toward an alternative security system: moving beyond the balance of power in the search for world security', *Alternatives: A Journal of World Policy*, 8, Winter 1982–83.

Jonas, S., 1991, *The Battle for Guatemala: Rebels, Death Squads and US Power*, Boulder, Westview Press.

——, 2000, *Of Centaurs and Doves: Guatemala's Peace Process*, Boulder, Westview Press.

Kabeer, N., 1994, *Reversed Realities: Gender Hierarchies in Development Thought*, New York, Verso.

Kaldor, M., 1999, *New and Old Wars: Organized Violence in a Global Era*, Stanford, Stanford University Press.

Kandiyoti, D., 1985, *Women in Rural Production Systems: Problems and Policies*, Paris, UNESCO.

——, 1991, 'Identity and its discontents: women and the nation', *Millennium: Journal of International Studies*, 20, 3.

Karlsson, S., 1996, *Amerikas bakgård – om USA:s utrikespolitik i Karibien*, Stockholm, Nerenius and Santérus.

Kearney, M., 1991, 'Borders and boundaries of state and self at the end of empire', *Journal of Historical Sociology*, 4, 1, March.

King, G. and C. L. Murray, 2002, 'Rethinking human security', *Political Science Quarterly*, 116, 4.

Kramer, F. V., 1993, *Biografía Política de Guatemala*, Guatemala, Flacso.

Krause, K. and M. C. Williams (eds), 1997, *Critical Security Studies: Concepts and Cases*, Minneapolis, University of Minnesota Press.

Kronsell, A., 2005, 'Studying silences on gender in institutions of hegemonic masculinity', in B. Ackerly, M. Stern and J. True (eds), *Feminist Methodologies for International Relations*, Cambridge University Press (forthcoming).

La Feber, W., 1993, *Inevitable Revolutions: The United States in Central America*, New York, W. W. Norton and Company.

Laffey, 2000, 'Locating identity: performativity, foreign policy and state action', *Review of International Studies*, 26.

Langness, L. L. and G. Frank, 1981, *Lives: An Anthropological Approach to Biography*, Novato, Chandler and Sharp.

Lapid, Y. and F. Kratochwil, 1996, *The Return of Culture and Identity in IR Theory*, Boulder, Lynne Rienner.

Lindholm Shulz, H., 1999, *The Reconstruction of Palestinian Nationalism: Between Revolution and Statehood*, Manchester, Manchester University Press.

——, 2003, *Palestinian Diaspora: Formation of Identities and Politics of Homeland*, New York, Routledge.

Lipchutz, R. D. (ed), 1995, *On Security*, New York, Columbia University Press.

Lisch, L., 2003, 'Impartiality, storytelling, and the seductions of narrative: an essay at an impasse', *Alternatives*, 28.

Lister, R., 1997, 2003, *Citizenship: Feminist Perpspectives*, Basingstoke, Macmillan.

Lugones, M. C. and E. V. Spelman, 1983, 'Have we got a theory for you!: feminist theory, cultural imperialism and the demand for "the woman's voice"'. *Women's Studies International Forum*, 6, 6.

Majawil Q'ij, 1994, 'El nuevo amanecer' ('New Dawn'), presentation of organization, Majawil Q'ij, 32 Ave. 1–56 Zona 7, Guatemala: 'Mujer maya: fuente de vida, resistencia y futuro', *Vóz y pensamiento Maya*, periódico de Majawil Q'ij.

Mama Maquin (Organization of Guatemalan Refugee women), 1994, *From Refugees to Returnees, Chiapas*, Mexico: Mama Maquin–CIAM.

Marchand, M. and J. Parpart (eds), 1995, *Feminism, Postmodernism, Development*, London, Routledge.

Marchand, M. and A. Sisson Runyan, 2000, *Gender and Global Restructuring: Sightings, Sites and Resistances*, London, Routledge.

Martínez de León, L. E., 1994, *La democracia de las armas*, Mexico, Centro de estudios de Guatemala/Claves Latinamericanas.

Martínez Peláz, S., 1994, *La Patria del Criollo*, Guatemala, Ediciones En Marcha.

Masters, C., 2002, 'In/securing subjectivity: hesitant engagements between feminists and poststructuralists', unpublished paper presented at ISA, New Orleans.

McClintock, A., 1993, 'Family feuds: gender, nationalism, and the family', *Feminist Review*, 45.

McSweeney, B., 1999, *Security, Identity and Interests: A Sociology of International Relations*, Cambridge, Cambridge University Press.

Melander, V., 1999, *The Hour of God? People in Guatemala Confronting Political Evangelicalism and Counterinsurgency (1976–1990)*, Uppsala, Uppsala University, Faculty of Theology.

Milliken, J., 1999, 'The study of discourse in international relations: a critique of research and methods', *European Journal of International Relations*, 5, 2.

Moghadam, V. M. (ed.), 1994, *Identity Politics and Women: Cultural Reassertions and Feminisms in an International Perspective*, Boulder, Westview Press.

Mohanty, C., A. Russo and L. Torres (eds), 1991, *Third World Women and the Politics of Feminism*, Bloomington, Indiana University Press.

Montejo, V., 1994, *Testimonio: Muerte de una Comunidad Indígena en Guatemala, Guatemala*, Editorial Universitaria, Universidad de San Carlos de Guatemala.

Morgenthau, H., 1973, *Politics Among Nations*, New York, Knopf.

Mudimbe, V. Y., 1988, *The Invention of Africa: Gnosis, Philosphy and the Order of Knowledge*, Bloomington, Indiana University Press.

——, 1994, *The Idea of Africa*, Bloomington, Indiana University Press.

Muppidi, H. 1999, 'Postcoloniality and the production of international insecurity: the persistant puzzle of US–Indian relations', in J. Weldes, M. Laffey, H. Guterson and R. Duvall (eds), 1999, *Cultures of Insecurity: States, Communities, and the Production of Danger*, Minneapolis, University of Minnesota Press.

Narayan, U. and S. Harding (eds), 2000, *Decentering the Center: Philosophy for a Multicultural, Post-Colonial, and Feminist World*, Bloomington, Indiana University Press.

Nelson, D. M., 1999, *A Finger in the Wound: Body Politics in Quincentennial Guatemala*, Berkeley, University of California Press.

Niarchos, 1995, 'Women, war, and rape: challenges facing the International Tribune for the Former Yugoslavia', *Human Rights Quarterly*, 17 April.

Ochberg, R. and G. Rosenwald (eds), 1992, *Storied Lives: The Cultural Politics of Self-Understanding*, New Haven, Yale University Press.

Okin, S. M., 1989, *Gender, Justice and the Family*, New York, Basic Books.

Olsen, K. and L. Shopes, 1991, 'Crossing boundaries, building bridges: doing oral history among working-class women and men', in S. Gluck and D. Patai (eds), *Women's Words: The Feminist Practice of Oral History*, New York, Routledge.

Palma, G., 1995, 'El rol del sistema educativo formal en la formación de las nociones de identidad nacional en la juventud de la Ciudad de Guatemala', paper presented at LASA.

Palme Commission, 1982, *Common Security: A Program for Disarmament*, Stockholm, Tidens Publishers.

Parker, A., M. Russo, D. Sommer and P. Yaeger, 1992, *Nationalisms and Sexualities*, New York, Routledge.

Passerini, L., 1992, *Totalitarianism and Memory*, International Yearbook of Oral History and Life Stories, Vol. 1, Oxford, Oxford University Press.

Pateman, C., 1988, *The Sexual Contract*, Stanford, Stanford University Press.

——, 1989, *Feminism, Democracy and Political Theory*, Stanford, Stanford University Press.

Paul, B. and W. Demarest, 1992, 'The operation of the Death Squad in San Pedro', in R. Carmack, 1992, *Harvest of Violence: The Mayan Indians and the Guatemalan Crisis*, Norman and London, University of Oklahoma Press.

Peterson, V. S., 1990, 'Whole rights? A critique of the givens', *Alternatives*, XV.

——, 1992, 'Transgressing boundaries: theories of knowledge, gender, and international relations', *Millennium: Journal of International Studies*, 21, 2.

——, 1994, 'The politics of identity in international relations', *The Fletcher Forum of World Affairs*, 17, 2.

Peterson, V. S. and A. Sisson Runyan, 1993, *Global Gender Issues*, Boulder, Westview Press.

Pettman, J. J., 1996, *Worlding Women: A Feminist International Politics*, London, Routledge.

Pin-Fat, V., 2000, '(Im)possible universalism: reading human rights in world politics', *Review of International Studies*, 26, 4.

——, 2003, 'Writing humanity through danger: human rights and September 11'. unpublished conference paper, International Studies Association Annual Conference, Portland, Oregon.

——, 2005, 'The metaphysics of the national interest and the "mysticism" of the nation-state: reading Hans J. Morgenthau', *Review of International Studies*, 31, 2, April.

Pin-Fat, V. and M. Stern, 2005, 'The scripting of private Jessica Lynch—biopolitics, gender and the "feminisation" of the U.S. military', *Alternatives: Global, Local, Political*, 30, 1.

Radcliffe, S. and S. Westwood (eds), 1993, *Viva: Women and Popular Protest in Latin America*, London and New York, Routledge.

——, 1996, *Remaking the Nation: Place, Identity and Politics in Latin America*, London, Routledge.

Randall, V. and G. Waylen, 1998, *Gender, Politics and the State*, London, Routledge.

Reardon, B., 1985, *Sexism and the War System*, New York, Columbia University Press.

——, 1993, *Woman and Peace: Feminist Versions of Global Security*, New York, SUNY Press.

Rehn, E. and E. J. Sirleaf, 2002, *Women, War and Peace: The Independent Experts' Assessment on the Impact of Armed Conflict on Women and Women's Role in Peace Building*, UN Development Fund for Women (UNIFEM).

REMHI/ODHAG, 1999, *Guatemala: Never Again!*, Mary Knoll, New York, Orbis Books.

Ricoeur, P., 1990, *Time and Narrative*, Vols 1–3, Chicago, University of Chicago Press.

Rigby, A., 2001, *Justice and Reconciliation: After the Violence*, Boulder, Lynne Rienner.

RIS (Review of International Studies), 2004, 30, 2.

Said, E. W., 1985, *Orientalism*, Harmondsworth, Penguin.

——, 1993, *Culture and Imperialism*, New York, Knopf.

Salazar, 1991, 'A third world women's text: between the politics of criticism and cultural politics', in S. Gluck and D. Patai (eds), *Women's Words: The Feminist Practice of Oral History*, New York, Routledge.

Sanford, V., 1997, *Mothers, Widows and Guerrilleras: Anonymous Conversations with Survivors of State Terror*, Uppsala, Life and Peace Institute.

Saravia, E. A., 1985, *Popol Vuh: Ancient Stories of the Quiche Indians of Guatemala*, Guatemala, Turismas.

Scarry, E., 1985, *The Body in Pain: The Making and Unmaking of the World*, Oxford, Oxford University Press.

Schirmer, J., 1993, 'The seeking of truth and the gendering of consciousness: the co-madres of El Salvador and the CONAVIGUA widows of Guatemala', in S. Radcliffe and S. Westwood (eds), *Viva: Women and Popular Protest in Latin America*, London and New York, Routledge.

——, 1998, *The Guatemalan Military Project: A Violence Called Democracy*, Philadelphia, University of Pennsylvania Press.

Schutte, O., 1993, Cultural Identity and Social Liberation in Latin American Thought, Albany, State University of New York Press.

——, 2002, 'Cultural alterity: cross-cultural communication and feminist theory in North–South contexts, in U. Narayan and S. Harding (eds), 2000, *Decentering the Center: Philosophy for a Multicultural, Post-Colonial, and Feminist World*, Bloomington, Indiana University Press.

Security Dialogue, 2004, 35, 3.

Sen, G. and C. Grown, 1987, *Development, Crises and Alternative Visions*, New York, Monthly Review Press.

Shaw, K., 2004, 'Creating/negotiating intercises: indigenous sovereignties', in J. Edkins,

V. Pin-Fat, and M. Shapiro, 2004, *Sovereign Lives: Power in Global Politics*, London, Routledge.

Shaw, M., 1994, *Global Society and International Relations: Sociological Concepts and Political Perspectives*, Cambridge, Polity Press.

Sherbakova, I., 1992, 'The gulag in memory', in L. Passerini, *Totalitarianism and Memory*, International Yearbook of Oral History and Life Stories, Vol. 1, Oxford, Oxford University Press.

Smith, C. A. (ed.), 1990, *Guatemalan Indians and the State: 1540 to 1988*, Austin, University of Texas Press.

Solares, J. (ed.), 1993, *Estado y Nación: Las Demandas de los Grupos Étnicos en Guatemala*, Guatemala, Flacso.

Solomon, J., 1994, *Institutional Violence: Civil Patrols in Guatemala*, Washington DC, The Robert F. Kennedy Memorial Center for Human Rights.

Sommer, D., 1991, 'Rigoberta's secrets', *Latin American Perspectives*, 18, 32.

Spelman, E. V., 1988, *Inessential Woman: Problems of Exclusion in Feminist Thought*, Boston, Beacon.

Spivak, G., 1988, 'Can the subaltern speak?', in C. Nelson and L. Grossberg (eds), *Marxism and the Interpretation of Culture*, Chicago, University of Illinois Press.

Stephensen, C., 1988, 'The need for alternative forms of security', *Alternatives*, 13.

Stepputat, F., 1996, 'Repatriation and the politics of space: the case of the Mayan diaspora and return movement', *Journal of Refugee Studies*, 7. 1.

——, 1999, 'At the frontiers of the modern state', in A. Arce and N. Long (eds), *Post-War Guatemala*, London, Routledge.

Stern, D., 2004, *The Present Moment in Psychotherapy and Everyday Life*, New York, HarperCollins.

Stern, M., 1991, *Security Policy in Transition, Sweden After the Cold War*, Gothenburg University, Sweden, Padrigu Papers.

——, 1993, 'Reading the project, global civilization: challenges for sovereignty, democracy and security', *Futures*, March, 25, 2.

——, 2001, Naming In/Security – Constructing Identity: Mayan Women in Guatemala on the Eve of Peace, PhD dissertation, Gothenburg University, Sweden, Padrigu Papers.

Sylvester, C., 1994, *Feminist International Relations in a Post Modern Era*, Cambridge Studies in International Relations, Cambridge, Cambridge University Press.

Terriff, T., S. Croft, L. James and P. Morgan, 1999, *Security Studies Today*, Cambridge, Polity Press.

Tickner, J. A., 1993, *Gender in International Relations: Feminist Perspectives on Achieving Global Security*, New York, Columbia University Press.

——, 2001, *Gendering World Politics: Issues and Approaches in the Post-Cold War Era*, New York, Columbia University Press.

Torres-Rivas, E. and B. Arévalo de León, 1999, *From Conflict to Dialogue: The WSP Guatemala Way*, Guatemala, Flacso.

Trinh, T. Minh-ha, 1989, *Woman Native Other: Writing Postcoloniality and Feminism, Bloomington*, Indiana University Press.

——, 1987, 'Difference: a special third world women issue', *Feminist Review*, 25.

UNDP, 1999, *Human Development Report*, New York, Oxford University Press.

UN Security Council, *13 October 2004*, Report of the Secretary-General on women and peace and security, S/2004/814.

Von Busekist, A., 2004, 'Uses and misuses of the concept of identity', *Security Dialogue*, 35, 21.

Wæver, O., 1995, 'Securitization and desecuritization', in R. D. Lipschutz (ed.), *On Security*, New York, Columbia University Press.

Walker, R. B. J., 1993, *Inside/Outside: International Relations as Political Theory*, Cambridge Studies in International Relations, Cambridge, Cambridge University Press.

——, 1998, 'The subject of security', in K. Krause and M. C. Williams (eds), 1997, *Critical Security Studies: Concepts and Cases*, Minneapolis, University of Minnesota Press.

——, 2004, 'Conclusions: sovereignties, exceptions, worlds', in J. Edkins, V. Pin-Fat and M. Shapiro, *Sovereign Lives: Power in Global Politics*, London, Routledge.

Walker, R. B. J. and S. Mendlovitz (eds), 1990, *Contending Sovereignties: Redefining Political Community*, Boulder, Lynne Rienner.

Walt, S., 1991, 'The renaissance of security studies', *International Studies Quarterly*, 35, 2.

Waltz, K., 1979, *Theory of International Politics*, Reading, Addison-Wesley.

Warren, K. B. (ed.), 1998, *Indigenous Movements and their Critics: Pan-Maya Activism in Guatemala*, Princeton, Princeton University Press.

Weber, M., 1918, 1994, 'The profession and vocation of politics', in M. Weber, *Political Writings*, Cambridge, Cambridge University Press.

Weldes, J., M. Laffey, H. Guterson and R. Duvall (eds), 1999, 'Introduction: constructing insecurity', in J. Weldes et al., *Cultures of Insecurity: States, Communities, and the Production of Danger*, Minneapolis, University of Minnesota Press.

Weldes, J., M. Laffey, H. Guterson and R. Duvall (eds), 1999, *Cultures of Insecurity: States, Communities, and the Production of Danger*, Minneapolis, University of Minnesota Press.

Wendt, A., 2004, 'The state as person in international theory', *Review of International Studies*, 30, 2.

Whitebrooke, M., 2001, *Identity, Narrative and Politics*, London, Routledge.

Whitworth, S., 1994, *Feminism and International Relations*, New York, St. Martin's Press.

Wibben, A., 2002, Security Narratives in International Relations and the Events of September 11, 2001: A Feminist Study, PhD dissertation, University of Wales, Aberystwyth.

Williams, P. and L. Chrisman (eds), 1994, *Colonial Discourse and Post-Colonial Theory*, New York, Columbia University Press.

Wilson, F., 1992, 'Ethnicity and gender in a modernizing world: an introduction', CDR Working Paper 92.3, Copenhagen, Center for Development Research.

Wilson, R., 1995, *Maya Resurgence in Guatemala: Q'eqchi' Experiences*, Norman and London, University of Oklahoma Press.

Woodward, K. (ed.), 1997, *Identity and Difference*, The Open University, London, Sage.

Worby, P., 1998, 'Organising for change: Guatemalan refugee women assert their right to land', in UNDP, *Women's Land and Property Rights in Situations of Conflict and Reconstruction: A Reader Based on the Interregional Consultation in Kigali Rwanda*, New York, UNDP.

Youngs, G., 1999, *International Relations in a Global Age: A Conceptual Challenge*, Cambridge, Polity Press.

——, 2000, 'Breaking patriarchal bonds: demoythologising the public/private', in M. Marchand and A. Sisson Runyan, 2000, *Gender and Global Restructuring: Sightings, Sites and Resistances*, London, Routledge.

Yuval-Davis, N., 1997, *Gender and Nation*, London, Sage.

Zalewski, M., 2005, 'Distracted reflections on the production, narration and refusal of feminist knowledge in IR', in B. Ackerly, M. Stern and J. True (eds), 2005, *Feminist Methodologies for International Relations*, Cambridge University Press (forthcoming).

Zalewski, M and J. Parpart (eds), 1998, *The 'Man' Question in International Relations*, Boulder, Westview Press.

Zartman, W. and L. Rasmussen (eds), 1997, *Peacemaking in International Conflict: Methods and Techniques*, United States Institute of Peace.

Zizek, S., 1989, *The Sublime Object of Ideology*, London, Verso.

Zur, J. N., 1998, *Violent Memories: Mayan War Widows in Guatemala*, Oxford, Oxford University Press.

Index